ABDUCTION

How Liberalism Steals Our Children's Hearts And Minds

Steven Feazel and Dr. Carol M. Swain

ISBN 978-1-63525-146-3 (Paperback)
ISBN 978-1-63525-147-0 (Digital)

Christian Faith Publishing, Inc.
296 Chestnut Street
Meadville, PA 16335
www.christianfaithpublishing.com

Printed in the United States of America

Steve Feazel and Dr. Carol Swain ring a warning bell for all parents to heed who want their children to embrace and cherish traditional values and moral living that will allow them to live happy and productive lives. The book reveals the dangers of a relative morality while providing practical action steps that parents can take to prevent their children from becoming conformed to the secular pattern of the world.

—Tim Wildmon, President,
American Family Association

A national wake-up call sounding the alarm on how sinful forces are undermining timeless spiritual values that are so important to maintain to nurture the success of future generations, this unique book provides positive insight that, if applied, can push back against a culture that places too little value on morality.

—Dr. Alveda King,
Civil Rights Activist,
Prolife Activist, Author,
Christian Minister

Steve and Carol take a historical approach to the demise of our culture and to the loss of the hearts and minds of our children. In knowing where to go, you have to understand where you have been. This work lays out the basis of how to recapture the culture wars and save our children.

—US Representative Marsha Blackburn (R-TN)

Steve Feazel and Carol Swain have performed a great service by exposing the people and institutions behind some of the most important threats to the innocence and moral and spiritual health of children today. These authors remind us that those responsible for the education of our young people frequently betray our trust by preaching to them the false catechism of me-generation "if it feels good, do it" liberalism. We owe it to our children and grandchildren to inform ourselves and to fight back.

—Robert P. George,
McCormick Professor of Jurisprudence,
Princeton University

Everywhere we turn, from our schools to Hollywood to the media to the courts, children's minds and souls are being usurped by the radical, secular left. Carol Swain and Steve Feazel tackle the immoral architects of the "New Morality" in this trenchant and timely book—and show parents how to fight back.

—Michelle Malkin,
Author of *Culture of Corruption* and *Who Built That*

At last, a book that gives parents hope in the cultural war to keep their children free from the destructive forces of a humanistic society.

—Melissa Ohden,
Abortion Survivor and Renowned Prolife Speaker

This powerful book will motivate you to become an agent of change for our nation's declining culture. It is easily readable, thought-provoking, and action-oriented. The authors bring light to darkness. Why don't you step up to the plate and join Dr. Carol Swain and Steve Feazel as they fight to save our nation by restoring Judeo-Christian values and principles to guide future generations?

—Suellen Roberts,
Founder and President of Christian Women
in Media and CEO of Global Media Summit

To my grandchildren Tanner, Zoey, Oliver, and Sawyer. May you embrace the values on which our nation was founded.

—Steve Feazel

For past, present, and future generations of America's children. For my sons Benjamin and Reginald; my grandchildren Chelsea, Destiny, Storm, Skye, and Tiara; and great-grandson Hezekiah.

—Carol M. Swain, PhD

Train up a child in the way he should go: and when he is old, he will not depart from it.

—Proverbs 22:6, NKJV

Whoever receives one little child like this in My name receives Me. Whoever causes one of these little ones who believe in Me to sin, it would be better for him if a millstone were hung around his neck, and he were drowned in the depth of the sea.

—Matthew 18:5–6, NKJV

The very power of [textbook writers] depends on the fact that they are dealing with a boy: a boy who thinks he is "doing" his "English prep" and has no notion that ethics, theology, and politics are all at stake. It is not a theory they put into his mind, but an assumption, which ten years hence, its origin forgotten and its presence unconscious, will condition him to take one side in a controversy which he has never recognized as a controversy at all.

—C. S. Lewis,
The Abolition of Man

CONTENTS

FOREWORD

Young people, especially teens and preteens, are the focal point of a cultural war raging in America. The prizes at stake in this struggle are the hearts and minds of our children. As it has for decades, the liberal Left is doing all it can to make certain that the worldview being adopted by our young people is the one that benefits liberal political candidates and liberal ideology. In *Abduction*, Steve Feazel and Dr. Carol Swain expose how Liberalism, aka the New Morality, uses culture in sinister ways to deceive young people into accepting a secular worldview that rejects traditional values and shuns the Christian faith.

The New Morality use public schools, colleges, the entertainment industry, and court decisions to capture the hearts and control the minds of young people who are, or are about to become, voters. Liberals embrace abortion, same-sex marriage, a godless culture, and a host of other morally bankrupt positions that contribute to degenerate living. These so-called "progressives" use any conceivable means, regardless how devious, to entice young people into rejecting traditional values held by their families. Feazel and Swain reveal this treachery of the Left and sound an alarm warning to parents to become more actively involved in guarding their children, who are at risk of being swallowed up by a hostile culture.

Abduction presents well-sourced, anecdotal accounts of how some people have successfully pushed back against liberal advances. It provides action steps that parents can take to build stronger bridges to their children and help them choose a worldview firmly grounded in traditional values and the Christian faith. It is time to take a stand and strive to prevent our children from being stolen by the ideas of a liberal political philosophy that makes no place for God and dismisses the principles of our Founding Fathers. This is your starting point for developing a winning strategy to fight the victorious fight for your children in the cultural war.

—Tony Perkins, President of the Family Research Council

ACKNOWLEDGMENTS

From Steve Feazel

I first would like to thank my wife, Edythe, who has traveled this literary journey with me. She has served as my initial editor and helpful advisor. She more than anyone is glad the project is done. She was always there, celebrating the highs and consoling during the lows. She deserves a great deal of credit for any success this book has. I would not have been able to do the project without her.

I have a deep appreciation and admiration for Dr. Carol Swain, who agreed to be the coauthor on this project. Her academic credentials are stellar, and her Christian faith is inspiring. Her contributions and collaboration have greatly enhanced the message of this book. Thanks to Sean Hannity for featuring her on his show that informed me of her values, conservative positions, and courage to speak out.

As one endeavors to take on a project of this magnitude, he benefits from the encouragement of friends and family. My brother, Jack, and dear friend, Jim Cummins, both provided great support for my efforts before they each left this world. A special shout-out to my son, Lance, who encouraged me at a dark point on this journey when he sent me a T-shirt on Father's Day that had the following words printed on it, "I'M A WRITER, WHAT'S YOUR SUPERPOWER?" We thank Christian Faith Publishing team for giving this project new life when it faced a dark hour.

From Dr. Carol M. Swain

I would like to thank Steve Feazel for convincing me to add this project to my overly busy schedule. I also owe a debt to Marcie Jameson, Mary Poplin, and Donna Willis who encouraged me throughout this process. . Mike Towle edited our final manuscript and Jennifer and Nathan Harden provided invaluable feedback at an earlier stage in the process. I have had long-standing support from Lee Beaman, Nan Bouchard , Pastors Sam Boyd, Jeff Dollar and L.H. Hardwick, Ken Harms, Mike Hardwick, Menda Holmes, A. J. McCall, William and Lisa Morgan, Steve Richards, and Dr. Ming Wang. I am also indebted to the congregants at Forest Hills Baptist Church, Grace Center, and Christ Church Nashville for their faithful prayers.

INTRODUCTION

CONSIDER THE FOLLOWING:

The female director of a small private school in Minnesota takes middle- and high-school students on a field trip to a sex novelty shop without parental permission (Minnesota 2015).[1]

The Boston Public School System distributes forty thousand donated condoms to teens. Parents who support the distribution of condoms complain about the sexually explicit messages on the wrappers: "One lucky lady," "Hump one," and "Tasty one" (Massachusetts 2014).[2]

The taxpayer-funded Adolescent Sexuality Conference teaches teens how to use meth to heighten their sexual experiences. Conference organizers distribute a pamphlet offering tips on oral sex and prostate stimulation (Oregon 2014).[3]

A judge sentences a female teacher to thirty days in jail for having sex with a male high-school student. The judge describes the teacher as "dangling candy" and asks, "What young man would not jump on that candy?" (Pennsylvania 2015).[4]

When Steve asked me (Carol) to coauthor a book about how liberalism corrupts our children, I hesitated at first because I already had a full plate of research projects. After initially declining, I reconsidered and decided to embrace this tremendous opportunity to help educate the public about the subtle campaign to steal the hearts and minds of future generations. Whether you are a single parent, married with kids, or a great-grandparent like me, you have a stake in protecting our children and preserving the best of our Judeo-Christian heritage.

I know what I am talking about. I am the mother of two sons, born while I was a married teenager. My children were not raised in a church. Perhaps as a consequence, their children—my grandchildren—have had an upbringing more secular than I would have preferred. There is plenty of evidence that our nation's culture is seeking to steal them. Steve and I have joined forces to fight for all our kids. They are the future of America.

We approach these and other issues from wholly different backgrounds. I am a black woman raised in rural poverty, who, by the grace of God, has achieved the American dream. A former high school dropout and teen wife and mother, I have risen to the height of tenured professor at two of America's most elite universities. I am somewhat younger than Steve and, therefore, have a different viewpoint on things: I was nine years old when Steve was entering college. As a child, I witnessed the civil rights movement that opened doors for people like me. Steve was raised in a white middle-class home but was no stranger to work; he paid his own way through college. With the encouragement of his family and good old-old fashioned persistence, he graduated from college and then earned two master's degrees. Although we have traveled different paths in life, we have joined forces for a common cause and with a common faith to benefit the youth of our nation.

Steve and I share a deep concern about America and the need to change the direction of the culture. We also share a strong conviction that readers of this book will play an essential role in helping to restore the Judeo-Christian foundation of our nation and its strong moral underpinnings. Only then will we have created a safe space for our children and their progeny.

I (Steve) stood at my book table at the Ohio Eagle Forum event in 2012, talking with a discouraged middle-aged woman. If the idea for this book had not already entered my head, she certainly could have inspired it. She told me the story of her daughter, whom she had homeschooled and raised in church. The woman cared for nothing in the world more than her daughter's well-being. After high school, her daughter went off to the local community college, a choice many families make for financial reasons. Little did she know what a costly choice it would be. After only one semester, the daughter came home and announced that she was now a confirmed atheist. It will not surprise you to learn that the woman, who had carefully raised her little girl to know and experience biblical values and the Christian faith, was devastated by her daughter's new direction in life. In the mother's eyes, eighteen years of careful love and instruction were destroyed in one semester. Mind you, this happened at a community college that is supported by tax dollars. She felt like she had paid for her own child to be stolen away. The story that mother told me is troubling, but it is not uncommon. It is a story repeated over and over across our nation as an increasingly secular and liberal culture launches a full-fledged assault on the hearts and minds of young people. Children who once embraced traditional values and the Christian faith grow up to become casualties of the culture war.

It hasn't always been this way. According to the Barna Group—a research organization that studies trends in American religious culture—until 1960 young Americans attended church at about the same rate as older Americans.[5] However, the cultural and political upheaval of the 1960s coincided with a decline in church attendance among young people, a trend that began with baby boomers and continues to this day. So what caused the change? Why did young people suddenly begin abandoning the faith of their parents? *That* is the question we hope to answer in this book.

My conversation with the disheartened mother hit me on a personal level. Her story was a reminder of my own heartache. My two sons, raised in a pastor's home, also became casualties of the culture war. They were not lost because of encounters in a college classroom but went astray due to the peer pressure of friends. In their adult years, there is some evidence that reclamation might be possible, but then there are the four grandchildren they gave my wife and me who will become targets of the liberal Left. I cannot stand by and do nothing. That's why I decided to write this book.

I (Carol) meet them on the college campuses of the most elite institutions in the world: bright young men and women whose parents have sacrificed much to get them a quality education that will establish them in their careers as influencers. Too often the parents are using their resources to support institutions committed to destroying their faith and indoctrinating their children with a secular worldview. The academic world is defined by cultural relativism. It is a world where there are no absolute truths, a world where the only norms and values that count are the institutional ones that celebrate a diversity of ideas and cultures and abandon ordinary Americans to the sidelines unless they embrace a particular feminist, racial, sexual, gender, or cultural identity. Also relegated to the sidelines are youth who have been raised in strong Christian homes. These young people must choose to organize and stick together or suffer the marginalization that comes with being a serious follower of Jesus Christ. We can do a better job of preparing them for the onslaught to come. We must be vigilant whether it is a Christian or secular educational institution. We must prepare our youth for the onslaught ahead.

CHRISTIANITY AND OUR NATIONAL CULTURE

In the 1860s, our nation fought the Civil War, which was anything but civil, as attested to by the gruesomeness of the battles and the great loss of life. Today, America is locked in another civil war. It is not a conflict where the two sides are distinguished by uniforms or the Mason-Dixon Line, or feared because of their military hardware. This civil war is a war of ideas; it is a struggle between two different concepts of morality. Many have termed it "the cultural war," and rightfully so because the prize at stake is control of the culture and all that goes with it—the welfare of the nation and the quality of life for its citizens.

We often hear or read in the media, "Why is our nation so divided?" Usually, the question is related to the political spectrum, but it goes far deeper. It goes to the core of our moral values. The currents of a New Morality seek to erode the national culture and reshape it into something far different from what the founders of the country ever conceived. The Founding Fathers drafted and signed the Declaration of Independence, and in it, they made reference to a divine deity four times. The Declaration states, "We hold these truths to be self-evident, that all men are created equal, that they are endowed by their Creator with certain unalienable rights, that among these are Life, Liberty, and the pursuit of Happiness."

Unalienable rights were regarded as rights that all men had from the hand of God, not from some form of man-made government. The very document that proclaims our birth as a free nation states that humans have been bestowed certain rights by the God who created us. By logic, this should mean that anyone who tries to encroach upon these rights would be going against the will of God. You cannot read the declaration of independence and conclude that the men responsible for it had no intent of allowing God to influence the culture, life, and law of this nation.

Our nation was established with a morality that came out of the Christian faith. It is not wrong to refer to this as America's Christian heritage. This Christian-based morality set the tone for our national culture. Life and law unfolded in harmony with a national Christian consciousness. The founders were careful not to designate any particular denomination as the official state church. They had witnessed the folly of this practice in other countries. Even though they chose no state church, they never wished for the influence of the Christian faith to vanish from the public arena.

This Christian influence had a significant impact on the shaping of our national culture, from which our values as a society were forged. You are what your values are. This is true for individuals, and it is true for a nation. In this traditional culture grounded in the Christian faith, what was taught to a child at church and in the family was reinforced by public institutions and national sentiment. The *New England Primer*, which served as a public-school textbook for nearly the first 125 years of the nation's history, was based solidly on the Bible and Christian teachings. It never entered anyone's mind to question its constitutionality.

"The times, they are a-changin'." We hear these words, we look around at our country, and we sadly have to say this is true. It is true because there is another morality surrounding us. This New Morality is called, among other terms, humanism, secularism, pluralism, situational ethics, relative morality, and postmodernism—none of them virtuous. In America's new civil war, it is traditional morality versus the New Morality, and the New Morality is gaining ground every minute. This book will document its surge and the dangers it poses to the nation, especially its young people.

A child is taught values at home and heads off to school and public life only to have his or her values attacked from sources that years ago would have affirmed those values. The New Morality is aggressive, active, resourceful, cunning, manipulative, deceitful, and very effective in its objectives. Our children are especially vulnerable to the onslaught, as they are exposed to the New Morality through various media, secular teachings at school, and peer pressure. Families witness a transformation of values in their children and wonder what happened. Parents end up not recognizing their own sons and daughters. Some families have seen severe rebellion. Others have seen tragedy as children have entered a dangerous subculture only to be lost forever.

The New Morality is fused to the liberal political agenda; they operate in tandem. There is a reason children are targeted, the goal being to reshape their morality and values: they grow up to be voters. If they are won over to the New Morality, then they are highly likely to vote for liberal candidates. Targeting our culture is the means by which the American Left gains political power.

It is time for us as a nation to look at the seriousness of this situation and ask, "Who's stealing our kids?" If the New Morality is allowed to advance unchecked by those who still embrace traditional morality, the scenario that will play out is not very comforting, especially when it comes to our kids, which includes babies (born and unborn) through adolescents.

Our kids are caught in the crosshairs. The New Morality is at the heart of the Left's strategic plan for victory. The New Morality feels time is on its side. Any victories it has winning over older adults are a bonus to the victories it gains among children and other young people. The New Morality aims at those who have not solidly established their values and who are therefore vulnerable to a time of questioning as they seek to develop their own identity. The New Morality seeks to replace parents as the main influencer in the lives of children. Isn't it odd that a fifteen-year-old must have a note from a parent to get an aspirin at school but that same child can walk into a drugstore and buy a morning-after abortion pill over the counter without Mom or Dad knowing about it?

In her book *The Death of Right and Wrong*, Tammy Bruce applies the term *Left Elite* to the New Morality that seeks to uproot traditional morality in the cultural war. Her words provide a clue to the seriousness of the battle pitting these conflicting ideas against each other: "Their moral vacuum, like the Energizer Bunny, wants to keep going, and going, and going until our culture and society looks just like them—vague, empty, and lost."[6]

A Sunday article on August 3, 2008, in the *Columbus Dispatch*, entitled "Atheists Bond during 'De-Baptism,'" pictured the national legal director of American Atheists dressed in some sort of ceremonial blue robe trimmed in gold. He was holding a hair dryer over the head of a nine-year-old girl as her mother looked on approvingly. The girl had a big smile and seemed to be enjoying the moment as others lined up to follow her. This was a "de-baptism" service; the hair dryer was as close as they could come to the opposite of water. It was their symbolic way of saying, "We're done with Christianity and now confirm to be nonbelievers." Frank Zindler, president of American Atheists, said the event is held to encourage atheists to come out of the closet so politicians will know of their growing numbers and see them as a group that can no longer be ignored.[7]

Christians are supposed to be silent in the political arena, according to liberals, who proclaim separation of church and state.

The liberals contradict the concept of separation of church and state by embracing atheists, whose political influence is more than welcome by those enthralled with the New Morality and who are willing to use children to accomplish their goals.

The headlines and TV news teasers give alarming reminders that our kids are becoming victims of a New Morality that, as glamorous as it might seem to those easily misguided, holds no true value or benefit for them. Ms. Bruce reminds us of a known fact that we must face, whether we like it or not. What we do today will determine the future of virtue. She writes, "The failure of a culture does not always happen on a battlefield—sometimes a great civilization collapses from within."[8]

Those of us who still connect with the traditional morality should not succumb to gloom and doom. It is not time to raise a white flag. Our kids are worth the fight, and we need to take the fight to the other side. When we consider the world we live in, it might appear that the New Morality, with its postmodern momentum, has seized the day, but it is not without vulnerability, and we are not without opportunity. Our side has won the day in the past; we can do it again if we are willing to fight to take back our culture. Let's guard our kids, and let's rescue those who have been stolen. Let's train others to wage war in a society that targets the most vulnerable.

In this book, we provide you with information and recommendations for actions you can take individually and collectively to help shift the culture from its current moral decline. As I (Carol) stated in my book *Be the People: A Call to Reclaim America's Faith and Promise*, it is time for "We the People" to stand up and take responsibility for the current state of affairs.[9] The decline did not happen overnight, and it will take a concerted effort by all of us to change the course of the nation by battling for the hearts and minds of our children.

CHAPTER 1

The Enemy Revealed

> The great enemy of the truth is very often not the lie—deliberate, contrived, and dishonest—but the myth—persistent, persuasive, and unrealistic.[1]
>
> —John F. Kennedy

There is a saying, "Know your enemy." It is good advice that is heeded by anyone serious about defeating an adversary. A high school football coach always gets a detailed scouting report on his team's next opponent. The team spends time studying film of the upcoming opponent's past games so they can observe their foe in action and identify the opponent's strengths and weaknesses. Preparation must be thorough, whether it is for the next football game or to counter forces looking to steal our children's future by reprogramming their values and beliefs.

Our present-day enemy is the New Morality. It needs to be thoroughly examined so we know what it is, where it came from, what it aims to accomplish, and what will happen if it succeeds. We can begin by defining and clarifying our terms.

Morality is an ethical system based on a philosophy that makes distinctions between right and wrong, and good and bad. People often proclaim, "You can't legislate morality." This is a false statement, because governments legislate morality all the time. Otherwise, we would not have laws banning prostitution, incest, murder, polygamy, and theft. Laws serve as strong deterrents to people who might otherwise contemplate engaging in activities prohibited by civilized society. They also can create an atmosphere of leniency, which influences people who once followed traditional morality to engage in conduct opposed to such standards.

When we refer to traditional morality, we mean the mores, folkways, and morals associated with natural law and a Judeo-Christian biblical worldview with its standards of right and wrong. We associate much of this with natural law.

Natural law is the universal sense of right and wrong that men can discern through human reasoning even without knowledge of the God revealed in the Bible. In Romans 2:14–15, the apostle Paul wrote, "When Gentiles, who do not have the Law [since it was given only to Jews], do instinctively the things the Law requires [guided only by their conscience], they are a law to themselves, though they do not have the Law. They show that the essential requirements of the Law are written in their hearts; and their conscience [their sense of right and wrong, their moral choices] bearing witness and their thoughts alternately accusing or perhaps defending them" (AMP).

The New Morality rejects the idea of absolute right and wrong. According to this belief, which is aligned with liberal political thought, morality is relative, depending on the individuals and cultures involved. Every act and decision must be judged in light of the context and circumstances in which each takes place. It is connected with postmodernism, which argues against an objective reality. In this system, all moral views are relative, and there is no overarching narrative to explain life. Rather, there is a series of narratives, called metanarratives, that form the basis of our reality. The New Morality emerges most prominently from the secular humanism and material naturalist worldviews. Material naturalists, such as the late Bertrand Russell, view human beings as "accidental collocations" of atoms. Its adherents place their faith in science. Scientism permeates academia and has held great sway over some of our US Supreme Court justices and national leaders who preach tolerance as the highest virtue as long as it doesn't pertain to Christianity.

Professor Mary Poplin describes the current metanarrative embraced by much of Western academia and the media. Her description helps explain why the intelligentsia no longer acknowledge God:

> After the Enlightenment, and particularly in the twentieth century, we humans finally matured and no longer needed to socially construct God or gods or any supernatural entities to understand our lives or guide our behaviors. We have now evolved enough to go it on our own, armed only with human reason and scientific evidence to steer the course of progress and break away from limiting rules and regulations.[2]

According to Poplin, the academic and media elite consider secular-humanistic worldviews vastly superior to religious worldviews. This is certainly the dominant worldview that young people encounter in public and private secondary schools and on university campuses in much of the nation. Clearly, we can do a better job of preparing our youth for the onslaught that awaits them. Fortunately, as Poplin demonstrates, the timeless truths of Christianity offer a vastly superior quality of life and source of hope than competing worldviews that often bring suicide, drug abuse, and degradation of minds and bodies.

TRADITIONAL MORALITY'S COLONIAL ROOTS

The New Morality wants to replace traditional morality as our culture's main influence. *Traditional morality* is the term we apply to the moral conscience the nation had when it was established by the Founding Fathers. This traditional morality was a natural extension of the founders' education, religious faith, family values, and personal convictions. It was not something impulsively thought up in the moment simply to "form a more perfect Union." They regarded it as a key foundational stone for the republic they would create, as evidenced by the declaration of independence.

Traditional morality did not emerge out of a vacuum. It was the cultural norm of the day after years of Christian influence, and it was enthusiastically practiced in colonial times. A 1609 charter for the Virginia colony contained these words: "The principle effect which we can desire or expect of this action is the conversion...of the people in those parts unto the true worship of God and Christian religion."[3]

The Massachusetts Charter of 1629 reveals an evangelistic mission for the colony:

> Our said people...be so religiously, peaceable, and civilly governed that their good life and orderly conversation may win and incite the natives of... that country to the knowledge and obedience of the only true God and Savior of mankind, and the Christian faith, which...is the principle of this plantation (colony).[4]

The founders of the colony of Massachusetts, which later became the state of Massachusetts, believed their fellow citizens had a responsibility to convert the Native Americans to Christianity. Today, the only thing our political leaders would help them do is set up a casino.

The 1662 North Carolina Charter expressed a sentiment similar to that of Massachusetts' founders, stating, ...being excited with a laudable and pious zeal for the propagation of the Christian faith.[5] Other colony charters carried expressions that clearly showed their allegiance to Christianity. The colonial documents of the original thirteen colonies give overwhelming evidence that the Christian faith was embraced, practiced, and influential in the daily political operations and culture of the day. As time went on, many colonies formed their governments out of the language that was written in their original charters. Connecticut drafted the "Fundamental Orders of

Connecticut," which was the first constitution written in America. The words in this remarkable document are very revealing:

"Well knowing when a people are gathered together, the word of God requires, that to [maintain] the peace and union of such a people, there should [be] an orderly and decent government established according to God."[6]

These words give us tremendous insight into how our political ancestors conceived of government and the guidelines upon which it should be founded. The words "government established according to God" are quite striking, mainly because they are words that would never be associated with government today; instead, they would likely be stricken from all public records. The American Civil Liberties Union (ACLU) would spend their last dime to make sure of that. Historically, it cannot be denied that the first constitution created on our national soil unashamedly proclaimed that "orderly and decent government" was achieved when it was based on God. To these founders, God was a welcome guest as they formed the framework of their government and their lawmaking.

These sentiments were also expressed in the 1643 New England Confederation that comprised the following colonies: Massachusetts, Connecticut, Plymouth, and New Haven. Their founding document said, "We all came into these parts of America with one and the same end and aim, namely to advance the Kingdom of our Lord Jesus Christ."[7]

As colonies took the next step in formalizing their governing organization, God and faith were not cast to the sidelines. Scholars such as George Marsden have noted that natural law was a belief system that unified Christians and deists.

> Our founders strictly maintained the religious formalities of the day, including the laws requiring church attendance...but the England from which the settlers came was itself a mix of religion and the secular. This after all, was the age of William Shakespeare, whose plays reflected the

sophisticated, Renaissance, this-worldly humanism of the day.[8]

Even the authors of *The Godless Constitution* begrudgingly admit
that the omission of explicit references to God in the Constitution
was not an oversight, but rather the outcome of a long debate between
Christians who wanted God referenced and those who wanted to
keep politics and religion separate. They concede that almost "everyone who participated in the debates about the Constitution shared a
concern about the health of religion."[9]

GOD ONCE COULD GO TO SCHOOL

The colonials were very concerned with education because lit-
eracy was a high priority. They wanted succeeding generations to be
able to read so they could read the Scriptures for themselves. The
Bible was used by many colonial educators as a reading textbook.
The New England Primer was a textbook widely used at the nation's
founding and for some 125 years afterward. It closely ties lessons to
biblical truths and the Scriptures. To study this textbook was to virtually take a Christian catechism.

Residents of the colonies had higher learning as a goal. Colleges
were established; Harvard was the first. During the times of the
Founding Fathers, Harvard was light years removed from what it
is today—a bastion of aggressively liberal thought and culture. A
glimpse into those early years of our nation's first colleges tells much
of what was valued by society and what effect they must have had on
those early students who shaped the culture. The rules for Harvard
students in 1636 included the following:

> Let every student be plainly instructed and ear-
> nestly pressed to consider well the main end of his
> life and studies is to know God and Jesus Christ
> which is eternal life (John 17:3) and therefore to
> lay Christ in the bottom as the only foundation

of all sound knowledge and learning.[10] In 1790, some fourteen years after the Declaration of Independence was signed, the rules still required Harvard students to attend worship services.[11]

Harvard's original motto was "Truth for Christ and the Church."[12] Today its motto is simply "Truth," and it is debatable if that really fits.

These mottos are amazing when contrasted with a twenty-first-century news story about two Harvard coeds who were trying to launch a new student magazine at the school that would feature nude photographs of students, along with articles advocating an acceptance of sexual promiscuity. Of course, they claim it's all protected by free speech.[13]

Such a proposition certainly would have rendered speechless the likes of John Adams, John Hancock, and other Harvard alumni who signed the Declaration of Independence.

Other early American colleges also emphasized the importance of the Christian faith to a proper education. In 1693, the College of William and Mary in Virginia held the following purpose for its students: "The youth may be piously educated in good letters and manners, and that the Christian faith may be propagated."[14] In 1792, William and Mary's rules stated that, "the students shall attend prayers in chapel at the time appointed."[15]

Yale's rules for students in 1787 esteemed a Christian lifestyle: "All the scholars are required to live a religious and blameless life according to the rules of God's Word."[16]

The Dartmouth College charter of 1754 contained some interesting words that mirror those of Yale: "All the scholars are required to live a religious and blameless life according to the rules of God's Word."[17]

In 1754, King's College, which later became known as Columbia University, held a unique admission requirement: "No candidate shall be admitted into the College…unless he shall be able to render into English…the Gospels from Greek…It is also expected that all students attend public worship on Sundays."[18] In America, higher education was once synonymous with religious education. Until the "late 1800s, most universities, even many of the state universities, had mottoes, seals, and buildings embellished with biblical texts."[19] This includes 104 of the nation's first 119 colleges and universities. In 1890, 316 of 415 colleges and universities were affiliated with Christian denominations.[20] Unlike today, the leading voices of that bygone era had biblical knowledge to shape and reinforce the traditional morality that is rapidly crumbling in the wake of the New Morality.

FROM THE MOUTHS OF THE FOUNDERS

Many of the Founding Fathers were graduates of colleges that stressed a Christian character, and their worldview was shaped by the spiritual principles they encountered in these halls of higher learning. They took their faith into the political arena and with them in their fight for liberty. The accounts of today's biased history revisionists are totally bogus when they try to portray the founders as a bunch of deists and atheists who had no fondness for the Christian faith or lacked the desire to have it influence public life.

John Dickinson, a signer of the Constitution and governor of Pennsylvania, leaves no doubt that the founders believed the rights they claimed came to them directly from God:

> Kings or parliaments could not give the rights essential to happiness…We claim them from a higher source—from the King of kings, and the Lord of all the earth. They are not annexed to us by parchments and seals. They are created in us by the decrees of Providence, which establish the laws of our nature.[21]

John Quincy Adams responded to a criticism that Americans were being swept away in anarchy by declaring that laws of a higher power were providing guidance:

The people of the North America union, and
of its constituent states, were associated bodies
of civilized men and [Christians], in a state of
nature, but not of anarchy. They were bound by
the laws of God, which they all, and by the laws
of the gospel, which they nearly all, acknowledged as the rules of their conduct.[22]

The words of Mr. Adams do not seem to be those you would
expect from a deist or atheist.

The religious fervor of Americans, as it pertained to government, had an irritating effect on the British. Sir Richard Sutton read
in Parliament a copy of a letter from a Crown-appointed governor
in the colonies. The letter contained the complaint of the governor,
who said when you ask an American, "Who is your master?" the
answer is, "He has none, nor any governor but Jesus Christ."[23]

Patrick Henry gave his famous speech, in which he shouted,
"Give me liberty or give me death!" Few know that in that same
oration, he also made direct reference to God, calling on His help in
the approaching war with the British.[24] A national leader making a
similar plea to deity today might be labeled a religious fanatic.

During the colonial era, deists worked with devout Christians
to achieve shared goals. The word *deist* comes from *deus*, the Latin
word for *god*. It connotes a belief in God based on rational reason,
rather than a need and belief in a supernatural being involved in
the day-to-day affairs of men. God is seen as a watchmaker who set
everything in motion and then abandoned His own creation.

Thomas Paine, the author of *The Age of Reason*, is one of the
more famous deists who openly denigrated Christianity, even though
he frequently quoted the Bible and its stories in his other writings.
Likewise, Thomas Jefferson and Benjamin Franklin, both widely recognized as deists, pushed for an American seal that would illustrate
important moments in the Bible, such as Moses's parting the Red Sea
and the children of Israel being led by a cloud by day and a pillar of
fire by night.[25]

Clearly, our nation was founded, shaped, and guided by men who knew the Bible and saw religious faith as a positive force for our society. Because of these men's education, training, and faith, the nation did not immediately stray from its biblical roots. It would take a series of US Supreme Court decisions to set the stage for the New Morality.

BIBLES AND CONGRESS

During the Revolutionary War, some uniforms even testified to the faith in God that American patriots held. The state of Massachusetts formed its own navy during the war and stated how the uniform for officers was to look:

> Resolved, that the uniform of the officers be green,
> and that they furnish themselves accordingly, and
> the colors be a white flag with a green pine tree
> and the inscription, "Appeal to Heaven."[26]

Can you believe that was from, of all places, the state of Massachusetts, which is now one of the most liberal states in the nation? An inscription with the words *Appeal to Heaven* actually appeared on a military uniform. This is from the same state that in recent years led the charge for same-sex marriage and endorsed the liberal agenda, demanding separation of church and state wherever it could be proclaimed.

In an incredible story from the Revolutionary War, Congress, in September 1777, ordered twenty thousand Bibles from Europe for the Continental soldiers because not enough copies could be found across the colonies.[27]

On October 12, 1778, the Continental Congress passed a resolution clearly stating it regarded religion and good morals as essential to a sound foundation for good government and recommending the various states should take note of the same:

Whereas true religion and good morals are the only solid foundations of public liberty and happiness: *Resolved*, That it be, and it is hereby earnestly recommended to the several states, to take the most effectual measures for encouragement thereof.[28]

In 1789, at the request of both houses of Congress, President George Washington issued a proclamation for "a day of public thanksgiving and prayer to be observed by acknowledging with grateful hearts the many signal favors of Almighty God especially by affording them an opportunity peaceably to establish a form of government for their safety and happiness."[29]

Interest in making the Bible more readily available to the people was again taken on by Congress. In January 1781, Robert Aitken, publisher of *The Pennsylvania Magazine*, petitioned Congress to sanction a publication of the Bible he was preparing at his own expense. Aitken said the Bible would be "a neat edition of the Holy Scriptures for the use of schools,"[30] and Congress seemed to agree. After inspecting Aitken's Bible project, Congress said it "highly" approved "the pious and laudable undertaking of Mr. Aitken, as subservient to the interest of religion as well as an instance of the progress of the arts in this country."[31]

Such an action would have no chance today. It would be attacked as a violation of the mythical separation of church and state, a topic we deal with in more detail in a later chapter. When the Bible was printed and ready to be circulated, it had a page that bore the endorsement of the Congress:

Whereupon, Resolved, That the United States in Congress assembled...being satisfied from the above report, of his care and accuracy in the execution of the work they recommend this edition of the Bible to the inhabitants of the United States.[32]

HERE COMES THE NEW MORALITY

Yes, in our history as a nation, we had a Congress that proudly endorsed a printed edition of the Bible. In light of this, how can anyone minimize the Christian heritage of our nation? The colonial history, the early educational institutions, key phrases in the Declaration of Independence, and the acts of the Continental Congress all gave clear reference to God and Christianity. It is not surprising that a traditional morality emerged in the nation solidly Christian in its origin. This traditional morality shaped the culture and values of a young nation as it expanded and grew over the ensuing decades. It was never seriously challenged until the mid-twentieth century, when a formidable system of contrariness emerged, the New Morality—an enemy within.

This New Morality encompasses a number of groups, movements, and ideologies united against the traditional morality and sharing a desire to weaken traditional morality's influence on society. The major distinction between the traditional morality and the New Morality is their respective center bases. The traditional morality is based on a belief in God; the New Morality does not believe in God or a Supreme Being—it believes instead in man as ruler of his own domain with his experience and knowledge. The traditional morality believes that because there is a God, there are absolutes and standards. The New Morality does not believe there are any absolutes; for it, there are no divine standards in place to affect morality.

In the traditional morality, life is the result of a Creator who esteems human life above all other life, for man's life is created with an eternal soul and made in the image of the Creator. In the New Morality, life exists because of random chance. Even though man may, at this moment in time, be the highest life-form on the planet, he is of no greater distinction than any other life-form that walks, swims, flies, or slithers on this earth.

As the beliefs and values of each of these two moralities are studied, simplistic is replaced by realistic. The great German philosopher Immanuel Kant wrote, "Two things fill the mind with ever new and increasing admiration and awe, the oftener and the more steadily we reflect on them: the starry heavens above and the moral law within."[33]

The New Morality does not believe that a moral law exists within a person. If there is no God, how could there be a moral law within? The founders believed in the inner moral law and believed it to be critical to the success of the republic they established. The moral law within—about which Kant wrote—is a constraining factor on the behavior of man. To believe it does not exist allows man to become devoted to his own selfish desires, lacking boundaries, lacking concern for others, willing to trample upon anyone in order to get what he wants.

HUMANISM, FORCE OF THE NEW MORALITY

The championing forces behind the New Morality are humanism and material naturalism. Humanism is the philosophy and intellectual thought system that powers the New Morality; material naturalism argues that only scientifically verified statements offer valid truth claims. Everything about man is the result of an accidental set of atoms that determines the reality he experiences. Science is the only reality that matters.[34] The beliefs of humanism are clearly stated in *The Humanist Manifesto I*, which was written in 1933: "Religious humanists regard the universe as self-existing and not created. Humanism asserts that the nature of the universe depicted by modern science makes unacceptable any supernatural or cosmic guarantees of human values."[35]

The New Morality devalues human life. Have you ever played out the logic of this major distinction between the two moralities— the Creator and the "by chance" issue? Pretend for a moment that humanism is true and life has come about by chance. Darwin is correct (still pretending), and man has emerged simply from the evolutionary process as the dominant life-form. Man would be the top dog, but he still would be a dog. He would not trace his origin back to God, the Supreme Creator. There would be no divine standard, no God-established absolutes to obey. In this existence, life is what you make it while you are alive, because once this life is over, that's all there is.

If this were true, then abortion would be no big thing. The same goes for euthanasia. Putting Grandpa down like you did Rover when he got sick would be well within the realm of acceptability. I (Steve) watched my mother suffer from the effects of Alzheimer's disease. I would visit her in the nursing home, and she would not know who I was. She had no quality of life. Little by little, she was dying, and nothing was going to change that. Every day she stayed alive in her apparent misery, she consumed resources. And some in our society would even say that she had no real right to go on living. When she finally died, I did not feel a sense of loss because that already had been felt years earlier. She, however, held the sanctity of life given to her by God, and God alone would decide when her life would end, not me—and certainly not some bureaucrat.

Humanism leads us to conclude that we should discard the weak and senile. In this view, there is no reason for someone like this to continue to live. We might even say it is our duty to euthanize people who are suffering, Dr. Kevorkian style. As the New Morality gains more influence and humanism increasingly becomes the prevailing thought of the day, that coldhearted reality comes ever closer.

We see glimpses of this reality already in the form of the Affordable Care Act—known to many as Obamacare. Government-designated bureaucrats now have the power of life and death in their hands. Think of the implications: when an elderly person has a terminal health condition and the federal budget is tight, the government actually has a financial incentive *not* to keep that person alive. Only an underlying moral conviction of the worth of human life would motivate us to do the right thing for him or her. Increasing government control of our health care system puts the lives of the weakest in the crosshairs of a political bureaucracy. If we allow secular humanism to win the day, the results will be dire.

We have every reason to be concerned about where the New Morality leads. In America, we see a disregard for human life at every stage of development, particularly at the beginning and ending stages of life. Unless we revive and reinvigorate traditional morality, there will be nothing that can stop us from following the slippery slope of euthanasia and physician-assisted suicide. This grisly reality is already claiming healthy bodies in formerly Roman Catholic nations, such as Belgium and the Netherlands.[36]

THE BASIS OF LAW

The contrasting concepts of "by God" or "by chance" have an effect on law. After all, the big question is, "What is law based upon?" The Founding Fathers believed law was based upon God. The following quotes verify this:

Samuel Adams: "In the supposed state of nature, all men are equally bound by the laws of nature, or to speak more properly, the laws of the Creator."[37]

John Quincy Adams: "The laws of nature and of nature's God...of course presupposes the existence of a God, the moral ruler of the universe, and a rule of right and wrong, of just and unjust, binding upon man, preceding all institutions of human society and of government."[38]

Alexander Hamilton: "The law of nature, 'which, being coeval with mankind, and dictated by God himself, is, of course, superior in obligation to any other. It is binding over all the globe, in all countries, and at all times. No human laws are of any validity, if contrary to this.'"[39]

James Wilson (signer of the Constitution and a Supreme Court justice): "In compassion to the imperfection of our internal powers, our all gracious Creator, Preserver, and Ruler has been pleased to discover and enforce his laws, by a revelation given to us immediately and directly from himself. This revelation is contained in the holy scriptures."[40]

The founders saw law as descending from God, which they felt was a protection for mankind. If law and rights came from God, then what person or man-made system could take them away? Hamilton actually believed that no human laws had any value if they were in conflict with the natural law given by God. James Wilson, a Supreme Court justice, implied that law should harmonize with the Holy Scriptures. Do you think he could get a seat on the bench today?

If law is not based on God, then what is the alternative that the New Morality offers? Humanism and the New Morality have ushered in the age of sociological law. Francis A. Schaeffer, in his book *A Christian Manifesto*, gives an accurate description of it:

> By sociological law we mean law that has no fixed base but law in which a group of people decides what is sociologically good for society at the given moment; and what they arbitrarily decide becomes law.[41]

There is "no fixed base" for law. Law is just what a bunch of people in some legislatures say it is, backed up by a smaller bunch of lawyers in robes who concur. It traces back to no grand standard, no divine decree. This is the New Morality. What Schaeffer describes is exactly how liberal politicians see law today.

Abortion and same-sex marriage may be in total conflict with God's standards as presented in Scripture, but for liberals and the New Morality crowd, gaining acceptance for something that is contrary to God's law is just a matter of making a new law or getting a court decision in their favor. This is why things that many of us never thought we would see in our lifetime are happening. Things such as same-sex marriage, assisted suicide of the terminally ill, polygamy, even softening attitudes toward allowing sex between adults and children if a child does indeed consent—all of these are just a law away.

We have arrived at a time when those who are making the laws and interpreting them often have no regard for the godly standard the founders proclaimed and upon which those laws were based. Again, it's a slippery slope. We have seen same-sex marriage and abortion legalized. Already there are legal challenges demanding the legalization of polygamy, which many see as the next frontier for marriage.[42] Who knows what we'll see next?

The Founding Fathers knew that the freedoms they desired for the nation and its people could lead to chaos if they had no logical constraints. They wanted freedom, but they also gave it form. The form was the law. We were to be a nation of law, and the laws were to be made with the input of the people guided by the foundation of law, which the founders pointed out in numerous ways and on many occasions to be God.

The America we have today, with its New Morality and rampant socialism, is no accident. It has been decades in the making. On June 10, 1963, Rep. A. S. Herlong Jr. read forty-five Communist goals into the *Congressional Record of the Eighty-Eighth Congress.*[43] These numbered goals can be looked up on microfilm or found by a simple Internet search. Most interesting for understanding the New Morality are goals fifteen through thirty-two. Herlong copied the goals from Cleon Skousen's *The Naked Communist,* written in 1958.[44] Mr. Skousen, a former FBI agent and Brigham Young University professor, lectured widely on the Constitution and on faith-based topics related to Mormonism.[45]

Although some liberals have sought to discredit Skousen's sources, just reading these goals today makes him seem prophetic. Here are goals fifteen through thirty-two:

15. Capture one or both of the political parties in the United States.

16. Use technical decisions of the courts to weaken basic American institutions by claiming their activities violate civil rights.

17. Get control of the schools. Use them as transmission belts for socialism and current Communist propaganda. Soften the curriculum. Get control of teachers' associations. Put the party line in textbooks.

18. Gain control of all student newspapers.

19. Use student riots to foment public protests against programs or organizations which are under Communist attack.

20. Infiltrate the press. Get control of book-review assignments, editorial writing, policymaking positions.

21. Gain control of key positions in radio, TV, and motion pictures.

22. Continue discrediting American culture by degrading all forms of artistic expression. An American Communist cell was told to "eliminate all good sculpture from parks and buildings, substitute shapeless, awkward and meaningless forms."

23. Control art critics and directors of art museums. "Our plan is to promote ugliness, repulsive, meaningless art."

24. Eliminate all laws governing obscenity by calling them "censorship" and a violation of free speech and free press.

25. Break down cultural standards of morality by promoting pornography and obscenity in books, magazines, motion pictures, radio, and TV.

26. Present homosexuality, degeneracy, and promiscuity as "normal, natural, healthy."

27. Infiltrate the churches and replace revealed religion with "social" religion. Discredit the Bible and emphasize the need for intellectual maturity which does not need a "religious crutch."

28. Eliminate prayer or any phase of religious expression in the schools on the ground that it violates the principle of "separation of church and state."

29. Discredit the American Constitution by calling it inadequate, old-fashioned, out of step with modern needs, a hindrance to cooperation between nations on a worldwide basis.

30. Discredit the American Founding Fathers. Present them as selfish aristocrats who had no concern for the "common man."

31. Belittle all forms of American culture and discourage the teaching of American history on the ground that it was only a minor part of the "big picture." Give more emphasis to Russian history since the Communists took over.

32. Support any socialist movement to give cen-
tralized control over any part of the culture—
education, social agencies, welfare programs,
mental health clinics, etc.

If we take the time to study history and trace the decline of
our nation, we can see what has motivated and energized the New
Morality.[46] When we look at the individuals currently running our
national government and making our laws, we often find the disillu-
sioned hippies and radicals of the 1960s, only now with gray hair and
without the bell bottoms. But more importantly, we see the results
of their rejection of religious principles as the foundation of political
law.

JUST A MATTER OF JUDGMENT

The fact is, we human beings need some restraint on our
behavior. Paradoxically, it is when we are unrestrained that we are no
longer truly free. This is because freedom that allows expression in
action with little or no responsibility leads to chaos. Law that is based
only on the current fad or feelings of contemporary political leaders will not prevent freedom from drifting into dark self-indulgence.
Schaeffer clearly warns of this:

> The humanists push for "freedom," but having
> no Christian consensus to contain it, that "free-
> dom" leads to chaos or to slavery under the state
> (or under an elite). Humanism, with its lack of
> any final base for values or law, always leads to
> chaos.[47]

Frederick Moore Vinson is a former chief justice of the Supreme
Court who died in 1953 and is credited with stating his belief that
"Nothing is more certain in modern society than the principle that
there are no absolutes."[48] I wonder how he and Justice James Wilson

would have gotten along. Their basis of law and concept of morality are worlds apart.

We are in the midst of a war of these worlds. The man who championed the "no absolutes" concept for the New Morality is Joseph Fletcher, who wrote *Situation Ethics* in 1966. Fletcher's book is to the New Morality what the Sermon on the Mount is to the Christian faith. The basic principle of Fletcher's book is that "there is nothing which is universally right or universally wrong; there is nothing which is intrinsically good or intrinsically bad."[49]

No clear right or wrong, nothing intrinsically good or bad? To some ears, that sounds liberating. But nothing could be further from the truth. No absolutes, no set standards; it is all just a matter of judgment. Morality based on human judgment is a free-for-all, because who is to say that one person's judgment is any better than anyone else's?

Take, for example, the following judgment that came out of one of our nation's courts. In February 2002, Judge Conliffe of Jefferson County Circuit Court in Louisville, Kentucky, dismissed (as in "threw out") murder charges against defendant Monica Berger. And what had Monica done? She had stabbed her two-year-old son to death with a butcher knife. The judge's reasoning for dismissal was that poor Monica was actually mentally ill because she had stopped taking her Addison's disease medication. In fact, this disease affects the adrenal glands, causing fatigue, muscle weakness, loss of appetite except for cravings for salty foods, and sometimes depression and irritability, but not insanity.[50]

You and I might hear that story and think, *That's simply wrong.* But the New Morality asks us to consider the case not in terms of absolute right and wrong but in terms of relative circumstances—the situational ethics. Even murder is not a simple moral question for the New Morality crowd; at least, it wasn't when it came to mother Monica. The New Morality compels us to give more weight to the situation, the circumstances, and the various factors that come into play. You may have heard of "no-fault divorce." With these people, you get "no-fault life."

THE END JUSTIFIES THE MEANS

Situational ethics might sound progressive, modern, or intelligent. It might cause some people to feel smarter or more open-minded. But, in fact, it puts all of virtue in jeopardy. Where is the motivation for integrity, honesty, fidelity, and responsibility? Situational ethics ushers in an attitude of "the end justifies the means." Think about it. If one feels in his judgment that his cause or goal is in the best interest of others, or if he has rationalized that it is a benefit he himself deserves, then anything he does to achieve it is okay.

If you have to lie to gain an advantage in a business deal that will benefit your company, then no problem; lie. If you have to enact voter fraud to win an election for your party, no biggie; just do it. If you have to sleep with the boss to get the promotion, no sweat; make the hotel reservation. If you have to bend the lines of decency to produce a trashy film in order to make millions, then bend away.

Situational ethics in combination with sociological law is a dangerous mixture. It is not what the Founding Fathers had in mind. I remember being amused in 2004 when presidential candidate (and liberal favorite) Howard Dean, then the governor of Vermont, campaigned with the slogan "Let's take our country back."[51] The country, in its culture and values, had already largely moved toward the New Morality. If anyone should use the words "Take our country back," it should be those connected to the traditional morality.

A CHOICE

There are many powerful and influential people in America today who want you to believe that the Founding Fathers' original intent was to establish a purely secular government in which neither Christianity nor any other religion would have an influence on public policy, culture, life, or law of the nation. But history doesn't support their version of the events.

George Washington gave his inaugural address on April 30, 1789. His speech did not indicate that secularism had arrived in the United States of America:

> It would be peculiarly improper to omit, in this first official act, my fervent supplications to that Almighty Being who rules over the universe—who presides in the councils of nations—and whose providential aids can supply every human defect…No people can be bound to acknowledge and adore the invisible hand which conducts the affairs of men, more than those of the United States. Every step by which they have advanced to the character of an independent nation seems to have been distinguished by some token of providential agency… We ought to be no less persuaded that the propitious smiles of Heaven can never be expected on a nation that disregards the eternal rules of order and right, which Heaven itself has ordained.[52]

In his first official act as president, Washington paid tribute to the Almighty Being and recognized Him as one who "presides in the councils of nations." This does not sound like someone who advocated a secular government void of any influence from God. These are not the words of an atheist. After his address, Washington and the newly elected Congress went to a planned worship service that was arranged by the Senate.[53] Apparently, the first senators were not progressive enough to realize they were violating the Constitution that many of them helped to establish.

At the end of his second term, Washington gave his farewell address and proved once again that God was a welcome guest in the nation's government:

> Of all the dispositions and habits which lead to political prosperity, religion and morality are

indispensable supports. In vain would that man claim the tribute of patriotism, who should labor to subvert these great pillars of human happiness...The mere politician...ought to respect and to cherish them. A volume could not trace all their connections with private and public felicity. Let it simply be asked, where is the security for property, for reputation, for life, if the sense of religious obligation desert...? And let us with caution indulge the supposition that morality can be maintained without religion. Whatever may be conceded to the influence of refined education on minds...reason and experience both forbid us to expect that national morality can prevail, in exclusion of religious principle.[54]

Our first president stated that religion and morality are necessary for political prosperity and that religion is the basis for security of property, reputation, and life. These words prove religion was highly valued by Washington and that it was both practical and welcomed in political life. Liberal politicians of today who embrace the New Morality are actively working against the sentiments expressed by Washington. On September 25, 1789, Congress requested President Washington to proclaim a national day of thanksgiving and prayer:

Resolved, That a joint committee of both Houses be directed to wait upon the President of the United States, to request that he would recommend to the people of the United States a day of public thanksgiving and prayer, to be observed by acknowledging with grateful hearts, the many signal favors of Almighty God, especially by affording them an opportunity peaceably to establish a Constitution of government for their safety and happiness.[55]

On October 3, 1789, Washington gave the proclamation, and his words were profound:

> Whereas it is the duty of all nations to acknowledge the Providence of Almighty God, to obey His will, to be grateful for His benefits, and humbly to implore His protection and favor.[56]

President Washington claimed it the duty of all nations to acknowledge God and to obey Him. You think the mainstream media had trouble with George W. Bush's Christian faith? They would choke on their own disdain for the first George W. Where was the ACLU on that first inaugural day? Why didn't they ensure the separation of church and state? Why was this proclamation allowed? The simple answer is that no one alive at the time considered it unconstitutional.

The Congress and the president worked together to establish a day to give tribute to the blessing of God on the nation. In so doing, they did not provoke any opposition that said such an act was unconstitutional. Many of those who helped write and ratify the Constitution were the ones who affirmed the action. They evidently saw no conflict with the Constitution, so why do the judges today have a problem with it?

When Jefferson was president, the United States agreed to a treaty with the Kaskaskia Indians that included an annual salary for a Catholic missionary priest and funds for a church building.[57] Remember that the Senate must approve treaties, and they approved this one and others that were similar. Can you imagine the outrage from the political Left if something like this were tried today? For our Founding Fathers, it was just another day at the office. Other historical evidence reveals that the Founding Fathers saw no conflict with religion and government and desired no real separation between the two, as the liberal Left of the New Morality does today.

The Constitution does prohibit the establishment of a national church, but it was never intended to separate religious faith from political life. The original intent of the founders is made clear by their words and actions. The Founding Fathers are on record, over and over again, confirming that religious faith not only forms the moral basis of our Constitution, but also is critical to our ability to endure as a free society.

KIDS ARE THE TARGET

We have come a long way since Washington's inaugural address. The line is drawn. The cultural war is on: traditional morality versus the New Morality; law based on God versus law based on convenience of man; morals based on absolutes versus situational ethics; a Creator versus a world formed by chance. It is a war of ideas, and the territory to be won is the minds of the people. Adherents of the New Morality have chosen a strategy that, with the ally of time and opportunity, has served them well. The target of their evil intent is our children. They target the minds that are vulnerable because these young minds are still in the process of forming their values, ideology, and worldview.

It's all about political power. If the Left can win over our kids, they will control the culture and use it in a way that strengthens their hold on political power. This is not a new strategy. It has been employed by two notorious despots of the past. Adolf Hitler said, "He alone, who owns the youth, gains the future."[58] Joseph Stalin's take on education echoed this same sentiment when he stated, "Education is a weapon the effect of which is determined by the hands which wield it."[59]

The Founding Fathers knew how important education was for maintaining liberty in the future. They wanted it to be used for propagating the nation's foundational Judeo-Christian values and the principles of freedom. The nation now has been put at risk, as the Left has flipped this emphasis through taking control of public education. Chapter 3 will deal in depth with this issue.

The New Morality has succeeded in getting God expelled from schools at all levels. The expulsion of God from our schools may have benefited the liberal Left politically, but it has not benefited the country. Anne Graham Lotz, daughter of evangelist Billy Graham, appeared on CBS's *The Early Show* two days after the 9/11 attacks in 2001. The interviewer, Jane Clayson, asked Lotz to explain the difficulty people would have in keeping their faith in light of the horrible event. Lotz responded:

> For years we've been telling God to get out of our schools, to get out of our government, and to get out of our lives. And being the gentleman He is, I believe He has calmly backed out. How can we expect God to give us His blessing and His protection if we demand He leave us alone?[60]

The proponents of the New Morality peddle their moral bankruptcy under the guise of free thinking and open-mindedness, most conspicuously in our schools and colleges. God is ignored and often even ridiculed. Then tragedy strikes, and people look at God and say, "Why?" If we desire and value the blessing and protection of God, like our founders did, then the nation needs to do an about-face and come back to God.

The Left, with the New Morality, is stealing our kids and controlling the culture. If this continues, they will steer the nation toward disaster. The New Morality is a formidable enemy, but we can fight back against it. This fight will be challenging to parents, grandparents, and all who desire to see our youth embrace the heritage on which the founders built this country; but our kids are worth it. As the New Morality advances in our culture, we are seeing the death of decency and the vanquishing of virtue. We dare not stand back and do nothing.

MAKING A DIFFERENCE: CONSERVATIVE WEBSITES

The Internet has created an opportunity for voices to be heard that the mainstream media can't silence. There are some great websites that are operated by conservative organizations and some that have been founded by individuals who want to make a difference and push back against liberalism. A simple Google search ("conservative websites") can link you to many of these sites. We have provided a few important ones below, but there are many more. In any event, the consumer must be cautious and double-check the sources whenever possible. There are parody websites and articles that get shared and discussed as if they were true. The sources we list below do an excellent job of documenting the topics discussed:

> www.breitbart.com
> www.drudgereport.com
> www.frc.org
> www.heritage.org
> www.hotair.com
> www.humanevents.com
> www.michellemalkin.com
> www.nationalreview.com
> www.redstate.com
> www.theweeklystandard.com
> www.townhall.com
> www.winst.org
> www.worldmag.com

I (Carol) believe it is critically important to understand what the political Left finds important. In addition to perusing the *Wall Street Journal*, the *Washington Times*, and *The Economist*, I believe it is crucial for informed people to read *The New York Times*, the *Washington Post*, and other major news sources. Although you might not agree with their editorial stances, you will get a firm understanding of how the other side presents and supports its arguments. On many of these issues, the truth lies between the liberal and conservative viewpoints. On all these issues, we seek the biblical worldview.

TAKE ACTION

- Educate yourself about current events. Subscribe to organizational newsletters that can help you stay informed.
- Identify who in your community is working for positive societal changes, and give them your support.
- Learn the tactics of the political Left by reading Saul D. Alinsky's *Rules for Radicals*.
- Use your time, resources, and passion to work with like-minded people to develop strategies for regaining lost ground.

CHAPTER 2

Exposing the Myth

Congress shall make no law respecting an establishment of religion, or prohibiting the free exercise thereof; or abridging the freedom of speech, or of the press; or the right of the people peaceably to assemble, and to petition the Government for a redress of grievances.

—The Constitution of the
United States, First Amendment

A general Dissolution of Principles and Manners will more surely overthrow the Liberties of America than the whole Force of the Common Enemy.[1]

—Samuel Adams

A core strategy of the New Morality is to target kids. If kids can be convinced to embrace the New Morality, they will gradually grow to adulthood with humanistic values and situational ethics entrenched in their minds. The best place to get at the kids is where they are: in school. In this chapter, we will examine the concept of separation of church and state and its inroads into the education system.

Before the New Morality could hit schools with impact, it needed some credibility. They solved the problem by distorting view of the US Constitution, from which they concocted the concept of a separation of church and state, woven whole cloth from a faulty interpretation of the First Amendment's Establishment Clause ("Congress shall make no law respecting an establishment of religion"). Eminent scholars have documented that the founders "understood from the very beginning that the new country was to be a Christian nation,"[2] undergirded by a morality based on biblical traditions.

TARGET CHRISTIANITY

Separation of church and state is a cardinal doctrine for the New Morality. It is as important to them as the Virgin Birth is to Christianity. From the time of the Founding Fathers clear through the mid-1900s, schools had always had a positive and cooperative relationship with Christianity and its values. Proponents of the New Morality knew that in order to be a prevailing force in the schools, they would have to neutralize, or preferably eliminate, the influence of Christianity from the schools. If a newly manufactured concept of separation of church and state could be foisted on the public and pollute the culture, the New Morality would be armed with the weapon that would make it the meanest bully in school.

H. L. Mencken, a political writer prominent in the 1930s and 1940s, once wrote, "Honor is simply the morality of superior men."[3] Mencken embraced atheism and was not shy in his verbal attacks on Christianity. The meaning of his quote is that those in power have the privilege of shaping morality to their liking. If you are not governed by a higher principle, then ultimately "might makes right." Saul Alinsky, the father of left-wing community organizing, advised his adherents to use radical tactics to foment change. Infiltration, manipulation, and deception were Alinsky's preferred strategies for revolutionaries. Alinsky advised would-be revolutionaries to clothe their actions with moral garments.[4] In truth, the New Morality was set in motion decades before Alinsky arrived on the scene.

The New Morality crowd tries to sell their concept of separation of church and state as a constitutional truth. They try to proclaim it as the original design of the Founding Fathers. Nothing could be further from the truth. In 1883, Supreme Court Justice Joseph Story III offered an interpretation of the First Amendment's Establishment Clause that refutes those who argue that America was founded as a secular nation with a rigid wall between church and state:

> The real object of the amendment was, not to countenance, much less to advance Mahometanism [Islam], or Judaism, or infidelity, by prostrating Christianity; but to exclude all rivalry among Christian sects, and to prevent any national ecclesiastical establishment, which should give to a hierarchy the exclusive patronage of the national government. It thus cut off the means of religious persecution, (the vice and pest of former ages,) and of the subversion of the rights of conscience in matters of religion, which had been trampled upon almost from the days of the Apostles to the present age.[5]

As I (Carol) stated in *Be the People*,

> Certainly Justice Story's understanding of the purpose of the First Amendment was a much-closer rendering than (and superior to) that of groups such as the Secular Coalition of America or the Americans United for the Separation of Church and State, which maintain that the Constitution requires a strict separation of religion and politics necessary to ensure religious freedom for all faiths.[6]

Despite a unified and concerted effort, the liberal Left does not need to convince the majority of the American people that their take on this issue is right; they merely need to persuade enough judges to agree with them.

The New Morality's separation of church and state is nothing more than a rewrite of history combined with a sophisticated marketing plan. The traditional morality regards the concept of separation of church and state, as held by the New Morality, a falsehood. This issue is an important one. The traditional morality believes the nation was established on sound moral, religious principles that were to have enduring influence on life and law. The New Morality wants no religious influence on life and law in the country. To gain the upper hand on this issue today, one side must win the battle of history, and history is where we must go to fully understand this controversy.

When we study the history on this issue of separation of church and state, we need to realize the crux of the issue. The New Morality and its liberal Left politicos want to prove that the Founding Fathers envisioned a secular government and designed a Constitution that restricted the influence of religion in any form or fashion on public affairs. Religion should not to be taught or referred to in public schools, they claim. It should not be connected to any national motto, pledge of allegiance to a flag, national holiday, or public governmental practice; and it should not be referred to in or on any government building or display. The New Morality crowd contends that the founders wanted a purely secular government, devoid of any religious influence, especially Christianity. For them, the First Amendment created a wall to prevent religion from touching government.

THE HEART OF THE DEBATE

The traditional morality looks at history and comes to an entirely different conclusion. It believes that the "establishing clause" in the First Amendment—"Congress shall make no law respecting an establishment of religion"—refers to preventing the government from declaring a particular sect or denomination as the official national church, like Britain had with the Church of England. The amendment's next phrase—"or prohibiting the free exercise thereof"—was seen as a restriction on Congress, preventing it from being intrusive on the practices of religion. If there were any wall, it was not a wall to keep religion from influencing government and its subsequent policies, but a wall to keep government from interfering in the free exercise of religion.

The interpretation of what is meant by "establishment of religion" is at the heart of the controversy. The New Morality takes it to mean any reference or tribute to a religion or practice of any part of a religious activity. Thus, for them, a moment of silence at the start of a school day is unacceptable, because it could appear to be a suggestion for those believing in prayer to pray at this time. Yes, they do go that far.

The traditional morality believes that the "establishment of religion" pertains to Congress not officially sanctioning a particular denomination as the national church, giving it preferred status among all other denominations. Prohibiting this action was not regarded as a desire to remove all influence of religion on the operations of government and public life. The fact that no one denomination would receive national preference did not preclude religion from playing a valued and welcome role in the development of life, culture, and law in the nation.

These two conflicting views are at the heart of the debate regarding separation of church and state. What really should decide this debate is the original intent of those who wrote the First Amendment when it was first adopted. The question is, who has history on their side? You would think that a careful examination of history would put the matter to rest. It is more complicated than that. The New Morality group and its Left-leaning legions have become quite skilled at spinning the news to gain favorable opinion for their viewpoints. Guess what? They do the same thing when it comes to history. This should not be a surprise. After all, history is just news of years gone by. If you can spin the present, it shouldn't take much more effort to spin the past.

Alexis de Tocqueville was a French political thinker and historian who came to America in the 1830s to observe how it functioned as a democratic country. At that point in history, a functioning, democratically elected government was a relatively new concept. Tocqueville wanted to know why the representative republic form of government in America was working while the attempt of democracy in France was failing. To his surprise, he found that the link Americans had to their spiritual faith was a key factor to the nation's success. He observed a national morality prevailing in the country, as is evident in his words, "Liberty cannot be established without morality, nor morality without faith."[7] To a nineteenth-century Frenchman, the value of the Christian heritage of America was obvious; but today, Americans in the liberal Left seek to attack that heritage with vengeance. They even deny that such a heritage exists. The New Morality has voiced the words "separation of church and state" loudly and often, as if such were printed on the national currency. Some surveys have revealed that two-thirds of Americans believe that these words are found in the Constitution. You might be surprised to learn that the words "separation of church and state" do not appear in the Constitution or in any official documents related to the establishment of the United States of America.

The New Morality's approach to history on this matter is similar to the way the mainstream media approaches the present: research the subject, take the parts that seem to support your desired results, proclaim these parts as the final word on the issue, and simply ignore the rest. If, perchance, you uncover information that appears not to benefit your cause and it cannot be concealed, then spin it to the nth degree. The New Morality believes that distorting truth or presenting falsehoods constantly over time will one day result in those distortions being regarded as truth by impressionable minds.

GETTING IT WRONG

The New Morality went into history in search of a champion for its so-called "separation of church and state" claims. They believe they found one in the third president of the United States, Thomas Jefferson, writer of the Declaration of Independence. He emerges as the man the New Morality sees as the Founding Father who gave them the historical proof to substantiate their claim that a totally secular government was the will of the founders.

When Jefferson was elected president, he received a letter from the Baptist Association of Danbury, Connecticut, that conveyed positive sentiments on his election and presented a concern. The Danbury Baptists were concerned that religious rights they had might be regarded as granted by the State and not as unalienable rights from God. Their words to Jefferson state this: "But, sir, our constitution of government is not specific...Therefore what religious privileges we enjoy (as a minor part of the State) we enjoy as favors granted, and not as inalienable rights."[8]

The Constitution in the First Amendment proclaims "free exercise" of religion. The Danbury Baptists were calling for a point of clarification because they feared that it might be interpreted that the State (federal government) could change this free exercise of religion if it, indeed, decided that this liberty was a right based on governmental policy. In essence, the Baptists were asking, "Can the government intrude in our religious activity in the future?" They also had a concern that, as a minority denomination, they could be at a disadvantage if another denomination was chosen by the government as a national church. It is quite clear that they were asking, "What reach does the government have into religion?" and not, "What restrictions are on religion regarding its involvement in public life and government activity?"

This distinction is significant because today's advocates of a strict separation of church and state have used Jefferson's response to the Danbury Baptists' letter as the all-important document proving their belief, even though they actually flip-flop the concern of the letter. The Baptists feared the intrusiveness of a strong government, whereas the secularists of the New Morality want to turn the emphasis to religion not being allowed any influence on government policy or activity.

Jefferson's response to the Baptists contained a phrase that stated his understanding of why the Constitution declared that Congress could not make a law that would establish a national religion or any law that would prohibit the free exercise of religion. That phrase was "thus building a wall of separation between Church and State."[9] This one phrase, from a response to an inquiry letter—by itself hardly a heralded document on the scale of the Declaration of Independence or the Constitution—is what the New Morality hangs its mythical doctrine of "separation of church and state" upon. They point to the "wall" Jefferson referred to as what needs to ever stand to prevent religion from touching any part of government and public policy. They got it all wrong! The "wall" in Jefferson's mind was not to prevent religion from touching government but to prevent government from entering into a religion's activity.

Since this is the case, then why do those of the New Morality have so much momentum and seem to be advancing their cause at will? Why are more and more restrictions placed upon religion with regard to public affairs? How are traditional references to God that have been a part of our national heritage now under attack? These questions are perplexing in light of the fact that we live in a representative republic, where the voice of the people is heard through its legislatures and public opinion is constantly polled. The New Morality has made so much headway with their mythical separation of church and state because they do not have to convince the public or persuade lawmakers in order to win the day. All they have to do is to have one of their lawyers convince five other lawyers in robes who sit on the Supreme Court to see it their way.

ONE PHRASE OUT OF CONTEXT

The New Morality picked one little phrase from Jefferson's response and used it as a springboard to fabricate a national policy. They disregarded the context in which the phrase appears. This is common practice for those of the New Morality; if something goes against their cause or even proves it wrong, they just ignore it.

It will not be ignored here. Below is a larger portion of Jefferson's response, which presents the context and understanding that undermines the New Morality's cause:

Gentlemen, The affectionate sentiments of esteem and approbation which you are so good as to express towards me on behalf of the Danbury Baptist Association, give me the highest satisfaction…

Believing with you that religion is a matter which lies solely between man and his God, that he owes account to none other for his faith or his worship, that legislative powers of government reach action only, and not opinions, I contemplate with sovereign reverence that act of the whole American people which declared that their legislature should "make no law respecting an establishment of religion or prohibiting the free exercise thereof," thus building a wall of separation between Church and State. Adhering to this expression of the supreme will of the nation in behalf of the rights of conscience, I shall see with sincere satisfaction the progress of those sentiments which tend to restore to man all his natural rights, convinced he has no natural right in opposition to his social duties.

I reciprocate your kind prayers for the protection and blessings of the common Father and Creator of man, and tender you for yourselves and your religious association, assurances of my high respect and esteem.[10]

Notice that Jefferson used the words *natural rights*. The Founding Fathers often used that phrase to refer to unalienable rights, meaning rights that came from God and not from the hand of the State. This shows that Jefferson understood the Baptists' concern to be related to the possibility that government could one day pass a law that would infringe on their religious liberty. Jefferson was assuring them that this would not happen, because the Constitution prevented the government from doing this. The wall protects religion from the State, not the other way around. It must be noted that Jefferson paid tribute in his response to "the common Father and Creator of man." This is proof that he believed in God, who created man and the world, thus not having the thought that life came about by chance. Somehow, the New Morality fails to point this out as it enthusiastically misuses his other words.

Jefferson himself poses a problem for those who argue for the strict separation of church and state. Recall in chapter 1 the treaty Jefferson made with the Kaskaskia Indians. Under the terms of the treaty, the United States government supported a priest and paid for a church to be built. Jefferson's own actions as president contradicted the claims of a wall of separation. He also designated space in the rotunda of the University of Virginia for chapel services.[11] He welcomed religious schools to locate adjacent to, and on the property of, the university so that students could be involved in religious activities.[12] He endorsed the use of the Charlottesville courthouse for church services.[13]

In real-life practice, it does not appear that the New Morality's patriot of choice verifies their interpretation of his so-called separation clause. All these actions by Jefferson would be condemned by the New Morality activists of today and outlawed by their willing black-robed accomplices. No president today could do what Jefferson did without the ACLU taking action and liberal politicians yelling foul. Jefferson's actions reveal that he welcomed religion as a valuable participant in public affairs and did not see it in conflict with the operations of the government. His words give further evidence, as he once wrote that religion was "deemed in other countries incompatible with good government, and yet proved by our experience to be its best support."[14] He wrote those words in a letter to Capt. John Thomas in 1807. Why haven't we heard about this document but instead hear only about the letter from which the "separation-wall clause" was gleaned and its true meaning twisted around? Why haven't Jefferson's many words in favor of the active role of religion in American civic life emerged in this debate? Along with many other statements on the issue, Jefferson's letter to Captain Thomas disproves the New Morality's claim that Jefferson supported anything like the modern concept of separation of church and state.

TRUE INTENT

The same Congress that approved the First Amendment passed the act that created the Northwest Ordinance in 1789, when George Washington was president. The Northwest Territory would give the nation the states of Ohio, Indiana, Illinois, Wisconsin, and Michigan. Article 3 of the ordinance contains the following words:

"Religion, morality, and knowledge, being necessary to good government and the happiness of mankind, schools and the means of education shall forever be encouraged."[15]

The Congress of the United States approved an act in which religion and morality is said to be necessary to good government. Apparently, the New Morality liberals do not feel that way. Yet, amazingly, they continue to claim that the Founding Fathers were on their side. The last part of the above quote doesn't make things better for the separation advocates. The writers and approvers of the act linked religion and morality as topics to be taught in schools. One of the reasons the New Morality is so aggressive in forcing their concept of separation of church and state on society is that it wants to use that clout to change the school system to access the minds of our kids. The Northwest Ordinance proves they are way off base.

As pastor of a small church in northeast Ohio in 1980, I (Steve) asked the local high school football coach if I could serve as chaplain of the football team. The coach enthusiastically approved. It was one of the most effective ministries I ever had. Before every kickoff, the players and I knelt in front of the fans and opposing team and prayed. We did the same at the end of the game, win or lose. It never occurred to me that I was violating the Constitution. Clearly, neither would Jefferson or Washington have seen it that way. But that is how it would be seen today by the liberal Left. I was even invited to give a sermon to the graduates of the local public school at their baccalaureate service. You will not be surprised to learn that those services are not held anymore. To do so would be unconstitutional, according to the New Morality activists.

In what sense, if any, did the founders truly intend to "separate" church and state? It was only in this sense: the founders did not want a national church, that is a national denomination. It was this that they wanted to dispel in the Establishment Clause of the First Amendment, while still allowing religion to influence the government. They had seen the legacy of national churches in the European countries from which they and their ancestors came. The religious wars, the special taxation, and the sectarian rivalry all were undesirable to them. As we mentioned earlier, Supreme Court Justice Story wrote,

> The real object of the First Amendment was, not to countenance, much less to advance Mahometanism [Islam], or Judaism, or infidelity, by prostrating Christianity; but to exclude all rivalry among Christian sects.[16]

Could it be any clearer what the intention was by those who wrote the First Amendment? The issue of establishing an official religion was related to a particular denomination, not all religion in general. By the way, in case you are wondering who Joseph Story was, let us share some of his résumé highlights:

- Son of one of the "Indians" of the Boston Tea Party
- Harvard graduate
- Member of the Massachusetts legislature
- Member, US House of Representatives, 1808–09
- US Supreme Court justice (appointed by President Madison), 1811–45
- A founder of Harvard Law School[17]

It makes you wonder if the rogue activist judges the New Morality folks used to advance their religious separation ideas ever studied Mr. Story. How could they come up with the radical decisions they have made in this area? Story clearly outlines the original intent of the framers of the Constitution, yet modern-day judges can't seem to make decisions in line with it. One of two things has to be at work: either these judges have their own antireligious agenda to advance, or they are just plain ignorant of the facts. Given their level of education and career success, the latter does not seem feasible.

Jefferson wrote on this subject to a fellow signer of the Declaration of Independence, Dr. Benjamin Rush,

> The clause of the Constitution which, while it secured the freedom of the press, covered also the freedom of religion, had given to the clergy a very favorite hope of obtaining an establishment of a particular form of Christianity through the United States; and as every sect believes its own form the true one, every one, perhaps, hoped for his own, but especially the Episcopalians and Congregationalists. The returning good sense of our country threatens abortion to their hopes; and they believe that any portion of power confided to me, will be exerted in opposition to their schemes. And they believe rightly.[18]

It is helpful to study the issue as it was debated by those at the Constitutional Convention to see if, indeed, the focus was on competing denominations and not religion in general. Who better to voice the essence of the debate than George Mason, who was known as the father of the Bill of Rights? He suggested wording for the First Amendment:

> All men have an equal, natural, and unalienable right to the free exercise of religion, according to the dictates of conscience; and that no particular sect or society of Christians ought to be favored or established by law in preference to others.[19]

Mason's words reveal that the debate on the Establishment Clause was related to various sects (denominations) and not about generally shutting out Christianity. The historical evidence is overwhelming against the position taken by the New Morality people and their secularist cohorts, but it hasn't slowed them down on pressing their views. The New Morality desires cultural and political influence. Their ultimate aim is to silence people of faith and ban them from the public square.

MASSACHUSETTS, YOU NEVER LOOKED SO GOOD

An important item to be considered in the separation of church and state is the actions by the individual states after the Constitution was ratified. Today, those who call for a strict observance of total separation of church and state demand that the laws passed related to this issue in Washington, DC, are to be adhered to by all the states. If the Supreme Court rules on a case that involves one state, its ruling is to be considered the law of the land for the rest of the states. If one state cannot have prayer at a high school football game, then no school in any state can have such a prayer. In this way, liberals have sought to impose their will chiefly through the federal court system.

Jefferson believed that states were to have jurisdiction when it came to religious exercise. He stated that the "power to prescribe any religious exercise…must then rest with the States."[20] Many states had words in their constitutions that encouraged religious involvement and influence on civil affairs. Religion was welcomed, and there was a strong belief that it improved the quality of government for the people. An example of this comes from the Massachusetts Constitution during the founding era:

> As the happiness of a people, and the good order and preservation of civil government, essentially depend upon piety, religion, and morality; and as these cannot be generally diffused through a community, but by the institution of the public wor-

67

ship of God and of public instructions in piety,
religion, and morality: Therefore, to promote
their happiness and to secure the good order and
preservation of their government, the People of
this Commonwealth have a right to invest their
legislature with power to authorize and require…
the several towns, parishes, precincts, and other
bodies-politic, or religious societies, to make suit-
able provision, at their own expense, for the institution of the public worship of God, and for the
support and maintenance of public protestant
teachers of piety, religion and morality.[21]

Let's just look at some of the points made by these words:

1. *The preservation of government depends upon piety, religion,
    and morality.* The lawmakers in Massachusetts didn't think
    the US Constitution prevented them from having religion
    play a vital part in the operation of their state government.
2. *The people have a right to demand that their legislature require
    towns, parishes, and the like to provide for public worship of
    God.* The state government considered itself responsible
    for the encouragement and promotion of the worship of
    God. Such an action today would be declared unconsti-
    tutional. So why wasn't it considered unconstitutional
    back then? The answer is because back then it was clearly
    understood that the Establishment Clause pertained to a
    specific denomination receiving favored status and not to
    the removal of religion entirely from the civic scene.
3. *The government encouraged and promoted the teachers of
    piety, religion, and morality and called for them to be sup-
    ported and maintained.* One thing that the New Morality
    is strongly against is the teaching of religion to young peo-
    ple, but an original state in the years following the ratifi-
    cation of the US Constitution felt it was well within its
    parameters to do so.

For years, there was no challenge to this position. Religion was allowed to influence life, law, and culture with the blessing of the government. All this time, Americans had no notion that they were being unconstitutional. Convincing us of that erroneous belief took the liberal elite of the New Morality and a handful of high court judges who were willing to refashion American jurisprudence to achieve their own ends. Yes, history records that the commonwealth of Massachusetts willingly promoted the worship of God and the support of religious teachers. Isn't this the state that gave us Ted Kennedy, Michael Dukakis, and one of the most liberal senators ever to be in Congress, John Kerry, with Elizabeth Warren providing the encore? Maybe the citizens of this state should revisit their history for a reality check.

Some sixty-seven years after the drafting of the Constitution, Congress issued a statement in a House Judiciary Committee report clearly showing that separation of church and state was neither a practiced policy nor something even considered: At the time of the adoption of the Constitution and the amendments, the universal sentiment was that Christianity should be encouraged...In this age, there can be no substitute for Christianity...That was the religion of the founders of the republic, and they expected it to remain the religion of their descendants.[22]

The words "In this age there can be no substitute for Christianity" were proclaimed by Congress in the mid-1800s, which is clear evidence that a separation of church and state was never the original intent of the founders or a belief held by those who followed them into leadership and power.

CLOBBERED BY THE COURTS

It is a tragedy that the liberal Left and the New Morality have taken the First Amendment and turned it into a loophole to advance their socialistic and morally bankrupt agenda. They have been able to get a majority on the Supreme Court to see things their way, and practices and freedoms that were enjoyed by the American people for more than 180 years were erased. Chapter 10 will deal with the judiciary branch and its impact on American life. There is a long list of judgments handed down by courts in which they accepted the misinterpretation of the New Morality gang on this issue of separation of church and state. Here are only a few:

> It is unconstitutional for students to start their school day with a nondenominational prayer. *Engel v. Vitale*, 1962.[23]

> It is unconstitutional to require students to read the Bible in school. *Abington School District v. Schempp*, 1963.[24]

> If a student prays over his lunch, it is unconstitutional for him to pray aloud. *Reed v. Van Hoven*, 1965.[25]

> It is unconstitutional for a war memorial to be erected in the shape of a cross. *Lowe v. City of Eugene*, 1969.[26]

> It is unconstitutional for a public cemetery to have a planter in the shape of a cross, for if someone were to view that cross, it could cause "emotional distress" and thus constitute an "injury-in-fact." *Warsaw v. Tehachapi*, 1990.[27]

> Even though the wording may be constitutionally acceptable, a bill becomes unconstitutional if the legislator who introduced the bill had a religious activity in his mind when it was authored. *Wallace v. Jaffree*, 1985.[28]

> It is unconstitutional for a classroom library to contain books that deal with Christianity or for

a teacher to be seen with a personal copy of the Bible at school. *Roberts v. Madigan*, 1990.[29]

Artwork may not be displayed in schools if it depicts something religious, even if that artwork is considered a historical classic. *Washegesic v. Bloomingdale Public Schools*, 1994.[30]

It is unconstitutional for a kindergarten class to ask whose birthday is celebrated by Christmas. *Florey v. Sioux Falls School District*, 1980.[31]

If the Founding Fathers read these items, do you think they would say, "Yes, that's exactly what we had in mind when we put the Constitution together"? Not a chance. These court decisions are evidence that the New Morality has gained much ground in the culture war, and they did most of it without swaying public opinion or passing a single new law.

It needs to be pointed out that not all judges on the high court have remained silent on this issue, even though they are on the minority side. The late Chief Justice Rehnquist described the separation of church and state as a misleading metaphor:

> But the greatest injury of the 'wall' notion is its mischievous diversion of judges from the actual intentions of the drafters of the Bill of Rights… The "wall of separation between church and State" is a metaphor based on bad history, a metaphor which has proved useless as a guide to judging. It should be frankly and explicitly abandoned.[32]

The words "mischievous diversion of judges" tell me that the late chief justice got it. He understood what the Founding Fathers had in mind and that it is ridiculous to wipe out 180 or more years of practices that were a vital part of our culture and rooted in our heritage. The New Morality has found the Achilles' heel of our republican representative form of government to be the judiciary, and they have exploited it effectively.

Jefferson is the great hero of the separation-secularist crowd, as they selectively take words from his response to the Danbury Baptists out of context in order to legitimize their position. But Jefferson was not a fan of sweeping judicial power, a fact that is quite ironic since the courts have won Jefferson's modern-day secularist admirers nearly all their victories. Not surprisingly, antireligious activists usually fail to quote Jefferson when he speaks out about the judiciary system. Jefferson realized the dangers that the judiciary branch held when it was not accountable to an electorate, a point he strongly made in a letter to William Jarvis:

> You seem…to consider the judges as the ultimate arbiters of all constitutional questions; a very dangerous doctrine indeed, and one which would place us under the despotism of an oligarchy. Our judges are as honest as other men, and not more so. They have, with others, the same passions for party, for power, and the privilege of their corps…And their power [is] the more dangerous as they are in office for life, and not responsible, as the other functionaries are, to the elective control. The Constitution has erected no such single tribunal.[33]

Activists calling for a strict separation of church and state have a problem in making their case that this concept should be standard operating procedure. In 1862, Julia Ward Howe's "Battle Hymn of the Republic" was published. It became very popular during the Civil War, and it remains revered today. It was even sung at President Obama's second inauguration, in January 2013, by the Brooklyn Tabernacle Choir. Our republic has a hymn that mentions Christ by name and is filled with religious proclamations. Why is it still sung now at national events, and why was it ever allowed to be accepted, if separation of church and state is the rule?

In 1884, the Washington Monument was completed, and the pyramid cap on the obelisk overlooked the US Capitol. Few people know that two Latin words are engraved on the east side of the cap: *Laus Deo*, which translates "Praise be to God." These words are the first thing the morning rays of sun touch in the nation's capital each day. If separation of church and state is to be the norm in the nation and was so set by the Founding Fathers, then why did these words make it onto the Washington Monument?

The Pledge of Allegiance was altered in 1954 by Congress and signed into law by Eisenhower to include the words "under God" ("one nation under God"). This is one change the separation-of-church-and-state crowd has sought to reverse, but they've failed to gain ground at the Supreme Court level. You can be sure of this: they will try again when they think that they have the right combination of Supreme Court justices in their favor.

A couple of years later, in July 1956, Congress approved the motto of the nation, which we read on our currency: "In God We Trust." How did this get past the separation-of-church-and-state zealots? No luck for them at the Supreme Court level on this one, either, in three tries, but there is always the future and a new court.

Any honest look at American history, both in the days of the founders and even in relatively recent years, gives evidence that separation of church and state, as it is being promoted these days, has no basis in history or constitutional law. Yet liberals have successfully used this mythical concept to wreak havoc in our schools and to alter other cherished national institutions.

The Founding Fathers wanted government of the people, for the people, and by the people. Today we get government by the judges, for the Left elite, in spite of the people. The policy of separation of church and state, as it is now being carried out, has separated our country from its true heritage and the foundation of its greatness—and our children are deceived and no longer taught the truth in school.

MAKING A DIFFERENCE:
LISA ABLER AND VACATION LIBERTY SCHOOL

Political grassroots movements provide a great deal of inspiration for conservative people to become involved in politics. Millions of people saw their country being led away from the principles on which the founders had established it, and they wanted to take an active role in pushing back. One of those who took creative action was Kentucky mother and housewife Lisa Abler. She followed the format of Vacation Bible School that thousands of churches utilize each summer and created Vacation Liberty School. She designed a curriculum that features lessons on the principles of liberty as they were expounded by the Founding Fathers.

The lessons boldly proclaim the nation's connection to a Christian heritage. Students, from ages ten to fifteen, began getting factual information on the founders, the founding documents, and capitalism that they were not receiving in public schools.

Lisa put her curriculum online, and other towns began Vacation Liberty Schools. Lisa's first school, which was started in the summer of 2010 in Georgetown, Kentucky, had tremendous influence elsewhere, as similar schools appeared in other states. Word of her venture grew rapidly when Glenn Beck interviewed her on his television show, which at the time was on Fox News Channel. Thousands of children have been students of Vacation Liberty Schools since Lisa started her project in 2010.

The program has had its critics, who believe it is wrong to teach history to children in a way that directs them to vote a certain way. Have these critics not paid a visit to the public schools and college classrooms to see how liberals are directing our children in those places? More power to Lisa and all who run Vacation Liberty Schools.[34]

TAKE ACTION

- Take one of Hillsdale College's free courses on the Constitution or the Federalist Papers (http://online. hillsdale.edu).
- Encourage your children to visit the Constituting America website to learn more about the Constitution and the nation's founding (http://www.constitutingamerica.org).
- Get involved with groups and organizations that support traditional values and principles.

CHAPTER 3

Public Schools: Ground Zero

> It is an object of vast magnitude that systems of education should be adopted and pursued which may not only diffuse a knowledge of the sciences but may implant in the minds of the American youth the principles of virtue and of liberty and inspire them with just and liberal ideas of government and with an inviolable attachment to their own country.[1]
>
> —Noah Webster

It was Christmas season 1955. I (Steve) and members of my fifth-grade class were on stage for the evening elementary school Christmas program. Our parents were there, anticipating the performance. One of the songs sung was "Joy to the World," the Christmas carol that includes the phrase "the Lord is come." Nobody got upset; nobody got offended. There were no protests at the principal's office the next day. The ACLU did not sue the school or any of the teachers.

Even the Jewish kids in the class, of which there were many, were right there on stage, singing away with the rest of the kids.

Today, this Christian program would be considered unconstitutional, all because a parent, on the basis of separation of church and state, was successful in getting a school to stop leading Christmas carols.[2] Although we read about few outliers in different regions of the country, for the most part, Christian teachers know that all it takes is one complaint from an atheist parent or an adherent of a non-Christian religion to jeopardize their jobs and the financial health of the school system itself.

My (Steve's) wife, who attended elementary school in the 1950s, recalls that when she and her classmates had lunch, the principal came to the lunchroom to say grace, giving thanks for the food. Today, in some school districts, a student would risk being expelled if she raised her voice in personal prayer before eating. She would be ridiculed if she tried to utter the Lord's Prayer at her commencement speech. Christianity is not welcome in public schools, even in places, where other religions are accommodated. One example of this was reported by Bill O'Reilly in 2007, when San Diego schools made special provisions for Muslim students to have a time and place for prayers, while not affording Christians such favors.[3]

Indeed, the Christian world has changed significantly since the 1950s. The civil rights movement brought about needed change in America, ending racial-segregation laws in the South and voter suppression of nonwhites. Christianity itself took a blow when its critics around the world pointed to the glaring inconsistencies between the tenets of the Christian faith and the segregated and unequal living conditions imposed on black America. However, black America's struggle for civil rights emboldened antireligious political groups to assert rights-based arguments that would eventually spur the US Supreme Court to chip away at the Christian influence in public life. It was a sadly ironic turn of events, since the civil rights movement came about largely due to the leadership of black Southern pastors and Christian leaders, including, most notably, of course, the Rev. Dr. Martin Luther King Jr.

I (Carol) witnessed the end of the annual Christmas party at Vanderbilt University's law school, where faculty and staff would gather for festivities that included Christmas choirs and a decorated tree. The demise of the Christmas party occurred within two years of my arrival in 2000. A newly hired atheist professor expressed displeasure, and the annual event was ended and eventually recast as "Festivus" in a nod to a December 18, 1997, episode of *Seinfeld*.[4]

Attendance at the party dropped significantly after the Christmas celebration was ditched for the Festivus holiday, which mocks the materialism of Christmas. Some faculty who had been at the university for decades had participated in annual Christmas parties, and a few expressed embarrassment at the assertive stance of their brash new colleague who had zero tolerance for the law school's traditions. Protections for religious liberty have been so diminished that oftentimes a single person who complains has the power to suppress the religious expression of everyone else around.

UNCONSTITUTIONAL ACTS?

In 1999, a football coach in London, Ohio, was sued by the ACLU for having prayer with his high school team.[5] It's the kind of story with which we have become all too familiar. Even voluntary prayer is no longer protected in our schools. The New Morality equipped itself with the separation-of-church-and state clause from the Supreme Court and took off for the schools to make our children casualties in the cultural war. Any Christian influence on students was targeted. The Ten Commandments, which happen to hold historical as well as religious value, had to go. They could not be hung on a wall as a reference to Jewish history, even though they are engraved on the wall behind the bench where our Supreme Court justices sit. The Founding Fathers saw the schools of the nation as a place where religion as well as other disciplines would be taught. The Northwest Ordinance and statements in constitutions of the thirteen original states bear this out. Christianity's presence in the public school system was welcomed without contest all the way into the mid-1900s. A practice approved by the people of local communities for more than 150 years is now considered wrong.

The first blast from the New Morality came in the 1947 Supreme Court case of *Everson v. Board of Education*. The case focused on a New Jersey statute that allowed parochial students to be transported on public school buses. The Supreme Court struck down this statute, citing the Jefferson "wall of separation clause" as reason for its action.[6] This decision may not appear too devastating on the surface, but it set the stage for future decisions that would wreak damage on traditional morality as the cultural war began in earnest. What the court did was take a federal restriction and place it on a state.

The First Amendment says that "Congress shall make no law respecting an establishment of religion." The Constitution prohibits Congress from this action but does not limit a state. In fact, the states of Massachusetts and Connecticut continued to support state-established official churches after the Constitution was ratified. In 1833, Massachusetts became the last state to end such an arrangement.[7]

The Supreme Court made a power grab in this decision. It claimed it had power over religious activities in individual states as well as in the federal government. The Supreme Court, in effect, changed the law on its own. The New Morality crowd now had an effective strategy to advance their cause. From now on, it would be a full-court press.

When the court expanded the Establishment Clause to the states, it declared open season on the public schools. Fresh from their victory in 1947, the New Morality scored a second victory in 1948, with *McCollum v. Board of Education.* This case dealt with a school district permitting an organization formed by Jewish, Catholic, and some Protestant leaders to conduct religious classes at the school. The classes were elective, and a student could only enroll in the class if he or she had signed parental permission. Students were never required to take one of these classes. No religious teacher received any payment from the school district for his services. It all sounded harmless enough, but not to those of the New Morality bunch, who cherish the separation doctrine. The Supreme Court said it was wrong for Illinois to commingle "sectarian with secular instruction."[8] Isn't this interesting?

The school system in question is in Illinois, and from what territory did Illinois come when it gained statehood? The answer is the Northwest Territory—the same Northwest Territory that President Washington created in 1789. You remember—the one with the ordinance that encouraged the formation of schools and for religion to be taught at those schools. Some 159 years later, a Supreme Court told a state that was following the original instructions from Congress and the president that it was out of line to do so.

Once again, the court intervened in state law regarding religion, even though the First Amendment was written for the express purpose of restricting the federal government's power over religious activities ("Congress shall make no law respecting an establishment of religion, or prohibiting the free exercise thereof [italics added].")

The Supreme Court's ruling in the *McCollum* case was certainly "prohibiting the free exercise thereof " in an individual state. The court stopped a religious activity in a state, something that Congress was prevented from doing. We have to live with the fact in our nation that many judges, on the Supreme Court and elsewhere, do not believe they are bound to interpret the Constitution as the founders designed it. Instead, they misuse their position to advance the desires of the New Morality. Our public-education system has borne the brunt of many of these decisions. Our children suffer because of it.

In 1962, the New Morality fired its legal big guns again. In the case *Engel v. Vitale*, the Supreme Court made the decision that took prayer out of schools. The state of New York had a prayer at the beginning of the school day that said, "Almighty God, we acknowledge our dependency upon Thee, and we beg Thy blessings upon us, our parents, our teachers and our country."[9]

Student participation was totally voluntary. The prayer was voluntary and nondenominational. The court said that these two factors did not prevent the prayer from being exempted from the establishment clause. The court said that "prayer in its public school system breaches the constitutional wall of separation between Church and State."[10]

There are a couple of problems with this decision.

First, why from 1789 until 1962 was prayer acceptable in schools? In 1962, there suddenly were enough lawyers in robes on the Supreme Court to say otherwise. Could we as a nation have been so ignorant for all those years that we violated our Constitution by allowing prayer in schools? Evidently the Supreme Court thought so.

Second, there is an issue with the words *constitutional wall of separation* used in the court's decision. There is no place in the

Constitution where those words appear! The words *wall of separation* appear only in the response letter by Jefferson to the Danbury Baptists. The Supreme Court attributed words to the Constitution that are not there in what appears to have been a deliberate effort to give their position more validity.

The made-up constitutional principles of *Engel v. Vitale* formed the basis for many later court decisions that would limit or prohibit prayer in public schools. It is this case, however, that has fueled the New Morality's enthusiasm for attacking anything and everything that relates to religion in public schools. The attacks have gotten so bad that children who choose to say grace before lunch at school must not do so out loud.[11] To deny an individual child the right to pray out loud in a school cafeteria is a violation of the most basic rights guaranteed in the Constitution. The "free exercise" clause forbids the federal government from impeding religious expression and other forms of speech.

PRIVATE PARTS AND PUBLIC EDUCATION

The Supreme Court does not want any tax money benefiting any religion in the public school systems, but what our tax dollar does pay for in schools today is shocking. In New York City, there is a public high school for gays—your tax dollars at work, citizens of New York.[12] The objections to such a thing cannot be lightly dismissed as right-wing homophobia. It is not the school system's place to make such an endorsement nor to give special treatment to any group based on sexual orientation. Some administrators said it was necessary because gay students often felt out of place or picked on by other students. If this logic is to be continued, then we should see schools for fat kids, geeks, and whatever flavor of the month comes along. This logic could take us back to schools dedicated to particular races. Can you imagine the city funding a high school only for Christians? Forget about it! What the city of New York did was reintroduce school segregation. We passed the Civil Rights Act to prevent this. Yet gay activists are quick to use the Civil Rights Act to gain traction for many of their causes, including same-sex marriage.

There are many religions that do not accept homosexuality as an alternative lifestyle. To endorse it through a gay high school is to say to these religions, "You're wrong." What public school system has the right to do that? Because same-sex marriages were not legal in New York when this school was established, the creation of a gay high school effectively meant the school system endorsed sex outside of marriage. If this is okay for homosexuals, then would it not also apply to heterosexuals? Should a public school system make a value judgment in this area that goes against the values of many of the taxpayers who support it? No wonder today we have kids who can unroll a condom but can't read.

A high school in Amherst, Massachusetts, chose as its school play *The Vagina Monologues*. Teenage girls took the stage and talked about their female genitalia, with the freedom to use vulgar slang words in their descriptions, while other students, some as young as thirteen, and parents looked on from the audience.[13] The irony is that the people so concerned about the influence of religion or who fear a religious symbol might offend someone don't seem the least bit concerned about who they might offend when they put their love of vulgarity on parade.

TARGETING TRUTH

The efforts of antireligious crusaders have reached the point of absurdity. Steven Williams knows this to be a fact. Williams, a fifth-grade teacher at Stevens Creek School in the San Francisco Bay area, was not allowed to distribute copies of the Declaration of Independence to his students because it made reference to God. Williams sued the school. His lawyer said, "It's a fact of American history that our founders were religious men, and to hide this fact from young fifth-graders in the name of political correctness is out-rageous and shameful."[14]

Here's a lawyer who is right on the money. The school was treating the Declaration of Independence as if it were unconstitutional. We have reached an all-time low in our country when we will not allow history teachers to use the true founding documents written by our Founding Fathers because the students might be exposed to God.

Williams has also been prevented from using George Washington's journal, John Adams's diary, "The Rights of the Colonists" by Samuel Adams, and William Penn's "The Frame of Government of Pennsylvania."[15] The reason these items were not to be used is because they make reference to God. The position of the school, it seems, was that students must be denied the historical truth if it deals with religion and God. In other words, political correctness is more important than truth.

Historical truth is a problem for the New Morality because it offers clear evidence that our nation was born in harmony with Christian morality. The solution is easy for the New Morality. If you don't like the way history is presented, then just rewrite it. The New Morality has its regiment of revisionists in active service. Their accounts of history should be closely questioned, but instead it has become the source for history lessons in public schools. It has been said that the first casualty of war is truth. In the cultural war, truth is more than just a casualty or collateral damage; it is a prime target. The revisionists have taken deadly aim on American history. The New Morality's cause is weakened if people know the truth about American history and believe it strongly enough to make sure it is passed on to succeeding generations.

One of the most blatant examples of the revisionists ignoring historical fact to advance their distorted position is their treatment of Thanksgiving. We all are aware of the story of the first Thanksgiving, when Pilgrims and Native Americans feasted away in kindred friendship. But a talk radio show reported one day before Thanksgiving Day that the state of Maryland teaches that the Pilgrims had a feast of thanksgiving because they were thankful to the Indians for teaching them how to plant corn. How absurd; it's simply not true. They sailed in the *Mayflower* to a new world to seek religious freedom.

They wanted to worship without fear of persecution. There is no chance that they would leave God out of such a significant day; their entire culture and value system revolved around the Almighty.

During their first winter, half the Pilgrims died due to the severity of the conditions. The following fall harvest was bountiful, and the Pilgrims held a three-day celebration feast in 1621 as a thanksgiving to God.[16] It was not a multicultural feast to celebrate the diversity of two cultures living in harmony with Mother Earth. Let's fast forward to the presidency of George Washington. He proclaimed a Thanksgiving Day, saying the words "to be grateful for His benefits, and humbly to implore His protection and favor."[17] Note the capitalization of *His*; that means it refers to God. This needs to be pointed out in case it perplexes the revisionists.

America did not begin to celebrate Thanksgiving officially as a national holiday until President Lincoln authorized it. He made a proclamation that set the last Thursday in November as the official day for Thanksgiving. Lincoln did so with these words:

"I do therefore invite my fellow citizens in every part of the United States, and also those who are at sea and those who are sojourning in foreign lands, to set apart and observe the last Thursday of November next, as a day of Thanksgiving and Praise to our beneficent Father who dwelleth in the Heavens."[18]

Lincoln's own words are evidence that he regarded this holiday of Thanksgiving as a day of religious importance. Lincoln was fortunate that he did not live in our day, or he would be sued in federal court for making such a proclamation. Obviously, he was not aware of the so-called wall of separation.

You have to rewrite history to make Thanksgiving something that is not connected to God. This is exactly what the New Morality does. The National Education Association (NEA) passed a resolution that said, "Thanksgiving is the recognition of unity and the rich American diversity that was embodied in the settlement of America."[19] The NEA believes Thanksgiving must celebrate the coming together of people, which would include immigrants. Some even want to turn Thanksgiving into Immigration Day. This clearly shows that the intent of the New Morality is to get rid of God from any portion of our educational system, even if it means denying students the truth of their own country's history. It's one thing to forbid public schools to endorse a given religious faith, but to eliminate all historical references to Christian influence on our nation's history turns our history lessons into lies.

Textbooks reveal much on this issue, and what is learned should alarm us. Let's first go back to 1832, when Noah Webster wrote *History of the United States*. In it, he states,

> Almost all the civil liberty now enjoyed in the world owes its origin to the principles of the Christian religion…The religion which has introduced civil liberty is the religion of Christ and His Apostles, which enjoins humility, piety, and benevolence; which acknowledges in every person a brother or sister and a citizen with equal rights. This is genuine Christianity, and to this we owe our free constitutions of government.[20]

Webster was one of the first to call for a Constitutional Convention. Many of the delegates wanted him to lead the ratification efforts. He certainly had no problem giving Christianity the credit for the formation of our liberties and our constitutional form of government. His history book proclaimed the benefit of Christianity to government. The textbooks of today do not echo this belief.

Paul Vitz, a New York University psychology professor, has made a study of public school textbooks. He researched sixty widely used social studies textbooks and did not discover one that communicated the spirituality of the Pilgrims. About his study, he wrote, "Are public school textbooks biased? Are they censored? The answer is yes, and the nature of the bias is clear: Religion, traditional family values, and many conservative positions have been reliably excluded from children's textbooks."[21] Vitz believes textbook authors are obligated to present the truth and that the failure to do so is a neglect of duty by the writer.[22]

SEPARATION OF MOSQUE AND STATE, ANYONE?

History textbooks are not the only ones targeted by the New Morality as they expand their assault on public schools. In California, a textbook titled *Across the Centuries* came with "Islam simulation materials." These were needed because the state legislature required three weeks of Islamic studies for seventh graders. Sorry, Christianity and Judaism, you didn't make the cut. Somehow, some way, Islam made it under the separation-of-church-and-state radar. Is not the point to ban all religions from the public scene where tax dollars are at work? The textbook pointed out positive teachings of Islam and contrasted them against Christianity. Meanwhile, it's a safe bet that they didn't print the horrors of the Moors' invasion, the Battle of Tours, and the execution of Jews in Qurayza.[23] Liberal educators seem to go out of their way to paint Islam in the best light because it makes them feel enlightened and tolerant to do so. Meanwhile, they demand utter silence on the topic of Christianity's role in American history. Their standards of religious tolerance are utterly inconsistent.

In California, students not only had to endure the textbook, but also had to emulate being a Muslim. They had to take an Islamic name, pray in the name of Allah, simulate their own jihad (your guess is as good as ours on how they did this one), dress in Muslim garb, memorize Islamic prayers, and fast at lunch during Ramadan.[24] We wonder if they had to read the following words from the Quran:

> Then kill the Mushrikun [pagans]…wherever you find them, and capture them and besiege them, and prepare for them each and every ambush.
> —The Noble Quran 9:5

> I will cast terror into the hearts of those who have disbelieved, so strike them over the necks, and smite over all their fingers and toes.
> —The Noble Quran 8:12

That is because those who disbelieve follow false-hood, while those who believe follow the truth from their Lord. Thus does Allah set forth their parables for mankind. So when you meet (in fight Jihad in Allah's Cause), those who disbelieve smite at their necks till when you have killed and wounded many of them, then bind a bond firmly (on them, i.e., take them as captives). [The verse goes on to say the only reason Allah doesn't do the dirty work himself is in order to test the faithful-ness of Muslims. Those who kill pass the test.]… But if it had been Allah's Will, He Himself could certainly have punished them (without you). But (He lets you fight), in order to test you, some with others. But those who are killed in the Way of Allah, He will never let their deeds be lost.

—The Noble Quran 47:3–4

Can you imagine a public school teacher trying to explain those passages to his students? There is definitely a place in our schools for teaching students about other religions and cultures. But, once again, what we observe is the inconsistency and bias of the liberal approach to these topics: they see a kid at a lunch table offering a silent Christian prayer, and they are ready to file a lawsuit, but they show no concern when bureaucrats in California dedicate weeks of classroom time to the study of Islam. What we have is a double standard.

DEATH 101

The ultimate purpose of education is to help a student obtain the skills and knowledge needed to make a living and have a produc-tive life. Some in the public school systems of our great land have a different view. They advocate teaching lessons on what is known as "death education." This is for real. Samuel Blumenfeld, an author and expert on education topics, documents this dark side of the public classroom. He tells what took place when a school had what was called a "suicide talking day," which was held following the suicide of a student. That day, teachers and students discussed death in every class. Teachers assigned students to write their own obituaries and suicide notes.[25]

Blumenfeld follows the story of Tara Becker, one of the students at the school. She said they were told to trust their own judgment in deciding whether to live or die. It is absurd that a teacher would say such a thing to a teenager. Tara said that after that day, she herself even considered suicide as a solution to her problems and a way of liberating her spirit. Her story was documented in a video production by Phyllis Schlafly and became a subject on ABC's *20/20*. On that program, Tara reported that the students talked in class about how they wanted to look in their caskets (a good answer would have been, "Very old"). The TV show reported that 10 percent of public schools offer death education. Clearly, not all of them are conveying to students the value of life. In case you are curious to know what school Tara was talking about, it was Columbine High School in Colorado—where a shooting rampage by two of its students a number of years after Tara was a student in the death-education class killed twelve students and one teacher.[26]

In 1969, Johnny Mandel wrote the music and teamed up with lyricist Mike Altman in creating the song "Suicide Is Painless." It became the theme song for the motion picture *M*A*S*H** that went on to become a popular TV series about a medical unit in the Korean War. I don't think that a parent of a teenager who committed suicide would say that it was painless, but some teachers don't seem to be unnerved about it.

A Massachusetts school had a number of suicides, which led to an investigation by an education consultant. The consultant met with the teacher in charge of the death-education course. The teacher actually told the consultant that fewer suicides would not necessarily mean improvement had taken place.[27] If you think that is bad, it gets even worse. The teacher then conveyed that if students decided to take their own lives, it would be a tribute to their courage in making "an independent decision."[28]

This dysfunctional teacher and other New Morality disciples who masquerade as educators in public schools make homeschooling look good. Keep in mind that wherever courses like this are taught in public schools, you're seeing your tax dollars at work.

CAMP LIB

The public school system today serves as an indoctrination camp for liberals. It gets worse at the college level. The National Education Association (NEA), which is the public teachers' union, takes liberal positions on issues and endorses liberal candidates for political office. When these candidates win, you can bet they will not support any laws or actions that will go against the NEA. The NEA has become a special-interest group for liberal politicians who, in turn, protect it from needed education reform and policies that would require accountability for schools. There are many metropolitan school systems in which less than 50 percent of students who reach high school ever graduate. We have school systems that are making a failing grade but do not want the nation to see the report card. All the while, the teachers and administrators think they know best what your children should learn about history, the origin of life, faith, sex, and a host of other subjects and issues that will shape their values.

The New Morality gang is advancing teachings that are radical and detrimental to children and teenagers. And they are able to do it because they control the public schools. Vladimir Lenin, the late Communist dictator of the Soviet Union, said, "Give me four years to teach the children and the seed I have sown will never be uprooted." Like the liberal extremists who control our educational system, Lenin recognized that indoctrinating children is the key to gaining long-term political power. Public schools offer a perfect opportunity for liberal educators to shape the worldview of an entire generation.

Teachers' unions fear private schools. The NEA has resisted and fought against vouchers that would allow people of low income to have their children leave a failing public school for a private school. Public schools don't want competition because it will reveal their incompetence. The New Morality does not want your kids in private schools because many private schools do not teach their brand of morality. The District of Columbia enjoyed a successful voucher program, in which many minority children were excelling. Its success posed a problem for the NEA, which had a simple solution. The union called on President Obama to ride to their rescue. Obama decided that those in the program could finish, but no more students would be allowed to enroll, which meant the program would die in due time. Victory for the NEA.[29] It seems strange that a minority president would end a program that was benefiting minority children and giving them a promise of a better future. It's not so strange when you realize it's a liberal president who got a stack of campaign cash from the NEA teachers' union.

Milton Friedman, the late Nobel laureate and economist, obviously believed differently from the president on this educational issue when he stated,

> Our goal is to have a system in which every family in the U.S. will be able to choose for itself the school to which its children go. We are far from that ultimate result. If we had that—a system of free choice—we would also have a system of competition, innovation, which would change the character of education.[30]

The last thing liberals want for their NEA accomplices is competition. It is just too perfect a situation to have taxpayers underwriting the liberal indoctrination of children in schools where the children not only are required to go, but also are taught values that are adverse to those held by their families. Wherever school-voucher programs are put forth as an alternative to the current public-education format, the NEA and liberals team up to fight them vehemently. Liberals want a woman to have a choice when it comes to aborting her child, but they don't want mothers of children to have a choice about where their children should go to school.

The NEA not only dislikes private schools; it also is no fan of homeschooling. A unique homeschool case in 2013 became part of a court battle. It involved Uwe and Hannelore Romeike, devout Christians from the southwest part of Germany. They came to America in 2008, asking for political asylum so they could homeschool their children, since Germany does not allow homeschooling. Our nation's law says individuals can qualify for asylum if they can prove they are being persecuted because of their religion or because they are members of a particular social group.[31]

The German family was granted asylum in 2010 and now lives in Tennessee. Sounds like a wonderful, good-old-fashioned American story, right? Not so fast. Liberals in our legal system, including the Department of Justice, tried to overturn the asylum, based on the concept that the family was not facing real persecution, and deport the family back to Germany.[32] The family was finally allowed to have permanent-resident status in 2014. If the founders could look down on this, they would be astonished at those who fought against this family. Liberal forces were at work to deport a family who immigrated to America for the same reasons many of the first settlers came to these shores. The same people who want to deport the German homeschoolers are the same bunch who are okay with millions of illegal immigrants enrolling their kids in public school and partaking of our social services with no fear of being sent back to their own country. I guess the German family just doesn't represent a large enough voting bloc to make the liberals care.

PERSECUTION IN PUBLIC SCHOOLS

Colin Gunn is a Scotsman who now lives in Texas and produces documentaries. In 2011, he made a film called *IndoctriNation*. He took a used school bus and modified it into somewhat of a motor home, then loaded up his family for a trip around the United States so he could interview people about separation of church and state as it relates to public education. Gunn believes government schools are a detriment to today's children, and he makes a compelling case in his film.

Two people who appear in the film had experiences with their public schools that are noteworthy. One is a Mr. Liston, who had children in a public school in Charleston, West Virginia. He went to a school board meeting to complain about a book that his daughter was assigned to read. As he made his protest, he began reading from the book. When he read a portion of the book, the film editors had to black out his mouth and bleep out words because they were graphically obscene—so much so that one of the board members asked him to stop reading. Another board member said, in effect, that if an eleventh grader had to read those words as an assignment, then she, as an adult, should be able to hear them.[33] The Bible has been banned from school, but in the school Mr. Liston's kids attended, literary porn was acceptable. This school would likely be the first one to buy *Fifty Shades of Grey*.

The other person was a young teacher named Sarah LaVerdiere. Sarah came from a long line of teachers. She taught at an elementary school in Raleigh, North Carolina. She is a very dedicated Christian and had to walk a thin line to make sure her faith did not become apparent to her students. She said that if she ever read a scripture in class, she believed she would be fired that day. One late October day, she decided she could no longer teach at a school where she had to teach on values she did not believe in. She tendered her resignation and was allowed two weeks for her last day. The school board asked her to write a letter to the parents of her students explaining her resignation.

Her letter was lengthy and, in detail, gave a strong witness to her faith. The school board would not let her send it to the parents. The board then demanded that she resign immediately and leave the premises. She was allowed a few lines for the parents, which were, "[The school board] is asking me to move my resignation date because they are concerned my Christian beliefs will influence the students and parents."[34]

The children were removed from her classroom and sent to a special place on the playground. The principal watched her while she cleaned out her personal belongings from the classroom. She was then escorted out an exit where her students would not see her.

How would Declaration of Independence signer Benjamin Rush feel if he learned of Sarah's story, in light of his words in *Of the Mode of Education Proper in a Republic*, written in 1806? He wrote,

> The only foundation for a useful education in a republic is to be laid in Religion. Without this there can be no virtue, and without virtue there can be no liberty, and liberty is the object and life of all republican governments.[35]

Christian teachers are not the only targets of persecution in public schools; Christian students are as well. Attorney Robert Tyler of Advocates for Faith and Freedom, a legal organization in Murrieta, California, reports that there has been an increase of complaints by Christian students in public schools who are being picked on by teachers because of their faith. Tyler states, "We have seen a dramatic increase of phone calls nationwide as it pertains to kids in public schools who are facing hostility because of their faith."[36] He adds,

> The more that our kids are being told that there is no God, and the more hostile that these teachers are allowed to be, and the more disapproval that they have the ability to show toward Christ, the greater impact it will have on future generations and whether they believe in God.[37]

The Seminole High School gospel choir of Sanford, Florida, felt the persecution sting. The choir had been in existence for twelve years and was formed because of strong community support. It was invited to sing at a 9/11 memorial service at Central Baptist Church in Sanford in 2002. School-board members and community leaders were invited, along with the general public. When school officials learned that Seminole High's gospel choir was invited to sing, they banned the choir from participating. They went on to claim that voluntary participation by individual choir members would violate school policy.[38]

The latest intrusive venture by the federal government into local-level public education is Common Core. Common Core is described on an official website as providing

> A consistent, clear understanding of what students are expected to learn, so teachers and parents know what they need to do to help them. The standards are designed to be robust and relevant to the real world, reflecting the knowledge and skills that our young people need for success in college and careers.[39]

It sounds so noble and helpful; what could be the downside of such a project? The fact that the federal government is propelling itself into local community education is downside enough. Common Core would be a foothold for the feds in local education, and it's just a matter of time until their level of control grows. At the outset, forty-five states signed on for the program. However, as time has gone by, more and more states have opted out of Common Core upon learning more about its standards. Some of the opposition has been provided by the Home School Legal Defense Association. Its director of federal relations, William Estrada, voices the association's concerns:

> Our concern with the Common Core is two-fold…The first is that the success of homeschooling shows that kids do best when parents are in control of educational decisions. Common Core centralizes what kids are taught, how they are taught, and what they should learn, in the hands of a few educational bureaucrats at the national

level—completely cutting out parents, teachers, and local school boards...

The second major concern is that a national curriculum and national standards will eventually be broadened to include homeschoolers, which would eliminate the ability of parents to tailor their educational message to each specific child... It will eliminate the freedom of homeschool parents to choose their child's education.[40]

Many states have moved away from Common Core because its standards are below ones those states currently have in place.[41] We don't need Big Brother on our local school boards. It only make sense that if Washington sets the standards for schools, it will make them low enough for poorly performing schools to measure up so that success can be proclaimed, regardless of how untrue it might be. If your state has not pushed back on Common Core, start the effort yourself.

The educational system has been hijacked by the liberal Left and their cohorts of the New Morality. The words of Dr. Rush tell us that the loss of virtue results in a loss of liberty. Is not liberty the reason for our nation's existence? Then why would a group of people employ a political strategy that would include driving virtue and morality from our education system? They do it because it helps them gain and maintain power.

Our schools have forsaken the moral compass that the founders believed to be vital to public education. The results have been an increase in sexually transmitted diseases among teenagers, an increase in teenage suicides, half or more of high school students dropping out or not graduating in many metro areas, and an increase in drug use and violence among teens. It does not appear that education under the New Morality has fared very well. As poor as modern public education is, liberal educators still clamor for something to raise student achievement. That something, invariably, is more money. Author and conservative leader Phyllis Schlafly states so poignantly, "Our public school system is our country's biggest and most inefficient monopoly, yet it keeps demanding more and more money."[42] No amount of money will solve the moral problem our schools have. And that's mainly because it is a problem those in charge believe does not exist.

It takes courage to stand against the prevailing antireligious sentiment in our schools. News outlets were all abuzz about a YouTube video that went viral in June 2013 showing a valedictorian in a South Carolina high school ripping up his approved speech and instead saying the Lord's Prayer. Roy Costner IV took a stand against a restriction he felt was wrong, and the approving applause and cheers the audience gave in response indicate he was not alone.[43] It is time we take a stand like this young man did and make our voices heard in our local communities and in Washington, DC.

MAKING A DIFFERENCE: WISCONSIN VOUCHER PROGRAM

In June 2013, Wisconsin took a big step for school choice. Governor Scott Walker supported a school voucher program for the state, and it passed the state Senate by one vote. This program will allow children of low-income homes to leave failing public schools and attend private schools where they will be exposed to a better education. Many who favored school choice wish the program would cover more children. Wisconsin Senator Leah Vukmir (R) wished the program could be available to all Wisconsin students. She stated, "A parent who is not happy with their child in the school should have some ability—as taxpayers who are paying taxpayer dollars for those schools—to put their children in a school, public or private, or even to homeschool, and have resources covered for that."[44] School-choice advocates are grateful they have an ongoing example of how a school voucher program can work. They believe that success can lead to future expansion.

> When applications exceed the enrollment cap, lawmakers and voters will see the program's ben-

efits," said Brian Pleva, a Wisconsin government affairs associate for the American Federation for Children. "Once people realize that there's way more than five hundred or even a thousand students throughout the state that are making the income eligibility requirements, they'll see that there's a lot more people who would take advantage of this right, given the opportunity.[45]

Congratulations to Governor Walker and all the Wisconsin citizens who dared to fight the liberal monopoly of public education in what is traditionally a strongly Democratic state.

TAKE ACTION

- Run for a seat on the school board.
- Organize a group of well-qualified individuals who can review textbooks for historical accuracy and bias.
- Monitor public schools to ensure that Christian students are not being denied rights that members of other religions are being allowed to enjoy.
- Join the homeschooling movement and swap skills with other parents to ensure expertise is offered on all topics.

CHAPTER 4

Sexy Kids

> It is the duty of parents to maintain their children
> decently, and according to their circumstances;
> to protect them according to the dictates of pru-
> dence; and to educate them according to the sug-
> gestions of a judicious and zealous regard for their
> usefulness, their respectability and happiness.[1]
> —James Wilson

Chances are, when you wiped crumbs from your five-year-old's face, then walked her to the end of the driveway to meet the school bus that would take her to her first day of kindergarten, you were hoping to preserve her childhood innocence. But the New Morality has different intentions because the sexualization of your children is one of its highest priorities. It starts in public schools. It is disheartening to learn that one of the most dangerous things you can do to your children is to send them to a public school, where they will be exposed to an aggressive agenda designed to steal their innocence and undermine the values and principles instilled in them from Christian parents and dedicated Sunday school teachers.

Sex Ed in the Name of Tolerance

When it comes to the New Morality, sex education begins in kindergarten. Let us introduce you to GLSEN, which stands for the Gay, Lesbian, & Straight Education Network. This organization is in or is coming to a school near you. When you visit its website, you quickly learn that its target is K–12 schools.[2] GLSEN wants to indoctrinate kindergarten and elementary school students. Get them before they get to college; by then, they will be hopelessly steeped in political correctness and willing to accept almost any lifestyle as normal.

GLSEN would have you believe its only interest is changing antigay attitudes and making schools safe for children by ending bullying. How many kindergarten kids do you know who are worried about their sexual orientation? Tammy Bruce, a self-described homosexual female, reveals GLSEN's ulterior motive when she writes that though it cloaks itself in a mantra of tolerance, it is implementing programs in schools "aimed at nothing less than sexualizing your children."[3]

The Lesbian, Gay, Bisexual, and Transgender (LGBT) community has its own history month in October; and groups such as GLSEN and the Gay-Straight Alliance Network have designed lessons and other materials aimed at shaping your child's attitudes regarding sexuality. Now we have something else in October scarier than Halloween. Here is what GLSEN announced at the start of LGBT Month in 2015:

> LGBT History Month is an opportunity for educators to teach students about lesbian, gay, bisexual, and transgender (LGBT) people, history and events, which plays a significant role in creating positive school climates for LGBT students... GLSEN provides educator resources on LGBT History Month, including a timeline of events in LGBT history; an oral history curriculum project highlighting the stories of nine important people

in LGBT history; a resource to help high school educators support LGBT students and implement LGBT-inclusive curriculum while meeting reading and writing standards; and videos… detailing the experiences of LGBT people coming out during the 1950s, 1960s, and 1970s.[4]

They want our kids to be taught the accomplishments of people who have attained some success in life, then to identify them as people who were lesbian, gay, bisexual, or transgender in their sexual identity. If someone made a great discovery or created an invention of tremendous marvel, why does a child have to know their preference in sexual partners? The same thing is at work here as it is in the advertisements we see. Corporations hire sports and entertainment celebrities to pitch their products, hoping that we who hold those people in high esteem will buy the product based on the endorsement of the celeb. Kids see a professional athlete drinking Gatorade, and they want to be like him. In their minds, drinking Gatorade is a way to start.

The LGBT History Month, dressed in the spirit of tolerance, is nothing more than a marketing program to present the homosexual/bisexual lifestyle as something to aspire to. It is designed to encourage students to engage in experimentation and a questioning of their own sexual identity. GLSEN would like to increase the percentage of people who identify as gay from the miniscule 3.5 percent to numbers high enough to support their efforts to present the lifestyle as normal.[5] GLSEN is very proactive in its mission. On March 25, 2000, a statewide conference was held in Massachusetts at Tufts University. It was called a "Teach Out" and was cosponsored by GLSEN and the Massachusetts Department of Education. Teachers received continuing-education credits for attending, but students were also invited to attend, and they did.[6]

One of the workshops was titled "What They Didn't Tell You about Queer Sex and Sexuality in Health Class: A Workshop for Youth Only." This workshop was for youth ages fourteen to twenty-one, but some as young as twelve attended. Bruce describes the workshop, including all the indecent details; workshop presenters described how lesbians have sex, discussed dildos, and offered tips on how a fourteen-year-old would know if the dildo was too large or small. The kids were then offered gay "resources" about similar subjects.[7] Amazingly, state tax dollars were used to help make this possible.

The conference was presented in the name of tolerance. This workshop on "sexual how-to" wasn't really about tolerance; it was marketing. It was presented with the hope that some of the attendees would commit to this behavior. The presenters also explained "fisting" to the attendees. Fisting is defined as "a sex act which involves the insertion of a fist and forearm into the vagina or rectum of the partner."[8] One of the presenters described fisting as "an experience of letting someone into your body that you want to be that close and intimate with."[9]

Remember, this conference was cosponsored by the state Department of Education for educators and students of public schools. It was the Massachusetts citizens' tax dollars at work.

ABSTINENCE: A TARGET

It used to be that in high school, we had sex education; nowadays, it is "sexuality" education. The New Morality wants to present more than just biological facts when it comes to sex. They want comprehensive sex ed for our kids, and they want it early, even in elementary school. Today, kids as young as five can be taught masturbation, homosexuality, and anal intercourse at school.[10]

GLSEN is not alone as an educational force for new sex education in the schools. SIECUS is another provider of misguided morality. SIECUS stands for Sexuality Information and Education Council of the United States. This organization has assisted the Division of Adolescent School Health of the Centers for Disease Control and Prevention in Its School Health project.[11] The website of this organization is major propaganda for the New Morality. It states that abstinence is the only way to be totally safe from acquiring an STD or becoming pregnant.[12] But don't let this lead you to believe they are advocates and endorsers of abstinence programs. A quick tour of their website clearly reveals otherwise. In fact, the organization actively opposes abstinence-only education, particularly government-funded programs.

Since their inception, SIECUS has been tracking abstinence-only-until-marriage programs, advocating for an end to federal funding for these programs, and helping educators and parents keep these harmful programs out of their schools.[13]

SEICUS believes quality sexual education includes a contraceptive policy. At one time, the organization even went so far as to say that "while it is generally desirable for parents to be involved in their children's contraceptive decisions, the right of each person to confidentiality and privacy in receiving contraceptive information, counseling, and services is paramount."[14]

Notice that they said it is "generally desirable for parents to be involved in their children's contraceptive decisions" but that privacy in this matter is "paramount." Let us translate that for you: "Parents would want to know for the most part if their kids were using contraceptives and thus having sex. Most parents would try to curtail this activity in their offspring. If teenagers can have access to contraceptives without their parents knowing it, they will be free to have sex without Mom or Dad voicing disapproval." If SIECUS has its way, the government could replace parents as the primary influence on kids when it comes to decisions about sex.

SIECUS has four levels of age groupings for which they design their comprehensive sexual-education materials. Here are some examples of what they want each age level to learn:[15]

Level One: Ages 5–8
- Both boys and girls have body parts that feel good when touched.
- Vaginal intercourse—when a penis is placed inside a vagina—is the most common way for a sperm and egg to join.

- Some people are homosexual, which means they can be attracted to and fall in love with someone of the same gender.
- Touching and rubbing one's own genitals to feel good is called masturbation.
  [Did you get stuff like this in kindergarten through the third grade?]

Level Two: Ages 9–12
- Some people are bisexual, which means they can be attracted to and fall in love with people of the same or another gender.
- Many boys and girls begin to masturbate for sexual pleasure during puberty.
- Human beings have natural, physical responses to sexual stimulation.
  [How about in grades four through six—did anybody tell you about bisexuality?]

Level Three: Ages 12–15
- Understanding one's sexual orientation can be an evolving process.
- Talking openly about sexuality can enhance relationships.
- Masturbation, either alone or with a partner, is one way people can enjoy and express their sexuality without risking pregnancy or an STD/HIV.
- Young people can buy nonprescription contraceptives in a pharmacy, grocery store, market, or convenience store.
  [When you were in junior high school, did any teacher encourage you to masturbate with a friend?]

Level Four: Ages 15–18
- The understanding and identification of one's sexual orientation may change over the course of his/her lifetime.
- All people have the right to express their gender identity.

- Some people use erotic photographs, movies, art, literature, or the Internet to enhance their sexual fantasies when alone or with a partner.
- Some people continue to respect their religion's teaching and traditions but believe that some specific views are not personally relevant.
[In high school, did any teacher encourage you to shower with a friend?]

Does this sound like an abstinence program to you? Abstinence is actually targeted by the New Morality. There is no way they want it taught in public schools.

The governor of Louisiana authorized $1.6 million for an abstinence program to be taught in the state's public schools. The program was implemented to lower the teenage pregnancy rate. The money for the project was to come from the 1996 Welfare Act. When the ACLU got wind of this, they went to war. They claimed abstinence programs were Christian-based and that spending federal dollars on them was illegal.[16] The end result was that no federal monies were used and other funding had to be obtained.

Television host Bill O'Reilly calls the ACLU the most dangerous organization in America.[17] Considering this action in Louisiana, it could also be called the most disingenuous organization in America. Just because Christians support abstinence programs does not make them religious. By the same logic, if Christians supported a school-lunch program, no federal monies could be used to fund it because it would have to be deemed a religious activity. After all, many Christians are involved in feeding the hungry.

The ACLU action is a slap in the face to people who are not Christians and yet want their children taught abstinence in sex education. There really are parents like this: they know sex can result in a sexually transmitted disease or pregnancy and that abortion is not an extracurricular activity to be enjoyed. There are some people who believe in abstinence because of personal values, not because of a religious moral rule.[18] They want their first sexual experience to be with their married spouse as an action that says to the spouse, "You are special beyond anyone else in my life, and not doing this act with anyone else previous to you shows that I value you."

I (Steve) actually prefer another word that conveys the same intent as an abstinence program. That word is *deferment*. Sex is best experienced in the parameter of marriage. Sex is not wrong; it is not to be avoided. It is to be done in the marriage relationship. Sex is okay; just defer it until marriage. Inside its designed container of marriage, sex is a great and wonderful experience; outside marriage it can be tragically destructive, leading to teen pregnancy, economic hardship, or a life-threatening disease.

The federal Common Core curriculum also incorporates the New Morality values in sex education. In Georgia, a state opposed to adopting Common Core, one woman in opposition attended a meeting dealing with problems of the Common Core curriculum. Sex education was one of the topics. A photo was shown of an educator from Hawaii who was presenting some of the Common Core sex-education material to middle school students. The photo showed an easel with three points written on it. Those points were (1) oral sex, (2) vaginal sex, and (3) anal sex.[19] It also gave a graphic description of these three acts (which we have purposely omitted). Since when did it become imperative that a middle school kid become knowledgeable about anal sex?

Planned Parenthood is also taking an active role in indoctrinating our kids with a distorted and dangerous view of sex while using taxpayer dollars to do it. One example is the federal Personal Responsibility Education Program, or PREP, that has given six Planned Parenthood affiliates in northwestern states $20 million. The program says that it teaches abstinence but then goes on to define abstinence as avoiding sexual acts that risk pregnancy or STDs. Students are to be given cash payments that will encourage them to attend.[20] Some of the dollars that will help Planned Parenthood teach their promiscuous brand of sex education will come from the Affordable Care Act (also known as Obamacare).[21] It is a good business plan for them. More promiscuity now equals more abortion customers later on.

The American Life League (ALL), a pro-life organization, exposes Planned Parenthood's distorted sex-education program in a video called *Hooking Kids on Sex*.[22] It is highly graphic and not for the faint of heart. Planned Parenthood defends its actions, calling them purely educational. But the ALL video likens the strategy to a drug dealer who seeks to get a user addicted so he or she will be a regular customer. If Planned Parenthood gets a kid hooked on sex, it will have him or her as a potential customer for STD testing, birth control, and, if that fails, an abortion. Our kids' sexual health is being jeopardized for Planned Parenthood's wealth.

As I (Carol) reported in *Be the People*, the Girl Scouts of America is not your mother's group. It has joined forces with pro-gay groups and, since 2000, has allowed political correctness and alliances with groups such as Planned Parenthood to shift them from core principles that once emphasized God, nation, and traditional morality.[23] Kathryn Lopez has written,

> Girl Scout policy forbids sex on Girl Scouts time. But the book *On My Honor: Lesbians Reflect on Their Scouting Experience*,[24] published in 1997, is filled with coming-of-age stories sparked by gay encounters in the Girl Scouts. Along with an essay titled "All I Really Need to Know about Being a Lesbian I Learned at Girl Scout Camp" and various stories of "butch" counselors who "wore men's clothes and had slicked back short hair" is testimony to the prevalence of lesbians in Girl Scouting. One writer remembers, "By the time I was a junior counselor, Mic was assistant camp director and her gruff, deep-voiced directives no longer scared me. I didn't know that most of the counselors were lesbians." Others remember how sleepovers and camping trips were opportunities for same-sex sexual experimentation. Girl Scout staffers writing in the book claim that roughly

one in three of the Girl Scouts' paid professional staff is lesbian.[25]

Unfortunately, most parents don't know that the Girl Scouts has undergone radical changes since they were young. Its politically correct and feminist agenda can be destructive to the family.[26]

No one knows this better than Patti Garibay, who, after much frustration with the way the Girl Scouts were handling issues related to the Christian faith, started her own Christ-centered group for girls that would honor traditional values and provide character building and outdoor activities. Some twenty years later this group known as America Heritage Girls, based in Cincinnati, Ohio, has a number of troops in the nation and in other countries. The organization's mission is simply stated as, "Building women of integrity through service to God, family, community, and country."[27]

The male counterpart to American Heritage Girls is Trail Life USA (TLUSA). Its stated mission is "to guide generations of courageous young men to honor God, lead with integrity, serve others, and experience outdoor adventure."[28]

TLUSA does not apologize that its program is Christian-based and not "churchy." There is a strong emphasis on outdoor adventure and character building through interaction with male Christian mentors who teach biblical morals.[29] As Girl Scouts and Boy Scouts more and more compromise their founding values and become more secularized by today's culture, parents need to know there are real alternatives in American Heritage Girls and Trail Life USA. The Boy Scouts of America (BSA) resisted for years but finally caved to political pressure and accepted gay boys and men in 2015. As part of a settlement with a family whose son had suffered sexual abuse, a Santa Barbara court allowed BSA to keep its "perversion files" sealed. These files contain information about more than 1,200 child sexual-abuse cases that occurred between 1965 and 1985 and 1,900 additional reports from 1970 to 1991 that were not turned over to police.[30] These incidents occurred during the years the Boy Scouts officially banned gay troop leaders.[31] Clearly, BSA has long been infiltrated with men seeking youthful sexual partners. If the sexual abuse prob-

STEVEN FEAZEL AND DR. CAROL M. SWAIN

lem existed when there was a ban on gay troop leaders, how much more risk would children have been under if the ban were lifted?

From 2009 to 2011, Kevin Jennings, a controversial homosexual activist, was the nation's assistant deputy secretary for the Office of Safe and Drug-Free Schools at the US Department of Education. Scandals associated with Jennings include the following:

> "Brewstergate": the case of a young student, "Brewster," whom Jennings knew was having sex with an older man he'd met in a bus-station restroom;

> "Fistgate": a case in which Massachusetts public school educators, sponsored by GLSEN (founded and run by Jennings), instructed children as young as twelve about explicit homosexual practices, including such dangerous practices as "fisting";

> "NAMBLAgate": Jennings has repeatedly expressed admiration for the late Harry Hay, a member of the Communist Party and one of the most militant homosexuals of the past century. Hay was a sort of "senior statesman" in NAMBLA, the North American Man/ Boy Love Association;[32]

> "QueerSchoolsgate": Jennings wrote the foreword to *Queering Elementary Education* and has acknowledged that he developed the antibullying label as a way to present the pro-homosexual agenda as a safety issue;[33]

Under heavy pressure from Republicans in Congress, Jennings, who was appointed by then Secretary of Education Arne Duncan, resigned from his post. Unfortunately, he stayed long enough to implement changes that have made our schools anything but safe.

SEX, YES; LOGIC, NO

We live in a time when sexual disease is rampant. Many parents want their children to practice abstinence because of this issue alone. In her book, *Epidemic: How Teen Sex Is Killing Our Kids*, Dr. Meg Meeker shows the risks and danger of freely indulging in sexual activity:

- Nearly one in four sexually active teens is living with a sexually transmitted disease.
- Nearly 50 percent of black teenagers have genital herpes.
- Although teenagers make up just 10 percent of the population, they acquire between 20 percent and 25 percent of all STDs.
- Fifteen percent of all boys will be infected with the herpes virus by the time they're eighteen.[34]

Meeker also reports that every day, eight thousand teens become infected with herpes, for which there is no cure. Although this disease is not fatal, it is a nuisance that the infected will have to deal with throughout their life.[35] It is a disease that could even motivate a potential marriage partner to look elsewhere. And let's not forget that HIV/AIDS does not have a great ending. Any education program that encourages teenagers to have sexual activity gambles with their health and lives. Sexual promiscuity is a roulette wheel of tragedy for our young people. It could kill them.

The New Morality advocates argue that teens are going to have sex anyway, so we might as well tell them how to do it as safely as possible. Wait a minute. This is not the approach we use with alcohol and tobacco. We have programs that try to educate children about the dangers of underage drinking. We have SADD (Students against Drunk Driving) and other organizations that try to prevent teens from hitting the bottle before they are twenty-one. We even passed a law requiring twenty-one to be the legal age for alcohol consumption throughout the nation. An eighteen-year-old can vote, fight in the armed forces, and legally enter into contracts; but he or she still cannot buy a beer. We don't take the attitude that they will drink anyway, so let's just find a safe way for them to do it. We hit it head-on and try to lessen the number of kids who would choose to drink and disobey the law.

Americans have also declared war on tobacco and aggressively fight it on behalf of our children. Monies from the tobacco lawsuits were given to states so that they could fund programs encouraging kids not to smoke. After all, smoking can put one at risk for many diseases, such as heart disease and cancer, all of which can lead to death. We care about our kids, so we passed a law that makes it illegal for them to light up before eighteen. We have even passed laws to prevent tobacco companies from advertising on television. We have forced Big Tobacco to retire "Joe Camel," whose trendy marketing appeal might be too enticing for teens who want to be cool and thus could tempt them to start smoking.

We have an aggressive war on drugs. We lay out millions of government dollars to keep our kids away from drug use. Drugs are illegal, and we try to get our kids to "say no to drugs," as the slogan says. If we, as a nation, applied the same attitude toward sex that we do toward alcohol, tobacco, and drugs with regard to our kids, then abstinence would be the program of choice in our public schools.

There was a story on the news one evening about a young woman named Rebekka Armstrong. Rebekka was young and attractive—of course, most *Playboy* centerfolds are. There was something different about Rebekka, as the story revealed; she is HIV positive. A retrace of her sexual history found that she contracted the virus not during her life as a *Playboy* playmate but as a sixteen-year-old, from someone she met on vacation.[36] She now speaks to young people in schools on the subject of safe sex. Please note that her topic is "safe sex," not abstinence. Her website did not renounce the free-sex philosophy and was not telling kids to abstain from sex. What a shock. Her website contained nonnude sexy pictures of her scantily clad body in suggestive poses. In a video posted at the site, she offers a tutorial on condom use, which elicits laughter from her audience. But before the video ends, she notes that condoms aren't 100 percent effective.[37]

Let's review what we have here: playmate with HIV advocates "safe sex" as if she were a charter member of GLSEN or SIECUS; she strongly advocates the use of a condom but later states that you must realize they are not 100 percent foolproof. It adds up to teens are encouraged to have sex in an era when there is a real chance of acquiring a fatal disease. They are told to do so with the protection of a condom that will lower, but not eliminate, their chances of becoming infected. This is nothing more than playing sexual Russian roulette with our kids' lives.

The truth is, the New Morality wants your kid to become sexually active; it gives their cause more traction and power. Teens can get fatal diseases from sex, some of which lead to cervical cancer, but do we develop programs to get them to delay having sex? No. We spend government money on programs that encourage it, which sends a message: "Go ahead and have sex. We'll make it safe for you." The Gideons are barred from passing out Bibles to public school kids, but the government passes out condoms to our kids. By doing so, the kids get the message that they are expected to have sex.

A MATTER OF TASTE?

It was once reported that the state of Illinois was actually purchasing flavored condoms for distribution. Some 360,000 condoms were bought at five cents each in orange, lemon, grape, and cherry flavors.[38] We wonder if when the school lunch menu was printed in the local paper it also included what flavor of condom was to be given out on that day.

The truth is that condoms are not always foolproof. None claim to be 100 percent effective in warding off all STDs. The fact is that herpes and genital warts can be transmitted even when a condom is used, since it does not always cover all areas involved. If a condom breaks, all protection value is off. Have you ever wondered why we have not heard of a condom manufacturer, a school system, or a group like Planned Parenthood being sued because a kid used a condom and still got a disease or became pregnant? Why shouldn't the maker or distributor of the faulty condom be held responsible? Then they would have to pay for the expenses of raising the child. If the choice is for an abortion, then why not make the manufacturer and distributor pay the bill? Where are the trial lawyers when it comes to sex and our kids?

HOMOSEXUALITY 101

SIECUS unashamedly endorses homosexuality and attacks religion. It promotes homosexuality as a viable sexual alternative for your child. It makes reference to homosexuality in Level One, written for the five-to-eight-year-old age group. How is a kid's childhood enhanced by making him or her aware of such a thing as homosexuality? Some would say that it is so they will start developing tolerance at an early age. We believe they are too young to be put under the biased influence of educators who only want to further popularize the gay lifestyle. Here again, what is passed off in the name of tolerance is the first action to nurture future prospects for this lifestyle.

The GLSEN organization promotes two books that were created as textbooks on homosexuality for elementary kids. One is titled *Daddy's Roommate*, and the other is *Heather Has Two Mommies*. The books created a major controversy when parents objected. Defenders of the books say that their purpose is to get young children to grow up tolerant of homosexuals. They claim that such books aimed at this age will prevent less bigotry in later years. But is tolerance the real result? Through books like these, children are prematurely exposed to subject matter for which they are not psychologically or emotionally equipped. The surrender of their childhood for the sake of creating a society with less bigotry later is too high a price to be paid.

It is amazing that both GLSEN and SIECUS aggressively encourage and promote homosexuality in their sexual-education programs for public schools, because the issue is very controversial and contradicts religious teaching. Biblical Christianity forbids homosexuality, as does Judaism and Islam, and regards it as a sin. When a public school, which is not supposed to teach religion, endorses homosexuality in its sexual-education programs, it, in effect, is saying that Christianity is wrong. This is teaching religion. It is an effort to get a student to believe something that is adversely opposed to the religious faith that he or she is taught at home. At the very least, the public school should be neutral on this topic. David Limbaugh explains the mission of the homosexual advocates:

> It is no secret that gay activists are promoting the homosexual agenda in schools, with the idea that a transformation of students' attitudes about the behavior will lead not only to its acceptance in our society, but perhaps even an increase in the number of practicing homosexuals.[39]

In Level One of its guidelines, aimed at ages five through eight, SIECUS defines homosexuals as people who are "attracted to and fall in love with someone of the same gender." Someone should tell these five-to-eight-year-olds that this means many of these people will fall in love one night, then fall out of love, then fall in love with another person the next night, and so it will go, on and on. It is not unusual for a gay male to have more than one hundred partners in two years.[40]

Same-sex marriage continues to be hotly debated. Some states passed amendments to their constitutions to make same-sex marriages illegal, but their efforts became moot when in 2015 the Supreme Court ruled that same-sex marriage is legal. This means public schools that teach homosexuality is an acceptable alternative sexual lifestyle are endorsing sex outside of marriage. Many parents hold values that are opposed to this, and they teach these values to their children. When it comes to sex, the schools dare to teach values adverse to what is taught in the home. They have no right to do so.

An organization known as Advocates for Youth, a name that sounds wholesome enough, is actually dedicated to promoting gay, lesbian, bisexual, and transgender practices for teens and children. This group met to oppose federal funding for abstinence programs.

Pat Schiller, a longtime advocate of sex education, said, "Sexuality is a pleasurable experience whether you're two, six, or sixteen."[41]

Wayne Pawlowski, director of training for Planned Parenthood of America, said, "Boys should be encouraged to use condoms and masturbate at home so they will develop skills for future sex acts." Pawlowski also reportedly advocated that schools teach masturbation skills as part of sex-education classes.[42] If Mr. Pawlowski had his way, we would have to make report cards X-rated.

Homosexual advocates make various claims, which they expect us to accept as true without debate. Many in the media and the politically correct crowd are enthusiastic to comply. These claims are debatable; others can be put in the myth category. Some commonly repeated claims or myths are as follows:

- Ten percent of the population is homosexual. Research does not bear this out. The most recent data places the number of adults identifying as gay at 3.8 percent.[43]
- Homosexuals are born that way. No homosexual gene has been found, and the causes of same-sex attraction are still not well understood. [44]
- Homosexual relationships are no different than heterosexual ones. Research has shown that the average duration for a gay relationship is two years, and many gay men have more than one hundred partners.[45]
- AIDS is as much a risk for heterosexuals as it is for homosexuals. Heterosexuals can get AIDS through risky sexual behavior, but homosexual men are far more likely to contract AIDS.[46]
- Homosexuals are normal, healthy, everyday people. Studies show that homosexuals have a higher rate of suicide, drug use, and depression and that their many sexual partners put them at greater risk for sexually transmitted diseases.[47]

- Homosexuality is unchangeable. Simply not true. Many have changed. Focus on the family has reported on some who have made the change, and the ministry Exodus International has had success in helping homosexuals change to heterosexuality.[48]

Homosexuality has gone from being considered perverse and deviant behavior in past years to being a sexual orientation accepted by society and the Supreme Court. Could the same thing happen with pedophilia? Most people would say, "No chance." Be aware that the waters are being tested. The American Psychiatric Association designated pedophilia as a sexual orientation in the fifth edition of its Diagnostic and Statistical Manual of Mental Disorders (DSM-5) but retracted it when family conservative groups protested.[49] Sandy Rios, of the American Family Association, said, "Just as the American Psychiatric Association declared homosexuality an 'orientation' under tremendous pressure from homosexual activists in the early seventies, now, under pressure from pedophile activists, they have declared the desire for sex with children an 'orientation,' too."[50] How safe will our children be if some day in the not-too-distant future, pedophilia is once again given "sexual orientation" status?

REWRITING THE BIBLE

Christianity teaches that sex should be reserved for marriage. It is not surprising that those who desire to rewrite sexual education in the schools would take a shot at it. Christianity is seen as an obstacle to the New Morality and to those who support a free-sex philosophy. Their causes are more easily advanced if Christianity is neutralized or, better yet, eliminated. The view of the New Morality toward Christianity is clearly stated again by Tammy Bruce:

> A disturbing common theme among feminists and gays, meanwhile, was that if the average person continued to view religion positively, it

would mean, automatically, that feminists and gays were in trouble. The most threatening aspect of Christianity was its moral certitudes, which were the antithesis of the moral vacuum in which the Left Elite live.[51]

If you are wondering if this is just a religious Right radical sounding off, wonder no more. Bruce is a former president of the National Organization for Women's Los Angeles chapter and a self-confessed lesbian. However, she has a high regard for traditional morality and values. She is very much opposed to the tactics that the New Morality uses to undermine Christianity.

We have already looked at how the New Morality revisionists have sought to rewrite American history—and now they would like to try reworking the Bible. Debra Haffner, a past president and CEO of SIECUS, wrote an article titled, "The Really Good News: What the Bible Can Teach You about Sex,"[52] in which she tried to rationalize the controversial views of sexuality that SIECUS desires to teach kids in school. Their view of sexuality has received criticism from Christian sources, so what better way to fight back than to use the Bible to prove their warped views of sex?

When it comes to homosexual relations, Haffner refers to two verses in Leviticus and two verses in the New Testament:

> Do not have sexual relations with a man as one does with a woman; that is detestable.
> —Leviticus 18:22, NIV

> If a man has sexual relations with a man as one does with a woman, both of them have done what is detestable. They are to be put to death; their blood will be on their own heads.
> —Leviticus 20:13, NIV

Because of this, God gave them over to shameful lusts. Even their women exchanged natural relations for unnatural ones.
—Romans 1:26, NIV

In the same way the men also abandoned natural relations with women and were inflamed with lust for one another. Men committed shameful acts with other men, and received in themselves the due penalty for their error.
—Romans 1:27, NIV

What do we learn from these verses? Same-sex relationships are rejected by God in the Old and New Testaments. It was even regarded as a capital offense in the Old Testament. It is considered perversion. Why would the author use them to support her belief that same-gender sex is acceptable behavior? She argues that since there is not a large number of verses on this subject, it must not be a very important issue. She refers to the interpretations that some give these verses: "Most modern theologians believe that these passages about men having sex with men actually related to the rejection of nearby foreign cults. Such cults practiced sacred prostitution—often using male prostitutes—during religious observances."[53]

Who are these "most modern theologians"? We can guarantee you they are not evangelical theologians. They would be the same liberal theologians who don't believe in the virgin birth or the Resurrection. The "foreign cult" theory is a big reach, if not downright absurd. The author points to the relationship of Jonathon (son of King Saul) with David and infers that it was homosexual love when there is no evidence of this.[54]

One Old Testament story that deals with the homosexual issue is completely ignored by Haffner: the story of Sodom and Gomorrah. In the recent past, many states had what were known as sodomy laws (until the Supreme Court eliminated them, which made certain homosexual acts illegal. The term sodomy laws came from the name of the Old Testament town Sodom. The story tells of a man named Lot who lived in Sodom and was visited by two angels who appeared as men. He insisted that they stay in his house. When they did, the male folk of the town, young and old, surrounded the house and called out to Lot, "Where are the men who came to you tonight? Bring them out to us so that we can have sex with them" (Gen. 19:5, NIV).

The biblical account tells how God brought judgment on Sodom and Gomorrah by raining down burning sulfur. It is interesting that the author of the article failed to include this story. Somehow, I don't think that dropping burning sulfur on a town is the seal of approval for homosexual behavior.

Haffner doesn't quit with same-gender sex in the Bible. She also deals with adultery. When you read her words regarding this topic, you have to employ the Glenn Beck strategy of wrapping your head in duct tape to keep it from exploding. Not only does the Bible condemn same-gender sexual relationship, but also clearly regards adultery as a sin. Haffner disputes this strong position of the Bible by trying to make it a property rights argument. She claims that in biblical times adultery was tied only to a man having sex with another man's wife, concubine without his permission, not having sex outside of one's marriage.[55]

After reading Haffner's words, you might think that it was kosher to be a member of the Jerusalem swingers' club back in Bible times. Her interpretation is ludicrous. But what do you expect from someone who has embraced the New Morality with its relative moral code? She failed to cite the verse from the Sermon on the Mount, in which Jesus said, "You have heard that it was said by the ancients, 'You shall not commit adultery.' But I say to you that whoever looks on a woman to lust after her has committed adultery with her already in his heart" (Matt. 5:27–28, MEV). There is one theologian who disagrees with her interpretation, and He just happens to be the Son of God. Jesus gives a definition of adultery that even strikes a blow at pornography.

Another verse that didn't make it into Haffner's biblical review is Ephesians 5:3: "But among you there must not be even a hint of sexual immorality" (NIV). What GLSEN and SIECUS want to teach your kids about sex in public schools takes them way beyond a "hint." Lesbian, gay, bisexual, and transgender (LGBT) activists have a new arsenal in their war chest. The Supreme Court's decision in *Obergefell v. Hodges*, legalizing gay marriages in the fifty states. That decision creates a new environment in which the organization can operate. Nevertheless, the court's power grab and the unconstitutional manner in which it arrived at its decision ensure that *Obergefell* will become the new *Roe v. Wade*, as it has already sparked a massive resistance among God-fearing people.[56]

LGBT activists are now advancing their (not so) open-minded and tolerant ranks into the classroom for the indoctrination and intimidation of our children. The Queer Student Alliance, a student group that goose-steps right alongside LGBT leadership, is now charging into public schools and bullying children who choose not to celebrate the homosexual lifestyle.[57] Recent federal policies and the precedent set by the Supreme Court make their job easier.

Like a page straight out of Alinsky, children from the classrooms are selected, then isolated, then interrogated about whether they and their parents can speak the LGBT language and abide by all of their rules. Take the new gender-free-restroom bills the California legislature has decided to embrace that say any boy who decides to enter a girls' restroom or locker room can simply claim gender confusion that day and be exempted from any suspicion of bad behavior. In the wake of California's new law, children are experiencing gender confusion in spades.[58]

PARENTING THE GENDER-CONFUSED CHILD

Given what we have discussed, Christians are increasingly confronted with situations in which a child or close relative either joins the gay lifestyle or is suspected of being a part of that culture. What will you do if your son, daughter, or beloved grandchild tells you he or she is gay, bisexual, transgender, or same-sex attracted? Will you completely freak out or respond calmly? I (Carol) advise remaining calm while you collect information; you can freak out later. Unless you belong to a liberal Christian denomination, you will most likely grieve or experience shock or disappointment. Whatever you feel, you should calmly respond by asking your child, "Why do you think you are gay?" and listen carefully to his or her response. The reason might be something simple and easily addressed, or it could be quite serious. It could involve molestation or pressure from a peer or a teen or adult pedophile.

In today's culture, children are encouraged to question their sexual identities. They often are taught that male/female biological attributes associated with x and y chromosomes are not definitive markers of one's gender. This liberal "science" claims one's gender is a social construct that "varies across different cultures and over time."[59] Consequently, your daughter or son can be whatever gender he or she feels comfortable as on a given day.

When I was a child, I had a good friend named Patsy. I loved Patsy and wanted to spend my free time with her, but I never pondered whether I was "in love" with her or whether I wanted to marry her. Many people reading this chapter have had close relationships with members of the same sex. Did that make us same-sex attracted? No. Our world was so different: our early relationships with members of the same sex were a normal part of growing up. We were spared today's confusing situations in which children are led to question their sexual identities; many are pressured to engage in relationships to test their femininity or masculinity.

What should you do if your child expresses confusion about his or her sexual identity? First, do not panic or blame your parenting skills. Reassure your child of your unconditional love and your willingness to stand by him or her during this challenging time in their life. Bible-believing parents should seek counseling from Christian counselors, organizations, and fellow believers who have experienced similar family situations. It is critical not to compromise your biblically based values and principles.

Remember, our children have been exposed to ideas and temptations we never had. We must ground ourselves in God's Word. God's position on homosexuality does not change just because your son or daughter adopts a gay lifestyle. Parents in this situation should pursue prayer, friendship networks, and support groups. Ex-gays and same-sex-attracted persons who have overcome the temptation or chosen abstinence are the best evangelists for the gay community. When it comes to our children, we should never abandon them; at the same time, we should not condone unbiblical behavior or participate in events or situations that cause us great discomfort because of the open flaunting of the homosexuality lifestyle. Some resources that might help you in such a circumstance include Exodus Global Alliance and Parents and Friends of Ex-Gays (PFOX).

Whatever we do, we should not succumb to modern media and the temptation to help a gender-confused child transition from being a biological male or female to the imagined identity. In today's culture, we often hear of parents giving their children hormones to suppress normal development as a means for preparing them for a sex-reassignment operation where their bodies are permanently ordered.[60] It is one of the worst things that loving parents can do to their children. Studies show most children will outgrow gender dysphoria.[61] In fact, the American College of Pediatricians issued a statement blasting the practice of giving hormones to children describing this as a form of child abuse.[62] The mother who dresses her little boy as a little girl and sends him off to school is doing a disservice to the child and other students.

I (Steve) have worked with gays on various projects and have gotten along with them in an amiable way. Despite my commitment to the biblical teachings about homosexuality, I have never displayed contempt for them, and they showed no ill will toward me. We actually developed friendships. I don't approve of their lifestyle, and they disagree with my evangelical Christian position on homosexuality, but neither was cause for animosity. Christians have a right to their faith and belief that God's standard for sexual activity is between a man and a woman who are married to each other. No government entity, organization, or cultural trend has a right to force a compromise regarding this belief. Therefore, public schools have no right to determine the correct view or practice of sexuality to teach students. To favor the liberal approach of GLSEN and SIECUS in sex

STEVEN FEAZEL AND DR. CAROL M. SWAIN

education does a disservice to the students, especially those in lower grades, and it is disrespectful to taxpayers who disagree with these two organizations.

I (Carol) believe we are creating unnecessary gender confusion and angst among young people. Children in secondary schools are pressured into situations in which they feel forced to be in relationship with someone of the opposite sex or to tone down what are naturally occurring relationships with people of the same sex. Now children and parents alike are sometimes worried about friendships that fifteen or twenty years ago no one would have noticed.

MAKING A DIFFERENCE: CATHERINE WOOD, RELATIONSHIPS UNDER CONSTRUCTION

Catherine Wood is from Delaware County, Ohio. She is a small woman with a large vision. The state of Ohio allows for abstinence teaching in its public schools. Wood developed an abstinence curriculum for sex education to be used in the schools and founded an organization to present it. She has trained many who have gone into middle schools and high schools to teach abstinence to students. The curriculum must not proclaim any religious teachings related to the advocacy of abstinence. Even though Wood is a devoted Christian, she has been able to present materials and lessons that are mindful of this restriction while still having an impact on students' behavior. For the last few years, thousands of students from all over the state have made a pledge to save sex for marriage. Wood has stood up against the forces of the liberal Left regarding sex education in the public school. She is making a difference and saving many kids a lot of grief in life.[63] To learn more about Wood's work, visit http://www. relationships underconstruction.com/about-ruc.

Take Action

- Review the sex-education books and materials at your child's school.
- Debrief your children to learn what is taking place inside the classroom.
- Know whether schools in your city are dispensing birth-control pills, condoms, IUDs, or other sexual paraphernalia without the knowledge of parents.
- Speak with Christian counselors for advice about getting age-appropriate sex-education materials.
- Use resources such as Exodus Global Alliance and Parents and Friends of Ex-Gays (PFOX)[64] for information on how to support children and adults struggling with homosexuality, transgender dysphoria, or same-sex attractions. See also, Russell Moore, "What If Your Child Is Gay?" (2004).[65]

CHAPTER 5

Music Hits a Sour Note

> Modern music, headstrong, wayward, tragically confused as to what to say and how to say it, has mounted its horse, as the joke goes, and ridden off in all directions. If we require of an art that it be unified as a whole and expressed in a universal language known to all, if it must be a consistent symbolization of the era, then modern music is a disastrous failure.[1]
>
> —Baker Brownell, *Art Is Action*

Kids are into music. The people who make music and those who sell it know this all too well. The New Morality also knows this and makes sure that popular music is one of its allies in the cultural war. The advertising brains of Madison Avenue have long tried to influence our purchasing decisions by creating a clever jingle that will stick in our heads. Musical styles have no moral meaning one way or the other. Their content can convey positive, inspiring, and wholesome messages, or they can communicate messages that are degrading and disdainful. It all depends on lyrics and the image and actions of the performer. Today, like never before, some choose to change the moral behavior of our children by putting degrading songs in their brains and then laugh all the way to the bank. If you want to get a quick view of how far our society and culture has slid into the muck of indecency, you only have to look at the music industry in recent years.

WHERE DID HANNAH GO?

From 2006 to 2011, teenybopper girls embraced a TV music heroine named Hannah Montana, courtesy of the Disney Channel. Miley Cyrus, daughter of country singer Billy Ray Cyrus, gained stardom in the role. Miley Cyrus's character conveyed a wholesome image. After *Hannah Montana* became part of TV history, things changed for Miss Cyrus. She quickly went from being a role model to something you wanted your kids to shield their eyes from and avoid. She shocked the entertainment world in 2013 by "twerking"—which consists of sexually suggestive gyrations—with an older married man on national television. Cyrus had her coming-out party, which led to her coming out of her clothes. She did a music video for a song called "Wrecking Ball," in which she appears naked atop a wrecking ball and repeatedly licks a sledgehammer. On September 9, 2013, just one week after the video's release, it had logged more than 100 million hits on YouTube. Whatever wholesome image Cyrus had must have stayed with Hannah Montana, because a string of risqué photos and lewd performances followed. Her father, who gained fame with the hit song, "Achy Breaky Heart," must have again been experiencing a broken heart, as he admitted that it was a mistake to introduce his little girl to Hollywood.[2]

Cyrus followed the lead of Madonna and Britney Spears, who showed that pop fame is closely linked to skin exposure. As women like this gain fame—and millions in their bank accounts—countless numbers of young girls who are watching are all too willing to emulate. If lewdness helps a music star become popular, a high school girl might think the same will work for her as she seeks to fit in with the in-crowd. One thing is for certain: pop music has a powerful influence on the moral development of young people.

ABSURD, OBSCENE, AND LEGAL?

Aristotle declared, "Music has a power of forming the character."[3] If this is true, then we are in trouble when it comes to our kids. Some of today's music will only produce a degrading, despicable character because that's the kind of music it is. Music aimed at teenagers glamorizes promiscuous sex, drug and alcohol use, rape, and even murder. It usually doesn't show the negative repercussions these lifestyle choices produce.

Aristotle's fellow philosopher Plato also weighed in on this issue with a warning he first heard from a man named Damon: "When modes of music change, the fundamental laws of the state always change with them."[4] We see lyrics in music that were easily regarded as obscene a few years ago now being celebrated. The makers and sellers of popular music take pride in loudly spewing out shocking and vulgar lyrics. They are supported by various groups and individuals of the New Morality who believe that freedom of expression is a good thing, no matter how repulsive its content might be.

Obscenity laws have changed since music has changed, but they have not changed because the majority of people wanted the change or because legislatures made the change. They have changed because a handful of liberal, New Morality–embracing judges wanted them changed. The First Amendment is used as a loophole to pollute the minds of our youth and as a license to trash any positive moral character development that the youth might have. The late federal judge and US Supreme Court nominee Robert Bork expressed the sad reality of the situation our society now faces. He stated that current constitutional doctrine would make it almost impossible to prevent or punish music that is lewd, obscene, or filled with profanity. He goes on to contend that interpretation of the First Amendment has morphed from the protection of the expression of ideas to the protection of self-expression regardless of how vulgar and profane the self-expression is.[5]

Danny Goldberg is a dyed-in-the-wool liberal. In fact, he has been critical of the Democratic Party for not being liberal enough. He has enjoyed a successful career as a music-industry executive, working closely with performers such as Led Zeppelin, Bonnie Raitt, and Bruce Springsteen. He also served as an officer for the ACLU and as an active fund-raiser for liberal candidates, including the Clintons. With this background, we don't have to tell you what side he is on when it comes to the debate over today's music controversy. He was asked to testify on September 13, 2000, at a Senate Commerce Committee meeting chaired by Arizona senator John McCain concerning the subject of offensive lyrics in popular music.

One rap star whose latest album was in question at the time was Eminem. The album was filled with vulgar language and a sexual attitude that was degrading to women. It even took a shot at gay people.[6] Eminem also recorded a song on one of his albums in which the lyrics endorse raping a fifteen-year-old girl. In his testimony to the committee, Goldberg said,

> Angry, weird songs often make adolescents feel less lonely and more connected to other kids. Millions of these teens and young adults feel ostracized when politicians and academics who obviously have no real understanding of their culture make sweeping generalizations about their entertainment, conveniently overlooking the fact that every generation has embraced entertainment about sexual and violent themes. Gangsta rap is the direct descendant of the gangster movies of the 1930s and 1940s, the TV Westerns of the 1950s, and critically acclaimed films like *The Godfather*.[7]

It all sounds so nice and logical, but let's look closer. First of all, the gangster movies and TV westerns showed the bad guys losing; good beat out evil. In gangsta rap, the bad guys are seen as heroes. *The Godfather* was acclaimed—but mainly by an entertainment industry entrenched in the New Morality. "Angry, weird songs" are valued, it is said, because they help teens not to be lonely and to become connected to others. So are we to assume that this is a *good* thing? Many kids have connected with the wrong people. Haven't we all heard it said of someone, "He fell in with the wrong crowd"? Could it be that some of the adolescents who are described that way are now being tried as adults in court because they connected with people who were just plain angry and weird, who led them into a criminal act? How can Goldberg assume that others don't understand and know anything about teen culture? Teens are not the only ones who encounter the forces of the New Morality. Just because people don't agree with his take on the culture does not mean they don't understand it or know something about it.

Society has a right to constrain activity that puts itself at risk. Is this not the logic behind our drug laws? Could not the same logic apply to music that results in high-risk behavior by those who listen to it? There are people who, when they practice their religion, like to handle snakes. Some states have passed laws to make such a practice illegal, because it compromises people's welfare. For their own protection, these people are subject to restrictions on their freedom of expression. They have been censored, and the ACLU isn't running to their aid. We wonder how Mr. Goldberg would explain the way a teen could make a good connection with someone when hearing lyrics in a rap song that advocates raping a fifteen-year-old girl. Maybe he could explain the positive value that comes from a song by The Offspring titled "Beheaded," in which the group sings to listeners about cutting their parents' heads off, or from the song by DMX that describes having sex with a corpse.[8]

MUSIC FROM THE DARK SIDE

Music aimed at kids conveys endorsements of drug use and Satanism. Method Man sings lyrics in which he says as long as he pledges allegiance to the dark side, he'll never die.[9] Marilyn Manson claims that we're all stars in the dope show, in his song "The Dope Show." A group called GWAR performs lyrics that tell listeners to wipe their rear ends with the Holy Book.[10] Are we really supposed to believe there could possibly be some positive meaning in all these wonderful gems of artistic creativity as those in Mr. Goldberg's circle claim there are?

Those on the Left and in the New Morality like to say to the critics that lyrics are just words and have no effect on those who hear them. If this is true, how do we explain the rise in the teen-pregnancy rate and the fact that every eleven seconds a teenager gets an STD? How do we explain that violent crime, including murder among juveniles has greatly increased?[11]

In a documentary by Phil Chambers on teen music titled *Music to Die For*, he asks a teenage girl who was a fan of one of these shock-music groups, "What would you think of a band that sang about choking a woman to death while having sex with her?" The girl's answer was, "I think it would be kinda funny."[12]

Yeah, that would be a real knee-slapper. We wonder if this teen-age girl would like to share her sense of humor with the many parents who have had to bury a daughter who was raped, then murdered

CASE IN POINT

Human nature is fallen and bound by sin, Scripture tells us. That has always been the case. But our culture does change over time and can either discourage or encourage destructive behavior. American culture was, for many of its early years, much better equipped to repel any repulsive, vulgar items that threatened the moral character of its youth. The year was 1815, and the scene was the Supreme Court of Pennsylvania. A case involving Jesse Sharpless was being decided. Sharpless was on trial for having shown a painting to some young people of a man who was in an "obscene and indecent posture" with a woman.[13] This was a case of pornography being aimed at young people. The defense said it was a private viewing and, therefore, not an indictable offense.[14] The court did not agree with the defense's claim, pointing out that "many things occurring in private have a public effect and are therefore punishable."[15] The words of the court's decision are astonishing:

This court is...invested with power to punish not only open violations of decency and morality, but also whatever secretly tends to undermine the principles of society...Whatever tends to the destruction of morality in general may be punished criminally. Crimes are public offences not because they are perpetrated publicly, but because their effect is to injure the public. Burglary, though done in secret, is a public offense; and secretly destroying fences is indictable...Hence, it follows, that an offense may be punishable if in its nature and by its example it tends to the corruption of morals; although it be not committed in public...No man is permitted to corrupt the morals of the people: secret poison cannot be thus disseminated.[16]

MUSIC OVER MORALITY

The corporations that distribute today's vulgar and violence-ridden music have no difficulty putting profits over people. Former US Secretary of Education William Bennett and C. Delores Tucker, head of the National Congress of Black Women, together met with Time Warner executives to protest the music distributed to young people. They asked for one of the executives to read the lyrics to "Big Man with a Gun," performed by Nine Inch Nails. No executive would agree to read them, so one of the members of the Tucker-Bennett party took on the task.[17] The lyrics are very vulgar, with slang terms for male genitalia, references to oral sex, and pervasive profanity.[18] The song's content is totally degrading to women—hardly your basic "good, old-fashioned love song, coming down in three-part harmony." I (Steve) just can't remember any songs from when I was a teenager that were about male genitalia. It's difficult to see how these lyrics in question have any socially redeeming qualities. They certainly don't esteem women. The Time Warner executives responded with answers like, "Art is difficult to interpret," "What is art?" and "Who decides what is pornography and what isn't?"[19] If these lyrics are art, then this is art I would want my child to avoid.

After these lyrics were read, Bennett inquired of the executives if there was anything that was so deplorable they wouldn't sell it. Silence hung over the room. When the executives provided a couple of insipid responses, Bennett said "baloney" in a return volley that ended with Gerald Levin, the Time Warner chairman, leaving the room in protest to Bennett's choice of language.[20]

Music business corporations with executives who embrace the New Morality have no problem selling *any* music, regardless of how deplorable it is, as long as it makes big bucks. This is why we get raunchy rappers such as Snoop Dogg, whose song "Sexual Eruption" says he keeps a woman with him seven days out of the week, and all they do "is play in the sheets." Not exactly the words you'd want your fifteen-year-old daughter to hear in a love song.

Murder has been linked to gangsta rap. Some kids have allowed this kind of music to lead them to act out sexually; others have been motivated by it to commit murder. In 2013, a student-athlete named Christopher Lane was killed by James Edwards and two other teenagers. They said they did it because they were bored. The police thought there was more to it after they examined Edwards's tweets on his phone and realized his tweets were actually the lyrics of a song by Chief Keef. Keef's music is known as "drill music" that is mainly promoted through social media. Its lyrics are related to violence and criminal activity. Police believed there was a definite link between the lyrics and the death of the young Oklahoma athlete.[21]

There was also a shocking case in which the performer who sang about murder became the murderer. Four people who had been bludgeoned to death were found in Farmville, Virginia, in September 2009. Richard Alden Samuel McCroskey III, a twenty-year-old rapper who went by the name Syko Sam, was charged with the despicable crime. McCroskey specialized in a line of rapping known as "horrorcore."[22]

On his MySpace page, Syko Sam would rap about brutally murdering people and watching them die.[23] On a track called "My

Dark Side," he raps about killing people real slow and how good it feels to watch the victims take their last breath.[24] The aspiring rapper was from Alameda County, California, thus creating a coast-to-coast investigation on this bizarre case. The investigation found that Syko Sam befriended two of the victims through a subculture of violent, macabre music concerts. One of the victims was a sixteen-year-old girl, who investigators said was romantically involved with McCroskey. The other victims were her parents, as well as one of her girlfriends, who shared her taste for this absurd music style.[25]

THE RAPPER AND THE INCUMBENT

In 2008, America elected its first black president. In 2012, as the incumbent of the Oval Office, Barack Obama set his sights on reelection. He sought help from one of his friends, rapper Jay-Z, who was a corner drug dealer in Brooklyn before he amassed a net worth of $460 million from belching out lewd lyrics in rap songs.[26] Jay-Z values dollars over the welfare of American youth. His lyrics are vulgar and offensive to women. Yet he was given a platform next to the president of the United States, who claims to stand for women's rights. Gangsta rap promotes sexual promiscuity and hatred for law enforcement and is highly disrespectful of women.

But when one runs for president, money is needed for the campaign; and when the candidate knows someone who has $460 million, then scrutiny must be discarded. Jay-Z and the president enjoy their own mutually beneficial partnership. Jay-Z endorsed Obama for reelection and even hosted a fundraiser with his wife, Beyoncé, that generated $4 million for the incumbent. The president demonstrated his esteem for Jay-Z when introducing him by way of video at the Made in America music festival:

> To me, the idea of America is that no matter who you are, what you look like, or where you come from, you can make it if you try. Jay-Z did.

He didn't come from power or privilege. He got ahead because he worked hard, learned from his mistakes, and just plain refused to quit. That's the promise of this country; and all of us have the obligation to keep that promise alive.[27]

The president of the United Stated praises a man who rapped about raping and pillaging a village's women and children in a song called "Monster," which he did with Kanye West. Last we checked, raping and pillaging did not qualify one for role-model status, especially when women and children are the victims.

President Obama also regards Jay-Z's wife, Beyoncé, as a role model for his daughters.[28] The Mrs. of the family, Beyoncé doesn't score high marks with some of her lyrics on occasion. In her song "Partition," she is riding in the back of the limousine while she graphically describes a woman performing oral sex in the back of a limo, ending with the words that he "Monica Lewinksys" all over her gown. If Beyoncé is a role model for his daughters, then is the president planning on buying them a limo for graduation? A reference to giving oral sex in a limo is capped off by an ejaculation on the lady's (using the term loosely) dress. One has to take issue with the line that says he "Monica Lewinskys" all over her gown. Such an act would not be possible by a female, in this case the former intern to President Clinton. The name William Jefferson Clinton would be more biologically appropriate to use in the lyric. But why disparage a liberal ex-president when an unfortunate intern has been considered fair game to take the blame and is the preferred target of put-downs regarding Clinton's Oval Office scandal?

The president of the United States does not have the best interest of the children of our country in mind when he endorses and praises a leading producer of music who glorifies murder, rape, and hatred while disrespecting women. A president should speak out against such travesties that make no positive contribution to our culture and the character of our young people.

THE OBSCENE IS SEEN

The problem with today's gutter-inspired music is that kids don't just hear it; they also see it. Cable TV channels are not subjected to the same federal scrutiny as television broadcast channels. MTV has liberty to push the envelope on grossness and sex. It does so without apology, and kids are watching. The sexual content is so explicit that some have called MTV "porn for teens." It is an accurate description. Why would any corporation broadcast music and images that celebrate violence and high-risk sexual encounters? Simple, they make money from it. The values of America's kids are of no concern.

It is as if rap music executives are saying, "Some music is loud, stupid, excessive, vulgar, and appeals to the basic animal instinct. That's why we play it!" MTV appeals to the worst in human nature, freely admits it, and cashes in while your kids learn how to destroy their lives.

Bob Pittman, a former MTV chairman, said, "If you can get their emotions going, forget logic; we got 'em."[29] MTV is now showing more reality shows and fewer videos. The reality shows are just as deplorable in content as the music videos are. Kids still can get the videos on the Internet and even view them away from parental supervision on their smartphones.

Pittman also said, "At MTV, we don't shoot for the fourteen-year-olds; we own them."[30] MTV's target is the junior-high kid, and the network is proud of it. Chambers's documentary shows cuts and lyrics from various MTV videos, and the footage is not appropriate for fourteen-year-olds.[31] If the violence and sexual images from these MTV videos were part of a Hollywood movie, it would be rated R, and no fourteen-year-old would be allowed to see it. What Hollywood has been prevented from delivering to your fourteen-year-old through movies, MTV takes directly to the child via the protected pipeline of cable TV.

PART OF THE ACT?

(Steve): In December 2004, violence took center stage for real in the heavy metal music scene. Just a few days before Christmas, at a nightclub in my former hometown of Columbus, Ohio, thirty-eight-year-old Darrell Abbott, known as "Dimebag" Darrel and the lead guitarist for a group called Damageplan, was shot to death on stage by a crazed gunman as the group started its show. The gunman shot and killed four other people at the club before he was finally killed by police. People now were planning funerals instead of holiday activities.

What really got to me was the response concertgoers gave when they were interviewed about the ordeal. Some said, "We thought the whole thing was part of the act, at first."[32] Part of the act? True story—that's what they said. That says a lot about how far music has come, and it ought to shock us all. A crazed loon runs on stage and blows a performer away, and the fans think it's part of the act. Even if it was part of the act and the whole thing was staged, is that the kind of thing that should be done in a concert setting?

If you were at a concert in the sixties, seventies, or eighties, and someone came on stage firing lead, you would immediately know that it was not part of the act. But, of course, if such a thing were staged, some liberal would defend it as free speech and claim that the First Amendment protects it as freedom of self-expression.

Liberals who take a stand for free speech do so selectively. They say freedom is great for vulgar rappers, raunchy rockers, or irresponsible pornographers. But, they say, we cannot allow a teacher to have a Bible on her desk, allow a cross on public property, or risk letting a student bow in a silent prayer in his lunchroom. All these actions are not freedoms of expression to be tolerated, according to the extreme liberal view. There is always the chance that someone of a different faith or with different values might be offended by these acts. However, when it comes to popular culture, we must endure any offense and accept all kinds of vulgarity, grotesque violence, and indecent sexual acts from the entertainment industry. Liberals insist that those who create such material must have their freedom of expression.

THE PRICE OF FREE SPEECH

The New Morality folks who support the trash producers of the music and entertainment industry are the same ones who try to prevent conservatives and people of traditional values from speaking at certain universities. They are the same people who raise questions about groups such as Promise Keepers (a faith-based organization for men) being able to use the Washington Mall for an event to celebrate family values. Be sure of this: the New Morality does not seek equality for all but an advantage for its cause.

We are a free nation, but a nation that allows for unlimited freedom is on a path to destruction. Freedom works and thrives when the proper constraints are in place and honored. The Founding Fathers knew this and gave us free speech but not an unlimited freedom of expression that has no redeeming social values. We have laws against people driving drunk because such actions put innocent people at risk. Why can't a drunk driver mount a defense that his erratic driving pattern was just his artistic form of freedom of expression?

On February 1, 2005, in Columbus, Ohio, a nonsmoking ordinance went into effect, preventing smokers from lighting up in restaurants and in bars. The reasoning behind the ordinance was that secondhand smoke is considered harmful to those who don't smoke, and the city council members believed it was their responsibility to deny smokers their freedom of self-expression to protect the health of others. The city council censored the activity of smokers to protect others. But, of course, censoring the vulgar music industry that can influence teens to commit violence and risky sexual activity is a big no-no.

MUSIC BIGOTS

One thing the secular music industry believes is that it should not be constrained by censorship. Notice the word *secular*, because there is a part of the music industry that, for practical purposes, is censored. It is known as contemporary Christian music (CCM). It has music that parallels all the genres found in secular music: easy listening, light rock, rock and roll, heavy metal, pop, and even rap. You name it, it's there. But your teenager is not likely to hear any of it unless he or she goes hunting for it. CCM is relegated to Christian radio stations that came into existence so this music would have an outlet.

The cover of the July 16, 2001, issue of *Newsweek* showed a picture of smiling young people with the headline "Jesus Rocks." The inside article described the parallel entertainment universe that features Christian recording artists. It noted that fifty thousand people attended the Freedom Live festival in Tulsa, Oklahoma, and that various Christian rock groups were enjoying robust CD sales.[33] The article asked why the reader hadn't heard about all this and pointed out that mainstream entertainment considers "Christian entertainment as too marginal ever to outgrow its niche position."[34] It revealed that Christian pop music sales hit $747 million in the year 2000 and that for every ten albums country music sold, CCM sold seven.[35]

The article went on to say Christian music is growing, that in recent years it had experienced an increase in sales when secular music recorded a decrease. The popularity of Christian music had not gone unnoticed by the secular record companies. Many of them had created or purchased record labels for Christian music, and, as a result, CDs by Christian artists were not restricted just to Christian bookstores. They were also being sold in businesses such as Walmart.

CENSORSHIP IS NOT A FOUR-LETTER WORD

There are those who will argue that music does not really affect the behavior of its listeners and that fans don't really emulate their favorite stars' lifestyles. If this is true, then why do liberal politicians link up with rock stars to help drum up votes among young people? MTV sponsors Rock the Vote, an all-out effort to get young people to register to vote. We can assure you they are not looking to increase the conservative electorate.

The music industry, along with the film industry, cries out loud and strong that censorship should not apply to them and that the First Amendment protects them. Let's get one thing straight: in reality, we are a nation that uses censorship, and any society has a right to use it to protect the welfare of its people. Censorship is not saying that something is illegal, but that constraints are put in place so that age groups for whom the material is inappropriate are shielded from it. If there were no censorship in entertainment, it would mean that "anything goes" with network TV at any time. Network television cannot air vulgar and extremely profane language. It also cannot show nudity. This is censorship, and it is employed to maintain a standard of decency for the good of the public, especially children. The Federal Communications Commission can fine networks that break the rules of proper programming. Cable is not subject to the same rules, and thus we see what little or no censorship leads to.

It should be pointed out that tobacco companies cannot advertise on cable television. Their product is still legal yet restricted in how it can be marketed to the public. The New Morality calls for restrictions on speech that is derogatory to certain groups. They lobby for laws that prevent people from saying reproachable things about a group because of its race or sexual orientation. They want people's freedom of speech to be curtailed when it comes to making these disparaging remarks, but they want gangsta rappers to have carte blanche when it comes to their free expression. How can you call for laws against hate speech, but then allow for recording artists to sing (and we use that term loosely) about killing cops? Wouldn't singing about killing a cop be hate speech?

The difficulty with censorship is that it is very hard to regain lost ground. The New Morality and its musical-trash department own cable, and they are not likely to relinquish it or any part of it easily. They have the money to give their favorite politicos to make sure that they do not lose ground. However, public opinion is an influential factor, and it can have a tremendous effect on these same politicians. When the public is dead set against an issue, it is not wise to be on the side against them, no matter what interest group is channeling money your way.

If we, as a society, desire women to be treated with respect and we want young people to solve problems without violence, then it seems that a degree of censorship on material that advocates sexual abuse and violence would be in order. A political-science professor by the name of Stanley Brubaker argues that "in a republic form of government where the people rule, it is crucial that the character of the citizenry not be debased."[36]

Preventing Soil Erosion

I (Steve) enjoy a wide range of music. When I work out or drive my van, I may be tuned in to classical music, pop, or rock. I have a number of Christian CDs but am also a fan of mainstream rock. When I was about to go under anesthesia for my gallbladder operation, the nurse asked me what music I wanted to listen to. I asked for Meat Loaf but was told they didn't have any of his songs available, so I opted for the rock band Styx, from the eighties. The last thing I heard before the operation was the first lines of "Mr. Roboto."

Today there are Christian artists, such as Switchfoot or Lecrae, who have made rock or rap music with wholesome lyrics and have gained a strong fan base. They have proved that music can be edgy and still positive. Our Founding Fathers emphasized the value of morality and esteemed it as a positive factor in making democracy work. If such was true then, it is true now. Robert Bork gives credence to this thought, writing that morality is essential for free and democratic governments:

> A population whose mental faculties are coarsened and blunted, whose emotions are few and simple, is unlikely to be able to make the distinction and engage in the discourse that democratic government requires.[37]

There may be freedom to do something in a society, but that does not mean that it is a good thing to do for that society. A society never benefits when greed triumphs over virtue. It is a shame that the secular music industry does not adhere to this belief. The results are tragic for our children.

MAKING A DIFFERENCE: SPELMAN COLLEGE WOMEN

Spelman is the most famous black women's college in America, and its female students took action against the rap music genre. They protested the way women were portrayed as sex objects in rap videos and the disrespect aimed at women in the lyrics. Rapper Nelly cancelled a concert scheduled at the college when he learned a protest was planned. The students believed that rap music videos were too despicable to give the genre any credence. They pointed out that the videos portrayed black women as hypersexual and that the scenes were so explicit, they were a better fit for X-rated films. The students' target was BET, or Black Entertainment Television, a network that proudly broadcasts lewd videos. They also targeted other networks and radio stations that air this brand of rap music. The women admitted that their task would be daunting, but they planned a petition drive and made phone calls to the entities playing and broadcasting the material.[38] Even if they did not succeed fully in their mission, they deserve admiration for daring to make the effort, which may inspire others to do the same.

Take Action

- Look for the parental-advisory logo on music and DVDs to determine if they are appropriate for your child.[39]
- Use Scripture and scientific and medical information when you discuss the harmful effects of sexually explicit and violent lyrics with teenagers and young adults. Use secular research that supports your biblical worldview.

CHAPTER 6

Big Screen, Little Value

Movies can and do have tremendous influence in shaping young lives in the realm of entertainment towards the ideals and objectives of normal adulthood.[1]

—Walt Disney

It was April 20, 1999, and we watched our television sets in disbelief as the horror of the Columbine High School shootings unfolded. Eric Harris and Dylan Klebold entered their high school dressed in black trench coats and carrying loaded guns. They proceeded to shoot students, and when their massacre was done, twelve students and one teacher were dead. One of the movies that was a favorite of the two teenage assassins was *Natural Born Killers*.

This film made heroes of a young man and woman who went on a killing spree across the nation. The last scene has them escaped from prison, happily cruising down the open highway in their motor home with their new baby. They were the picture of the perfect family. Never mind that they had ruined many other families by randomly blowing people away whenever they felt like it. They would kill for the pure joy of killing. But, of course, that is only Hollywood; it's not real. Littleton, Colorado, and the bodies of teenage students in the halls of Columbine High School were real, and the pain in the heart of each parent who lost a child that day is real.

MOTIVATION TO VIOLENCE

The question lingers today: Does violence in movies motivate children to commit acts of violence? In response to this question, the Hollywood Left sends out figures such as the late Jack Valenti, former president of the Motion Picture Association of America, who claims that criticism of Hollywood is a threat to our liberties.[2] Others follow, repeating the claim that violence and sex in films do not lead to people participating in violent or sexual acts. Hollywood claims that films have no influence on behavior in society. Really? That must come as news to companies who pay motion picture studios for product placements in their films.

A James Bond movie *Moonraker* included an explosion scene in which a mob of people ran in panic from where the explosion took place. Debris flew all over the place, but firmly sitting on a lofty perch was a green-and-white cooler with the 7UP soft drink logo plainly in view. Who can forget the lovable ET downing Reese's Pieces as a sweet snack that was out of his world?

Merchandise that gets screen time in the movies usually isn't there by accident. Big bucks are paid for this kind of subtle advertising. Why would corporations pay large amounts of money for this exposure if movies have no influence on people's behavior? The answer is, films *do* influence behavior, and companies that pay to have their products in films know this. That's why there was a run on white suits after John Travolta gyrated his way through *Saturday Night Fever*. That's why countless parents had to divvy up the dough to buy their sons a Millennium Falcon after they saw it in *Star Wars*.

Films influence and motivate behavior. It's true that not everyone who sees a product placement in a film will go out and buy the related product. And likewise, not everyone who sees a violent film will become violent. But to insist that movies have no influence on the real world is silly nonsense.

Hollywood knows the power of its product, and so do special-interest groups. The antitobacco forces have tried to prevail on Hollywood not to have the heroes smoke or use tobacco products because it makes young people want to try them. The environmentalists have seen success in their lobbying efforts on Hollywood. Animated films such as *FernGully* and *Pocahontas*, as well as a slew of others, carried the "green message" to the screen. Hollywood needs to be aware that its political slip is showing. Robert Redford appeared in a film called *Sneakers* about a group of supertalented computer hackers who could gain access to almost any system they desired. The film ended with the news that the National Republican Committee was perplexed about why its bank account had been wiped out, when it was reported at the same time that certain environmental organizations had received major contributions.

The big screen is a showcase for violence, and Hollywood has sought to push the envelope as far as it can. Kids watch it. Even when the film is rated R, they find a way to see it. The more they watch it, the more they become desensitized to it. Violence and obscenity have become so commonplace that even the movie critics are no longer shocked. It is as if they now embrace it as an evolution in a progressive art form. Film critic and author Michael Medved related his experience upon seeing the film *The Cook, the Thief, His Wife, and Her Lover*. Medved took his wife to the screening of the movie and quickly realized that this should have been a solo trip for him. His brief account of some scenes from the film make you wonder what's going on in Hollywood:

> We see sex in a toilet stall, deep kisses and tender embraces administered to a bloody and mutilated cadaver, a woman whose cheek is pierced with a fork, a shrieking and weeping nine-year-old boy whose navel is hideously carved from his body… The grand finale of the film shows the main character slicing off—and swallowing—a piece of carefully seasoned, elegantly braised human corpse in perhaps the most graphic scene of cannibalism yet portrayed in motion pictures.[3]

What did the film critics think of it? They loved it, of course. *New York Times* film critic Caryn James said the film was "something profound and extremely rare: a work so intelligent and powerful that it evokes our best emotions."[4] Judging from Medved's account, we don't see any basis for our best emotions being evoked.

Medved reviewed the film on his PBS show *Sneak Previews* and spoke ill of its violence and absence of any significant moral value. A viewer sent him a piece of hate mail, berating him for his "moralistic high horse." This critic of the movie critic told Medved that his job was to comment on a movie's technical and production qualities and not deal with moral issues related to the film.[5] For this viewer, a film's moral and intellectual content was to be off-limits to critics like Medved. No comments were to be made about the message of the film. The thing that gets to our kids is the thing that the New Morality wants to be uncontested.

The defenders of Hollywood who say that there is no proof that violence in films inspires violence in real life should try to explain why a scene from *The Basketball Diaries* was edited out after the Columbine incident. The scene showed the character played by Leonardo DiCaprio having a dream where he walks into his classroom dressed in a long, black trench coat, carrying a rifle, and starts blowing away his classmates. Editing out the scene was proof that Hollywood could be sensitive to a hurt in our society and act responsibly in the face of it. However, as soon as enough time has elapsed for the issue to no longer be a primary concern, then Hollywood comes back out with the same old trash.

AMERICA, THE TARGET

Hollywood loves to bash America, especially when that America is linked to items that are not dear to the liberal political causes it supports. One of its favorite targets is big business, those corporations that employ millions of people and pay them wages from which these same people purchase movie tickets. In the film *Ernest Goes to Camp*, actor Jim Varney plays his zany Ernest character as a leader of camp kids who fight off an evil corporation that wants to turn the Native American–heritage campgrounds into a condo development.

Hollywood enthusiastically backed the Matt Damon film *Promised Land* to bash the fracking industry.

Hollywood loves to portray the large corporation and its leaders as evil, greedy, and corrupt. It is true that some corporations have corrupt histories, and their officers came under heavy scrutiny, but others have been stellar in their public service. Corporations give millions of dollars to construct new hospital wings and college buildings. But that's not what you often see on the big screen. A study showed that from 1945 to 1965 only 11 percent of feature films conveyed businessmen in a negative light. Between 1965 and 1986, 67 percent of the feature films placed businessmen in unsympathetic roles.[6]

Earlier, we looked at how children are exposed to revisionist history in public schools. The revisionists not only have the textbooks and the classroom lectures on their side, but they also have the big screen to help reinforce their distorted message. One thing the New Morality has learned and uses to its advantage is that there is no rebuttal in a movie theater. Put your movie out there, play loose with the facts, design it in a way that gains an audience sympathetic to the message, and, presto, you have reeducated the masses to your point of view.

Dances with Wolves, starring Kevin Costner, came out in 1990 and clearly gave a one-sided view of Native American history. When you watched that movie, you came away with the message that the white man was always wrong when it came to policies with Native Americans. As you viewed the film, you found yourself rooting for the Indians to kill the US soldiers, who were portrayed as ruthless and evil. Yes, there were incidents when the white man committed atrocities against Native Americans in the Western expansion, but a true account of history also tells of massacres Native Americans committed. There are also accounts that warring tribes tortured each other. One tribe that did this was the Sioux, the same tribe that came off so genteel in *Dances with Wolves*.[7]

Hollywood's bashing of America would not be complete without a focus on its favorite conflict: the Vietnam War. Medved gives a revealing explanation of why Hollywood is so taken with this war:

The deeper reasons for the special attraction to the Indochina conflict involve its unique status as the only war we ever lost and the unparalleled possibilities it provides to make America—and its military—look bad...Recent movies about Indochina almost always show American GIs perpetrating ghastly atrocities against innocent civilians—despite the painstakingly plain and well-documented historical record that shows that only a tiny minority of our troops ever engaged in such brutalities.[8]

Hollywood's treatment of the Vietnam War as an anti-America subject is insulting to the nation and the men who fought there who were just doing their duty. This war, with its political ramifications, was not a bright moment in our nation's history. One has to question, though, the motivation of those who gleefully display it to the public with the hope that many will hold contempt for our military and those who believe in maintaining a strong military.

SEX AND THE KIDS

The sexualization of our kids is a high priority for the New Morality, and for Hollywood. It presents the studios with a double benefit. They get to make big bucks from pedaling sex and, at the same time, help shape the culture toward the values of the New Morality. Hollywood is taking aim at younger ages. The slogan for Hollywood should be "Sex: It's Not Just for Teens and Adults." In the popular kids film *Shrek II*, the evil fairy godmother sang a song that included the words *sexy tush*. The donkey character, voiced by Eddie Murphy, had lines that referenced sex on more than one occasion. Watching the film, one wonders why such language would be in this film if the target audience is kids. When you think back to the mission of GLSEN and SIECUS, there is no wondering why.

When it comes to sex and Hollywood, I (Steve) could cite a number of films that, due to their sexual content, are not the best products to put in front of children and teenagers. But the one film that is a fair example of the depths to which Hollywood will sink to put sex on a silver platter (or screen) for your teenager is *American Pie*. In the movie business, a short descriptive line about a film is called a log line. The log line for *American Pie* is, "Four teenage boys enter a pact to lose their virginity by prom night."

Hollywood justified making the film by saying it is just doing a humorous takeoff on what high school adolescents really do across America. It is interesting to note that the official website for the film, produced by Universal Pictures, prominently displays the film's rating: R. Underneath the R rating, in a box, are the words that tell us why it is rated R: for "strong sexuality, crude sexual dialogue, language and drinking, all involving teens."[9] The words of note are crude sexual dialogue. These words belonged to the company that produced the film, not a film critic. The company spent millions in advertising to get your kids to watch it.

The warning for language is appropriate because the F-word and other vulgarities are liberally used in the film. The sexual-content warning is more than a warning; it's a two-word summary of the movie. The storyline was saturated with the topic of sex. Sex was portrayed as the all-consuming pursuit of every teenage male.

The film's first scene shows a teenage boy in his room trying to decipher a porn film that is scrambled on his TV. His mother comes in unexpectedly and surprises him. He panics and tries unsuccessfully to change the channel. His father enters the room and defends the boy to his mom, saying the channel is not an illegal channel. During this chaos, the viewers are treated to, or offended by, a brief glimpse of the boy's erection, which is covered by a tube sock.

At a party, the main teen-male characters discuss the topic of sex, and some take action. One boy and his steady girlfriend retreat to a bedroom, where it is obvious that she gives him oral sex. His back is to the camera when he ejaculates into a plastic cup filled three-quarters with beer. This is done in preparation for a later sight gag, during which another boy occupies the same room, anticipating sex with the girl he's with. Numerous other scenes in the movie depict equally explicit acts, all meant for laughs.

You might wonder why a movie about teen sex is titled *American Pie*. The reason is made very plain during a scene in which one of the boys comes home and finds a freshly baked apple pie on the counter and a note from his mother that she would be home late. The scene dissolves to a few minutes later, when the boy's dad, a porn-magazine distributor, comes home unexpectedly and sees his son lying on top of the counter with his groin thrust into the apple pie.

Before the film ends, one more despicable scenario had to be conveyed. One of the high school boys who ogled the portrait of his classmate's mother now meets her face-to-face when he wanders into the pool table room, where she is drinking scotch. He compliments her on her looks, and she offers him a scotch. We are later brought back into the room, where, even though they are not seen, the high school boy and his classmate's mother are having sex, which is discernible by their moans, groans, and breathy vocals. As if this is not enough, the music we hear in the background is Simon and Garfunkel singing, "Here's to you, Mrs. Robinson."[10]

I am sure that many people, as I do, find this film deplorable, but the executives at Universal Studios are not among them. For them, the film is fantastic—as in, financially fantastic. The budget for the movie was $11 million, and the film grossed more than $102 million in the United States. Worldwide, the amount was more than $235 million.[11] With a payoff like that, it's not surprising there was an *American Pie 2*, which featured the same characters on the same quest, but now as college students in the summer after their freshman year. The budget went up to $30 million, but the worldwide payoff was more than $287 million.[12] *American Wedding* was the third in the series.

In 2015, Hollywood released the film *Fifty Shades of Grey*, based on the book by the same name. The story is about a corporate billionaire who is a sadist and has a relationship with a young woman, whom he abuses sexually through bondage and beatings.[13] Is this the sort of thing teens and college-age adolescents need to see on Valentine's weekend, when it was released? The NFL launched an anti-domestic-violence program with special emphasis at the Super Bowl, and in the wake of that, Hollywood glorifies sadistic sex and abuse to women. Hollywood seeks to make millions on the sexual abuse of women and then drop a portion of its earnings into liberal candidates' campaigns, who then accuse conservative candidates of conducting a war on women. Can things get any more absurd?

Fifty Shades of Grey even had an impact on kids. Middle school kids are not old enough to see this film in theaters, but that did not prevent them from being touched by it. Parents of children in a middle school in Monessen, Pennsylvania, were shocked when they learned that their kids were given a word puzzle based on *Fifty Shades of Grey*. Four of the terms contained in the puzzle were spanking, submissive, leather cuffs, and bondage.[14] Is this what kids need to learn about in school? Taxpayers' dollars at work.

BLAME THE MEDIA, SHAME ON YOU

Parents of teenagers should worry about these films and the impact they might have on their children. The New Morality claims the media has no real influence on children. At least, that is what Karen Sternheimer states in her book *It's Not the Media: The Truth about Pop Culture's Influence on Children*. She believes that media should not be held accountable for any problems that affect kids:

> Blaming media for changes in childhood and social problems has shifted our public conversation away from addressing the real problem that impacts children's lives. The most pressing crisis facing American children today is not media culture but poverty.[15]

This statement not only shows Sternheimer's identification as a lefty liberal, but also that she is either not well versed on her topic or just plain chooses to ignore reality. Harris and Klebold, the two boys who shot up Columbine High School, were not eating meals paid for with food stamps. They were from middle-class families. Poverty was not a factor in the evil they chose to bring on others. Teens in middle-class and upper-class homes are taking their cues from pop culture and hitting the booze and hitting the sack without regard to the consequences.

Sternheimer actually goes against her premise when she writes, "We don't like hearing foul language blasting from the stereo of the car next to ours and cringe when young girls want to emulate sexy pop stars."[16] If the media and pop culture have no influence on children, why would a young girl want to copy the actions of Madonna, Miley, or Beyoncé? It is obvious: because she is influenced by them through the media and she wants to be like them.

Sternheimer wrote a sentence in her book that makes one who values virtue want to wrap his or her head in duct tape to keep it from exploding. Our comments appear in brackets throughout the quote,

> Even though most of us are not pedophiles [Does she expect a number of them to be in her reading audience, and are they just to be thought of as a minority group?] and do not directly harm children [Are we to gather that indirect harm is done to kids by most of us and is acceptable?], the insistence on children's inherent innocence version of childhood that many of us actively construct [So a childhood of innocence is not to be desired?] may do more harm than good [Does this mean we are to enhance a child's life by exposing them to sex and violence at an early age?].[17]

NOT JUST THE DOLLARS

Many say that Hollywood's actions are purely business motivated—that filmmakers only do what they do because it makes them money. This sounds, on the surface, like a logical argument. It is brought into question by an experience that Medved had, which I (Steve) have heard him tell in person and on the radio. He screened a movie and basically liked the film, except for the liberal use of the F-word throughout the production. He later spoke to the producer or director, one of the two, and told him that he liked the film but thought it would gain more box office success if it were not R-rated because of the language. This film principal responded by saying their research showed that Medved's analysis was correct, that they would gain substantially more box-office gross if they edited out the foul language and went for a PG rating. Medved inquired why they did not do this. The man said because they, the filmmakers, did not want to compromise themselves as artists.

So the use of the F-word is now art. When a teenager gets mad and reels off a volley of vulgar lingo, you can say he or she is just being artistic. Maybe it is wrong for us to be offended, for we could be in the presence of an emerging verbal Michelangelo. Medved's words provide a unique perspective on this ironic fact:

> Money is not the main motivation for their current madness. The leading figures of the popular culture, insecure and uncertain like all creative personalities, are driven by a deep-seated need to reassure themselves as to the significance of their own work. Contempt for "mere" commercial considerations is frequently expressed by those who long to view themselves as something more than entertainers or businessmen.[18]

An analysis of the business model of Hollywood gives validity to Medved's words. Hollywood seems bent on pushing the envelope with more violence and sex in R-rated movies, but these films, as a group, do not fare as well as G and PG films at the box office. Research by Robert Cain examined revenues related to film ratings, finding that R-rated films are less likely to succeed at the box office than those with G, PG, and PG-13 ratings. In fact, R-rated films return less profit than those targeting teens and family audiences.[19]

R-rated films are bad for the Hollywood bank account, but they help the New Morality forward their message and influence the culture. Most CEOs in successful corporations would cut back on the R-rated films if they were running studio production companies, but Hollywood just keeps the R films coming. In some years, there are more R-rated films made than G-rated and PG-rated movies put together. Hollywood can lose money on movies and still call their efforts "art." Try doing that with the company you work for and see how long your boss will be an "art" lover.

Medved cites a survey done among the American people regarding movies. The results revealed that 82 percent wanted less violence, 72 percent wanted less sexual content, and 80 percent wanted less foul language in films.[20] An overwhelming majority wants Hollywood to clean up its act, but Hollywood does not listen; it just keeps churning out the garbage. It is ironic that Hollywood won't listen to the American people, but every election year, the Hollywood stars and elite come forth and want the American people to listen to them.

THE ACCEPTABLE PREJUDICE

A favorite target of Hollywood is Christianity. There may be increased sensitivity to ethnic groups, special-interest issues, and different sexual orientations; but it is open season on Christians. Bashing Christians is not an abhorrent activity for Hollywood filmmakers; in reality, it is a legalized prejudice to be pursued with vigor. Hollywood defends its presentations of violence, foul language, and sexual content as merely their reflection of reality. In the movie *The Sum of All Fears*, neo-Nazi European industrialists are the villainous terrorists, even though in the Tom Clancy book upon which the film was based, the villains were Muslim extremists. The Arab-American lobbyists prevailed on Paramount Pictures not to use Muslims as the bad guys.[21]

The plot of the film was that terrorists wanted to set off a bomb at the Super Bowl. Based on the terrorist attacks that have been aimed at our nation, I'm inclined to think such an attack, as featured in *The*

Sum of All Fears, would more likely be carried out by Muslim terrorists than some neo-Nazi group. So much for art reflecting reality. Hollywood was willing to forego reality to be sensitive to Islam, but no sensitivity exists when it comes to Christianity. For that, bias and bigotry prevail. Hollywood has dared to produce films about personalities in the Bible that are totally contrary to what the Bible conveys about them. In *The Last Temptation of Christ,* Jesus is portrayed as confused, weak, and bewildered. Then there's the movie *King David,* which shows David giving up his faith in God at the end—something he never did in the biblical account. These films were protested by Christians who were offended by them, but Hollywood made no changes and allowed them to be released. The films did not enjoy box-office success.

It was refreshing to see Mel Gibson's provoking film *The Passion of the Christ* rock the Hollywood world. The road to getting this production on the big screen was not an easy one. No studio wanted to back the project, and distributors were not lining up for consideration. The Hollywood mainstream was not interested. After all, the film didn't show Jesus as a weakling. It didn't show biblical heroes rejecting God. On the contrary, it put Christianity in a positive light.

In order to make the film, Gibson had to fund it and direct it himself. Eventually, he found a distributor. The cultural impact was enormous. Many churchgoers bought tickets in advance through their churches. It became one of the highest-box-office-grossing films of all time. Imagine that—a film that treasures Christianity instead of trashing it scores at the box office and brings many people out to the theaters who probably avoid going to the movies the rest of the time. The film became an all-time blockbuster.

It was interesting to note the criticism Gibson and his film received as its release date approached. Hollywood and the news media said the film was anti-Semitic and degrading to Jews. *Boston Globe* journalist James Carroll wrote, "Even a faithful repetition of the Gospel stories of the death of Jesus can do damage exactly because those sacred texts themselves carry the virus of Jew hatred."[22]

I can't believe the lies in this statement. Carroll would say that no one should ever make stories faithful to the New Testament because they would always put Jews in a bad light. Using that logic, we should tell the History Channel to stop running documentaries on World War II because it puts the Germans in a bad light. I guess Gibson's film is a case in which a movie should not have reflected reality, which Hollywood claims to be so committed to doing. When the film *Corpus Christi*, which portrayed Jesus Christ as a homosexual, was released, Hollywood didn't worry that many Christians would be offended, nor did I see James Carroll write articles condemning this film as damaging to Christians.

All the noise about Gibson's film being too anti-Semitic was a smoke screen. The real reason people opposed it was that it was pro-Christian and could influence people toward traditional values. The critics went with the anti-Semitic approach because they felt they could get more traction with it in our politically correct society. Gibson proved that high-quality films with a pro-Christian message can attract an audience and be successful. Hollywood should take heed, but I'm not holding my breath. The major studios still control what gets made and what does not, for the most part. They also have cozy deals with distributors that determine what gets on a large number of screens. It should be pointed out that in the year when Gibson shook the Hollywood world with *The Passion of the Christ*, the Academy Awards gave the Oscar for best picture to Clint Eastwood's *Million Dollar Baby*, a film that championed assisted suicide.

If we are to believe what Hollywood puts out, then we would believe that Christians are crazy, kooky, crooked, mentally unstable, prejudiced, stupid, homicidal, greedy, sex addicts, and hypocrites. Hollywood has sent out this message on countless occasions. Most of the time, films that are degrading to Christianity don't pull in great revenues, but they are still out there, with propaganda that sooner or later reaches our kids. Over time, these kids make judgments and form values that affect their behavior and life. If their conclusions about Christianity are based on the Hollywood doctrine, then they will reach those conclusions by way of misinformation that is purposely designed to distort the truth. Sadly, that is the result many in Hollywood desire.

A CHRISTIAN CHARGE

There are Christian filmmakers who are making a valiant attempt to produce movies with a Christian message on the big screen. Alex and Stephen Kendrick have been successful in getting their films on the big screen, even if the number of screens and run times has been lower than major Hollywood studios are able to secure. Their film *Courageous* was successful, and their release of *War Room* in 2015 fared well at the box office. Other Christian film companies are getting some traction, but the fight to gain theater screens is a difficult one. Dinesh D'Souza has produced successful documentaries that have exposed the negative aspects of liberalism and have been critical of Barack Obama. His documentaries have had outstanding ticket sales. However, given the topics of his films, we don't think he's anticipating any Oscar nominations.

Christian families need to support Christian films at the box office, especially when the films measure up in quality production and a sound gospel message. Theaters will want to book more of these films when they realize the public is willing to purchase tickets for them.

MAKING A DIFFERENCE: TED BAEHR

There is one name at the forefront of film media as it relates to traditional values. That name is Ted Baehr. Mr. Baehr is the founder and publisher of *Movieguide: The Family Guide to Movies and Entertainment*, wherein he provides reviews on current films and entertainment from a family-values perspective. Parents can ascertain from his reviews whether a film is right for their family or children. He is also chairman of the Christian Film and Television Commission, which interacts with the secular entertainment industry by lobbying for films that have family values. Mr. Baehr does not take the approach of retreating from the world and carving out a Christian segment of entertainment. Instead, he stays active on Hollywood turf to influence the industry to realize the Christian-and-family-value audience is a market to be considered. Mr. Baehr's *Movieguide* is available online at www.movieguide.org and in print. Mr. Baehr is a noted author on the topic of media and culture through numerous books and articles. He is a cultural warrior who is not afraid to stand up to the powers of Hollywood and be the voice of values for all of us who share his sentiments.

TAKE ACTION

- Check the Kids in Mind website (www.kids-in-mind.com) before you take your children to a movie.
- Read the Summit Medical Group's finding on the harmful impact of R-rated movies on children under age thirteen, available at http://www.summitmedicalgroup.com/library/pediatric_health/ hhg_r-rated_movies.

CHAPTER 7

Invader in a Box

Television has been the single greatest shaper of emptiness.[1]

—Ravi Zacharias, author
and Christian apologist

Donald Wildmon wrote a book in 1985 titled *The Home Invaders*. He was speaking of television. Much of what was said about the film industry in the previous chapter can be applied to this chapter about television because much of it is produced by the same companies and individuals. Perhaps the biggest difference is the sheer volume of programming on television, with its sitcoms, dramatic series, reality shows, and cable-channel offerings. Television has been around since the 1940s, and the country has undergone a major cultural change since. Television is our electronic window to the world. Sometimes what it shows us is truly wonderful, but often the view is not inspiring. Dr. Wildmon took television to task some thirty years ago for questionable programming. If we were heading in the wrong direction thirty years ago, we are miles down that wrong path today.

THE POWER BOX

We might regard our TV sets as electronic windows to the world, but the New Morality sees it as an avenue of opportunity by which to invade our homes. Television is powerful, and the New Morality knows it, using it frequently to advance its agenda in both subtle and blatant ways.

Television survives because of advertising purchases by corporations. There are those who say that television's purpose is to inform and entertain, but its ultimate purpose is to make money. Programming is the means to attracting an audience, and when that audience is attracted, the programming is then rented out to corporations via commercials. The bigger the audience, the more broadcasters can charge for airing a commercial.

High ratings mean more money. Shows that pull a low rating are cancelled in the hope that they can be replaced by new shows that will achieve higher ratings. Put simply, money is at the heart of the matter when broadcasters decide what to air. What gets high ratings gets the interest of TV executives. If violence and sex get high ratings, then there will be programs with violence and programs that are sexually oriented, or programs with both. Even if such programs are criticized for their adverse effect on society, they will be defended at all costs—if they are moneymakers.

The unique thing about television is that it is in the home. Think about it. It is always there, and you turn it on and search for a show to watch. It is unlike the movie theater, where you have to make a choice regarding what film you want to see, and then you have to get in the car and go to the theater. It's much easier with TV; just turn it on and start watching. There is little effort or forethought involved. For the last half of the past century and on into this new one, people have been turning on the television and watching. While viewers are doing so, the New Morality is infiltrating their minds with its values, and it is doing it right in their homes.

Television has such a great impact on the viewers that it boggles the mind. This became abundantly clear to me when I (Steve) had an entertainment lawyer visit the creative-writing class I taught at a college. He told the students about the time back in the 1960s when his boss took him to a room in the network studios where a soap opera was filmed. In this room, there were wedding presents, some of which were very valuable, sent in by viewers for the characters on the show who were getting married in an upcoming episode. The characters were not real-life people, and their wedding was not real. Yet hundreds of people sent wedding gifts to them. What does this say? It says television is powerful. Corporations know that TV is powerful, and that's why they spend millions of dollars on advertising. TV is a medium through which messages can be sent to motivate viewers to take particular actions. If this were not true, corporations would not be spending big advertising bucks on it.

THE LINK THAT IS NOT MISSING

Surely, this does not come as a surprise to you. We bring it to your attention anyway, because there are those in the entertainment industry who argue this point to the contrary. Violence and sexual content attract viewers, resulting in higher ratings. To protect these money-making programs from their critics, TV executives claim that violence and sex on TV do not affect the behavior of the viewers in any way. The overriding question is, Do violence and sexual content in TV programs lead to more violence and sexual promiscuity in real life? A yes answer would be detrimental to the financial interests of the TV networks.

Victor Cline, PhD, from the University of Utah's department of psychology did an extensive study on TV violence and its link to violence in society. He found that there are twenty years of behavioral studies that relate exposure to violence in the media to violence in real life. He makes the statement, "I do not think that any fair reviewer…can deny that the media are one important contributor to the violence problems in our society."[2]

Critics of TV violence point out that repeated exposure has a cumulative effect. The more violence one sees, the less appalled by it he is. Dr. Cline was in total agreement with this concept. He found in his research that repeated viewing of violence desensitizes the viewer to the point that the shock element no longer exists. He went on to point out that the "capacity to empathize with the victim" is lost.[3]

In a study conducted by the University of Pennsylvania, children were asked, "How often is it all right to hit someone if you are mad at him?" Those children who watched a large amount of TV responded that it was almost always okay to hit someone who made you mad.[4] Studies also reveal that children who are heavy viewers are likely to have more fear in their lives than those with limited TV exposure.[5]

An article in *Children's Advocate* in 1997, by Jean Tepperman, gives powerful evidence that TV violence does contribute to more violent behavior in the real world:

> Since 1955, about one thousand studies, reports, and commentaries concerning the impact of television violence have been published. The accumulated research clearly demonstrates a correlation between viewing violence and aggressive behavior." That statement, made in 1992 by the American Psychological Association, summarized its comprehensive review of research on the effects of media violence. Other organizations including the American Medical Association, National Institutes of Mental Health, and the US Centers for Disease Control came to similar conclusions. One key study that showed the connection between media violence and real violence was one by Dr. Leonard D. Eron. He followed a group of young people for twenty-two years and found that those who watched more television at age eight were more likely, at age thirty, to have committed more serious crimes, to be more

aggressive when drinking, and to punish their children more harshly than others. Others have repeated Eron's study and found similar results throughout the United States and other countries as well.[6]

The TV networks disagree with the studies that show that TV violence leads to violent behavior in children—and later on, when they become adults. They have even commissioned their own studies, which—surprise, surprise, showed no link of their violent programming to violent behavior. The inconsistency of the TV networks is seen in their praise of an episode of the sitcom *Happy Days*:

> A network official will take great satisfaction in pointing out that an episode of *Happy Days*, in which the Fonz gets a library card, apparently spurred thousands of children to do the same thing within days. But in almost the next breath, the same executives will say TV does *not* influence viewers' behaviors. The stance is an effort to wriggle out of addressing questions in the impact that TV sex and violence have on viewers.[7]

TV networks are willing to take the praise for the good behavior they encourage, but refuse to bear responsibility for the violent behavior that their programs induce. Often their response to those who dislike violent or sexual content programming is, "Turn it off." This answer seems reasonable, but the issue is more complex than this simple action. Wildmon shows how faulty this concept is when he makes comparisons stating that if he doesn't like crime in the street, should he just stay in his house; or if he doesn't like drunken drivers, should he stay off the highways?[8] He goes on to say, "Whether I watch it or not, I have to live in the society which television influences."[9] If TV violence influences violent behavior in society, as many studies conclude, then all of us who live in society are at risk of being victims of that violent behavior.

Frank Mankiewicz wrote in his book, *Remote Control,* that he could not find a police chief serving any major city in the nation who did not believe that much of the crime his force dealt with originated on television.[10] It is absolutely absurd that TV network executives would believe their surplus of violent and sexually oriented programming has no influence on viewers but, at the same time, will charge big bucks for advertising to corporations that know, from their own studies, communicating on TV does motivate viewers to specific behaviors.

THE NETWORK FOOTBALL FUMBLES

Network television must contend with something filmmakers don't: the Federal Communication Commission (FCC). The FCC acts as the watchdog of the airways and has the power to fine TV and radio stations that violate its regulations. Given what is allowed to appear on TV these days, one would gather that their regulations are not all that strict. As true as this might be, there still are codes that prevent nudity and certain profanity and vulgar words from being aired. TV executives walk the line between developing violent and sexually oriented programming that will bring in a large audience while not violating FCC regulations. They do their best to push the envelope, hoping to gain more ground by testing what the FCC will allow them to air. Sometimes they go too far.

Perhaps the most famous FCC violation in recent memory was the halftime show at the 2004 Super Bowl. It was broadcast by CBS that year. Janet Jackson was the musical star of the show, along with a young Justin Timberlake. The two gyrated their way through a rock duet that was accented by sexually suggestive groping. The song ended with Timberlake pulling on Jackson's outfit in an aggressive, violent move that exposed one of her breasts. The incident became known as Nipplegate. No matter what it was called, it was expensive to CBS; the network had to pay an FCC fine of $550,000, though the Supreme Court later overturned the ruling.[11]

The National Football League was none too happy with the incident and protested to the network. They were not alone. In a survey, 68 percent of viewers said they saw the Jackson exposure, and of those, 31 percent said they were offended by it.[12] Bernard Goldberg accurately wrote, "If you get in bed with MTV, as the NFL did, you had better expect to have sex. That's the business MTV is in."[13] Mr. Goldberg wanted to convey that the NFL should not connect with the low morality of the entertainment world, so he used MTV as a synonym to identify with the deviant behavior in the music industry even though MTV had no direct involvement in the production.

Jackson and Timberlake tried to explain the incident as a wardrobe malfunction. Yeah, right. The only malfunction was what happened in the brains of the people who thought this thing up and the brains of those who went along with it.

The television industry holds an annual award show, for which they present Emmys to the winners. They should have an award for ABC called a "Dummy." ABC, which at the time carried *Monday Night Football* (it has since been carried by ESPN), and in light of the Jackson-Timberlake halftime fiasco, you would think they would be careful not to come close to doing anything similar. The following football season, ABC put on a promo for a *Monday Night Football* game that sent shock waves throughout the industry and into the homes of many viewers. Sex was once again visiting the NFL.

Star wide receiver Terrell Owens was paired in a skit with blonde star, Nicollette Sheridan, from the ABC hit show *Desperate Housewives*. In the skit, Sheridan hits on the football-uniform-clad Owens, trying to get him to forget playing in the game for the opportunity to play with her. Her words don't persuade him, but she is finally convincing when she opens up the large white towel, exposing her body to him. At least, that's what the viewers are led to believe, because all they saw was a view from the back of the female star, where the towel stayed in place.

The NFL prides itself on the fact that its product is entertaining to the whole family, and you can imagine that a large number of boys watch games with their fathers. The NFL is not served well when parents are afraid to watch games with their children. When you want to watch football with your family, you should not have to worry about whether or not there is going to be something that you do not want your kids to see. In case you are wondering, the FCC did not hit ABC with a fine for that skit, as they judged it did not go too far.Competition for Indecency

Why do major broadcast networks take chances? It is because they have competition from the cable industry. The FCC governs the airways; therefore, its regulations do not apply to cable channels, which send their signals through cables, not over the air. Cable channels can present programs containing nudity, gross violence, and profanity that broadcast networks cannot. When cable television was first introduced, the big networks still held the major share of TV viewers. As the years went by, cable's market share increased. It is now estimated that 85 percent of the population has cable, either by line or satellite dish.[14]

The networks are feeling the loss of viewers to cable and are willing to take major risks on programming, even if it might run afoul of the FCC. Some executives at networks believe they should have the same programming freedom as cable has. On the contrary, it would be better if cable had the same limitations as the networks. A Senate bill was introduced in 2005 by West Virginia senator John D. Rockefeller, a Democrat, and Texas senator Kay Bailey Hutchison, a Republican, to bring cable under the same control as the networks.[15] The bill went nowhere.

MTV: MUSIC TV OR SEX TV?

The programming freedom that cable enjoys has not been good news for parents. Cable's freedom from a watchdog like the FCC has given the New Morality a direct path to the minds of our kids.

One cable channel in particular had a huge impact on teenagers during the last two decades of the twentieth century: MTV. The *M* stands for *music*, and this cable channel made it possible for music videos to have a public outlet regardless of content. All the things that were discussed in chapter 5 regarding the violence and vulgarity in music now are available for kids to see and not just hear.

In recent years, many similar music-themed and youth-targeted channels have flourished. Often these channels are part of a basic package. That means they are not special pay channels; if you pay for basic cable, you get them whether you like it or not. As Robert Bork noted, the images your child might see in a music video on MTV may or may not illustrate the song lyrics. A rap video, for instance, could depict guns, killings, and graphic sex—all skillfully produced.[16]

Music videos were only the starting point of MTV's programming. It now produces reality TV and other shows that are not music related yet convey the same messages of sex and indecency that are celebrated in the music videos. One of MTV's groundbreaking reality shows was called *The Real World*. A description of it is given by Bryan Kemper:

> This is a show that places seven young people in a house, rigged with cameras in every room, to record their lives for six months. Nothing is sacred—not even the shower. In one of the recent opening shows they show the young adults discovering that the shower is a "double shower" so they can shower in groups, which they do. They have had episodes where the other roommates peek through the windows to witness group sex going on in the shower. The latest group had to be twenty-one or over because MTV wanted to film the show in a casino in Las Vegas. In the first episode, they showed them together nude in a hot tub and then three of them getting physical in the bath tub while others sat and watched. These scenes have been so graphic that they had to blur out sections of the screen to show them. To welcome the cast to the house they are greeted with a large bowl of condoms.[17]

MTV developed its own soap opera, which was all about teen-agers and all about sex. The show was called *Undressed*. Kemper's monitoring of this show produced this description: "Every story was about kids having sex in different situations, including their schools, homes (while parents are gone), and even in the school parking lots."[18] He went on to state, "There are episodes about group sex, sexual partner swapping, sexual fetishes, homosexuality, and much more. The plots always seem to be promoting casual sex as the norm and any variation as a great thing."[19]

If your teenager is taking in a steady dose of shows like these, he or she is being conditioned to participate in similar activities, with all the risks that accompany them. Television producers are only too happy to help further the sexual education of your teenager if you let them. And if these values happen to be contrary to your values on this topic, you should not be surprised. Executives and producers of youth-oriented programming know that bawdy content will get higher ratings. No doubt they would point out how much they care about your teenager as they lead him down the path of promiscuity because they endorse the use of condoms and also tell the kids how to contact Planned Parenthood.

Another cable show that enjoyed popularity was *Sex in the City*, which was broadcast on the HBO cable channel. Here is the synopsis of the first episode:

> At a birthday party for thirty-something Miranda, Carrie and her friends vow to stop worrying about finding the perfect male and start having sex like men. Carrie experiments with an old flame and meets Mr. Big; Miranda warms up to Skipper; Samantha has a one-night stand with a man Charlotte wouldn't sleep with on the first date.[20]

With this episode, a new show was launched to convey the idea that women should have sex just for the sheer pleasure of it, with all caution cast to the wind. Here was a show that was celebrating female promiscuity in an age when STDs were rampant. How many parents were thrilled to have a show that their daughters could watch that would glamorize women who chose to have sex indiscriminately? And many youth did find a way to watch it. The show no longer runs on TV, but it lives on via Netflix and other Internet-streaming services.

Cable also has pay channels, which are channels that do not come with the basic package and are available at an additional cost. Many of these are movie channels, such as HBO, Starz, and Cinemax. These channels show movies as you would see them in the theater. There is no editing to cut out profanity, violence, or sexual scenes because FCC regulations on this kind of content do not apply. What is shown in the theaters is now easily available at home.

When you first sign up for cable via satellite dish, the company gives you a few months of some pay channels for free, hoping you will decide to add them to your package. I (Steve) watched the movie *Dr. Dolittle* on HBO one Friday evening. This is a decent film about someone who is able to talk to animals. It is a film that the whole family can enjoy and a film that is acceptable for children to watch. Eddie Murphy is great as Dr. Dolittle, and there is some good comedy in the story. The film ended, and the credits rolled. I started doing other things, going in and out of the room. It was now around 7:10 on Friday evening, and I left the HBO channel on, using it as audio wallpaper.

The next film that came on was *Eyes Wide Shut*, starring Tom Cruise and Nicole Kidman. This film struggled to get an R-rating because it was basically a porn film that should have been rated "X." I came into the room and caught a glimpse of one scene in the film—an orgy in a mansion that had a satanic feel to it. In the scene, people are in hooded black capes with masks, and they pair off to have sex. Of course, with the masks, no one knows with whom they are having sex. I hit the off button. The nudity and profanity are plentiful in the film, so I've been told, and here it all was, available during primetime viewing on a Friday evening. What if there were parents whose kids were upstairs with their friends watching the kid film *Dr. Dolittle* while the grown-ups talked and had coffee downstairs? As time rolled on, the kids would soon have been watching a movie that could be described as "sex from the dark side."

TAKING IT TO THE LIMIT AND BEYOND

Cable's freedom from FCC regulations has motivated broadcast networks to "take it to the limit." One network aired a Victoria's Secret runway show, which presented gorgeous women parading around in skimpy, stylish underwear. Why do you think this show was put on TV? Do you think there was a great need in America, where women were saying, "I want to buy new underwear, and I just wish some company that sells it would put a show on TV so I could see what new products are out there"? Or do you think there were a bunch of guys sitting around at work during lunch saying, "I want to get my wife some new stylish, high-ticket underwear, and I wish that someone would put a show on TV that would show me what is available so I can buy it for her"?

The reason that show aired was not to present an infomercial but to get high ratings by showing lots of unclothed women. The show came under a great deal of criticism, and the special was not repeated in following years, only to later reemerge. But it's not always a matter of showing skin. Networks can convey a lot of sexual content through the storylines and dialogue in their sitcoms. *Friends* was a highly popular sitcom for NBC; at the peak of its popularity, its six stars each sought a salary of a million dollars per episode. Watching this show, you get the message that casual sex, homosexuality, and pregnancy out of wedlock are all OK—just the things you want your teenager to embrace.

The sitcom *Will and Grace*, which was popular in the early years of this century, featured a young single woman who had a gay male roommate. This Emmy Award-winning show was very positive for the homosexual agenda. Its success and impact are noted on the Classic TV and Movie Hits website:

By 2005, *Will & Grace* had been nominated for 49 and won 12 Emmys. From 2001–2005, *Will & Grace* was the second-highest-rated comedy among adults 18–49, second only to NBC's own *Friends*, which usually preceded it on the Thursday night schedule. It has also been heralded as responsible for opening the door to a string of gay-themed television programs such as *Queer Eye for the Straight Guy* and *Boy Meets Boy*. *Will & Grace* has won several GLAAD Media Awards for its fair and accurate representation of the gay community.[21]

Did the producers and network executives check with Christians, Orthodox Jews, and Muslims to see if this show offended them? I don't think so. A comedy show that makes us laugh and feel sympathetic toward a character who is homosexual is presented with the hope that it will make the public more accepting of this lifestyle. It is a weapon the New Morality uses to gain more ground. It seems to be working. Bork revealed how dangerous TV has been for the morality of the nation. While TV began by offering a relatively apolitical and traditional view of social norms, it now follows the politics of the Left, which has affected the way sex, authority, and even good and evil are presented on the small screen.

Robert Bork believed TV was dangerous for the morality of the nation. He felt it had become the electronic tool of the Left. They moved TV from a nonpolitical medium that held traditional values on social issues to subtly and openly challenging these values as they communicated their liberal agenda. Their success has brought about changes in sexual behavior, attitudes toward authority, and confusion regarding the concept of good and evil. Recreational sex is portrayed as commonplace and totally acceptable. Gays and prostitutes are seen as victims of some factor of social injustice. Adultery, pornography, and sex work, which ranges from strip dancing to prostitution, are no longer condemned. As far as the liberal Left is concerned, those who engage in such are not to be the target of any code of sexual morality that would restrict their behavior. Television today has established the relative morality of the sixties as the values to push on the public.[22]

Morality is not the only area that television seeks to influence. It also desires to alter people's political views. The show that clearly verifies this is *The West Wing*. This show was about the operations inside the White House. Viewers got a taste of what it is like inside a presidential administration as it tries to advance its political objectives. The hero of the show is the president, a Democrat, and the episodes have no problem favoring liberal Democrat viewpoints over Republican ones. The president's name is Josiah Bartlet, portrayed by Martin Sheen, himself a staunch liberal in real life. Ben Domenech, the conservative pundit who founded the web magazine, *The Federalist*, describes this fictitious character in an accurate way:

> Bartlet, by any measure, is Hollywood's version of a liberal Gipper, and Sheen plays him to the hilt. He's an undiluted liberal Democrat from the Northeast, with a Founding Father in his bloodline and a passion for economics. He's emphatically pro-abortion rights, pro-gun control, a champion of gays in the military, and a vociferous fan of campaign finance reform—though there's no word yet on how he actually got elected with such left-of-center views...Bartlet is [Bill] Clinton without the skirt-chasing flaws, a man with a common touch, a huge heart, and an aura of adult responsibility. He is a president designed to satisfy any liberal's wildest dreams.[23]

When it comes to Emmy Awards, *The West Wing* won its fair share, and it has been a favorite show of the media. Domenech presents an interesting perspective on this success:

> Of course, it's a bit of a stretch to imagine *The West Wing* getting the laudatory praise and awards it's received if the chief executive had been, say, a

pro-life, school-prayer-advocating Republican. Indeed, most of the partisan quibbling between conservatives and the White House staff that take place on the show are reduced to one-sided shouting fests, with the TV counterparts of Congressional Republicans getting the short end of the intellectual stick.[24]

Imagine that—conservatives and Republicans getting the short end of the stick from network TV.

ENDORSEMENT OF PORN

Television has news programs as well as entertainment, and there is a news-related issue that is appropriate to address in this chapter.

The issue concerns this one question: Why does TV news endorse pornography? Every TV news organization would likely protest this charge. But what else do you call it when a *Playboy* Playmate of the Year is invited on a news show to be interviewed so she can sing the praise of Playboy Enterprises and its philosophy, thanking it for giving her such a big showbiz break? This has been done on local news, network news, and even Fox News. If this is not endorsing pornography, then what is it?

And, more importantly, what does it say to our kids, especially the girls? A teenage girl could conclude that a porn career is a path to legitimacy and respect. Playmate centerfolds are sex objects, and why would a respectful news organization make any effort to feature that on its program? When viewers protest the content on television, be it by voice or boycott, TV executives claim that such a protest is dangerous. Instead of taking those concerns seriously, they dismiss those who are concerned with the moral impact of television as mere fanatics who want to force their morality on the rest of the country. Medved gives a befitting response to this position:

> Nowhere in the Constitution is it written that TV viewers must sit quietly on their couches and passively accept whatever the industry chooses to place on the air; the right to protest degrading material is not limited to those favored few who are asked to report their viewing on a Nielsen box.[25]

Some families may have strict rules regarding TV viewing, but nowadays so many programs can be watched directly on smartphones. This makes all kinds of extreme programming available for kids to watch while they are away from home. It's harder than ever for parents to monitor the media their kids are consuming.

One cannot minimize the impact TV has in the cultural war. With the advent of cable, we have content coming into our homes that would never have been considered possible thirty years ago. The immediate future doesn't show signs that it will get any better. TV is a favorite weapon of the New Morality. It is one that is sure to impact your children.

BAD ADS

Television delivers not only questionable programs for young people to view, but also commercials that discard values and present deceptive messages. Teenagers are a demographic group that advertisers target. Teens have money to spend, even if they get it from their parents. When it comes to fashion, teens want to wear the cool stuff. Label identity can be a big item. What you wear can put you in a particular social group. Some teens have no problem paying more than ninety dollars for a pair of jeans that look like they have been worn for years. Teens have insecurities that make them susceptible to advertising, which feeds on their feelings.

Susan Carney explains that advertisers create insecurity in teens about something—their appearance, for instance—and convince them that they have a problem that needs to be fixed. The advertiser then offers their product as the solution. "The message is that teens aren't good enough the way they are," Carney states. "Many kids unwittingly buy into that message, and as a result, end up being hypercritical of themselves because we don't fit a certain 'image' that they believe is necessary for their happiness."[26]

Many teens buy into this philosophy of getting the right image and then become disappointed when the payoff does not meet their expectation. Failure to gain the sought-after image could lead to the teen developing a sense of low self-worth, but the advertisers won't lose sleep over that.

Underage drinking is a serious problem among high school and college students. Alcohol ads on TV register with the under-twenty-one crowd. Those who appear in the ads may be over twenty-one; but the fun, excitement, and coolness portrayed in the ads is very attractive to teens and college students who are not yet twenty-one. Consuming an adult beverage makes some feel like adults. Drinking alcohol is perceived as a way to take that first desired step into social popularity. The effect of alcohol ads on teens has been documented by a research study at the School of Community and Global Health at Claremont Graduate University in California. It reported a significant correlation between exposure to advertising and alcohol use, particularly among girls, and liking the ads led to alcohol-related problems, such as an inability to do homework, getting into fights, causing others embarrassment, or neglecting responsibilities, particularly in boys. The study also found that "for both boys and girls, the more they were exposed to the ads and liked them, the more their alcohol use grew from seventh to tenth grade," which, of course, makes them more vulnerable to have alcohol-related problems later on.[27]

It is important to note that ads not aimed at those under the legal age to drink still have an impact on that age group, the members of which seek to consume the product even when it is not legal to do so. Alcohol advertisers may put the drinking age on screen as evidence that they are being responsible, but they secretly delight that their brand is making a mark on those who will be future customers. All that it takes on a college campus is for one twenty-one-year-old to buy the booze and bring it back to where all can have at it, even if they are under the drinking age.

Advertisers are notorious for using sex appeal in their commercials, but Planned Parenthood is bold enough to air ads encouraging young people to have sex. It took some heat over a racy ad that promoted the use of condoms for safe sex. Planned Parenthood decided to run the ad on MTV (birds of a feather?). The ad shows a young woman using power tools and saying that her dad told her to always use the "right tool" for the job. Later, she is seen bursting into a bedroom, where a young man waits under the covers. She rips off her work clothes down to a skimpy outfit and dives under the covers. Words convey the idea that the condom is the "right tool" to be used in their sex encounter.[28] Planned Parenthood does not provide the whole truth when it comes to condoms. Using them does not eliminate all STDs. Some can be transmitted by body contact in areas not covered by a condom.

Another Planned Parenthood commercial that ran on some Missouri stations focused on birth control. A young girl goes to a Planned Parenthood facility with her boyfriend to get birth control pills. Their marital status is not revealed, but all indications are that this couple is not married. Other young faces appear in the ad voicing lines of support.[29] Some of these people look high school age.

Planned Parenthood has a "birth control" web page where it answers questions. One question deals with parental consent. Planned Parenthood explains that different states have different laws regarding this consent but also reveals that some states allow teens to get pills without their parents signing an approval.[30] As a parent, you might not want your child to be sexually active in his or her teen years. But Planned Parenthood does, and it is willing to spend millions of dollars to convince your child to go its way.

Why does Planned Parenthood want your teen to be on birth control? They want as many teens as possible to be sexually active because they know teens can be negligent and reckless. They can forget to take a pill, or they might gamble that the condom is not needed on a certain occasion. More sexually active teens always means more abortions in the future for Planned Parenthood.

Making a Difference: Parents Television Council

The Parents Television Council does a tremendous job of alerting parents to objectionable television programming. Its website gives a clear guide to program content and provides helpful news articles about the television industry as it relates to family viewing. Its declared mission, "To protect children and families from graphic sex, violence, and profanity in the media, because of their proven long-term harmful effects."

In addition to its operating board, the organization has an advisory board that comprises many distinguished names from the entertainment industry, business world, and public sector—people such as actors Tim Conway and Connie Sellecca, former US Secretary of Education William Bennett, and film critic Michael Medved. The organization takes an active role in lobbying the industry to generate family-friendly programming and raises objections to indecent content. Advertisers are notified when it is believed that content is highly objectionable. The council's leadership knows that many advertisers do not want to be associated with programming that is considered indecent to many viewers. The Parents Television Council is to be commended for its work as a watchdog of this type of media. More parents should become familiar with the organization's work and share it with others. For more information, visit w2.parentstv.org.

TAKE ACTION

- Set limits on the number of hours your child watches television, and make sure you know what they are watching and when.[31]
- Learn to use your television's V-Chip technology. The V-Chip, which comes standard on all TVs made since 2000, gives parents and caretakers the ability to block unwanted programs from their home.[32]
- Study the impact of TV and video violence on children. Use your knowledge to help other parents protect their children.[33]

CHAPTER 8

Children, Stolen and Gone

Train up a child in the way he should go, and
when he is old he will not depart from it.
—Proverbs 22:6, NKJV

Too many of today's children have straight teeth
and crooked morals.
—Unknown High School Principal

As the New Morality advances, many of our kids have become casualties of the cultural war. Some of these casualties are obvious, like when we lose our children to acts of direct violence. Other casualties are less obvious. We see them when our children are drawn away from the church and from traditional values associated with strong Christian backgrounds and church upbringings. In this chapter, we discuss both the overt and the subtle ways children are targeted. We address gun violence, pornography both inside and outside the church, and what appears to be an effort to normalize pedophilia.

We see the direct casualties all too often on the evening news. We all remember when twelve teenagers and an adult were gunned down by two students at Columbine High School in Littleton, Colorado, on April 20, 1999. It was a horrifying day in our nation's history. And it is a day that we seem to be reliving over and over. Twenty children and six adults were killed at Sandy Hook Elementary School on December 14, 2012, by a young man who killed his mother before the massacre. On October 1, 2015, eight young adults and a teacher were gunned down at Umpqua Community College in Oregon. At Umpqua, the gunman lined up students and inquired about their faith. Students who hesitated at the gunman's question or refused to answer he wounded, and those who confessed to being Christians he shot dead.

In each of these cases, the killers committed suicide. Although many voices nationwide were quick to blame guns and call for greater gun control, in most of these tragedies, when medical records have been opened, the killers either were using or withdrawing from psychiatric drugs.[1] In the case of Adam Lanza, the Sandy Hook shooter, no drugs were reported in his system. But he was documented to have been suffering from untreated mental illness during the years he was being raised by a mother who purchased weapons for him and accompanied him to gun ranges.[2] She became his first victim.

Data from the Centers for Disease Control (CDC) and from the National Center for Health Statistics shows that the overmedication of our children is a serious problem in America. It is one that we believe makes them even more susceptible to committing acts of violence. According to the CDC, "As many as ten thousand toddlers may be receiving psychostimulant medication, like methylphenidate (Ritalin)."[3] Impoverished children on Medicaid are far more likely to be prescribed medication by the doctors who treat them. The percentage of children prescribed drugs has been increasing at a rather alarming rate. The CDC reported a "five-fold increase in the number of children under eighteen on psychostimulants from 1988–1994 to 2007–2010, with the most recent rate of 4.2 percent."[4] Similarly, the National Center for Health Statistics reports that "7.5 percent of U.S. children between ages six and seventeen" take medication for "emotional or behavioral difficulties."[5]

Whether it's the impatience of ill-equipped parents, the indifference of medical doctors, overworked day care providers, or a greedy pharmaceutical industry, something is broken in our society. In the high-profile cases of young people who have committed horrific acts of mass violence, we often learn that they were heavily medicated. Too many children have grown up on a steady diet of violent television shows, movies, and video games. In many cases, the killers have committed suicide as their final act of violence. While Hollywood is quick to side with politicians calling for greater gun control, Matt Philbin of *NewsBusters* has pointed out the hypocrisy of their doing so. During the first week of October 2015, the top ten movies featured 334 separate acts of violence, with 121 of these involving guns. Philbin's on-screen body count was thirty-nine deaths attributable to gun violence.[6] Researchers have also noticed an increase in gun violence in PG-13 films.[7]

TRAINING FOR VIOLENCE

In chapter 6, it was pointed out that Eric Harris and Dylan Klebold were fans of the movie *Natural Born Killers*. You can add to this that they liked playing the video game *Doom*. It falls into the game world genre known as "first-person-shooter," in which the player sees lifelike, 3-D graphics of people he can shoot and kill.[8] When gun violence occurs, liberals are quick to blame the guns but almost never examine the other factors in our culture—most of all, poor parenting—that are priming our kids for violence.

There are those who are quick to say that what Harris and Klebold did was a deplorable tragedy and in the same breath say that the entertainment industry, movies, and video games cannot bear any responsibility for such acts. While it's true the entertainment industry did nothing that can be legally connected to the Columbine tragedy, it does not mean that it had no influence on the behavior of Harris and Klebold. The violent films and video games that the two teenage gunmen enjoyed helped to shape their values and motivate them toward their horrific actions. These might be legal forms of entertainment, but are they good for our culture? Study after study has shown that kids who partake of a steady diet of violence by way of film and video games have a higher risk of committing a violent act.[9] We have parents who are weeping on their way to funeral homes while entertainment executives seem oblivious to the harm caused.

Many of those lost in the Columbine tragedy would be college graduates today and would have gotten married, started their careers, and maybe even presented their parents with a grandchild. Those twelve never got this future. It was stolen from them by two young men influenced by the forces of a New Morality bent on profiting from entertainment that undermines decency and virtue.

Lieutenant Colonel Dave Grossman wrote an article titled "Teaching Kids to Kill" that appeared in several periodicals, including the *Saturday Evening Post*. Grossman had a unique job during his military service: he trained people to kill. He reported that there is a "natural resistance" in humans to want to kill another human. He wrote that during World War II, it was learned that only 15 to 20 percent of the riflemen would fire at an enemy soldier. The problem was that World War II soldiers were trained to fire at bull's-eye targets and none were ever attacked by bull's-eye targets. When the training was changed so that soldiers fired on man-shaped silhouette targets that would come into view, then fall when hit by a shot, the percentage of soldiers who were ready to kill went up to 90 percent.[10]

Grossman, who taught this subject at West Point, contends that violent video games are having the same effect on kids as the military's training-to-kill programs have on new recruits. His words articulate the seriousness of this reality:

> Today the data linking violence in the media to violence in society is superior to that linking cancer and tobacco. The American Psychological Association (APA), the American Medical Association (AMA), the American Academy of Pediatrics (AAP), the Surgeon General, and the Attorney General have all made definitive statements about this. When I presented a paper to the American Psychiatric Association's (APA) annual convention in May 2000 (Grossman, 2000), the statement was made that: 'The data

is irrefutable. We have reached the point where
we need to treat those who try to deny it, like we
would treat Holocaust deniers.'[11]

The liberals and their garrisons of trial lawyers have gone after
the tobacco companies in the name of protecting our kids. The
cool-looking Joe Camel in his leather jacket is gone and will never
again influence our children to light up. Meanwhile, the violence
and sexual content in movies, cable programming, music, and video
games continue unchecked. If tobacco companies that produce a
legal product can be extremely restricted by law in how they can
promote their merchandise, the same can hold true for the entertainment industry's products that undermine the well-being of our
children. This strategy by the New Morality to use entertainment
to win over the young is effective, and liberals know this. If a trial
lawyer went on the attack mode against the entertainment industry,
seeking restraints on it similar to those on big tobacco, he would be
accused of shooting his own.

President Bill Clinton stated in his radio address on April 24,
1999, just a few days after the Columbine shootings, "A former lieutenant colonel and professor, David Grossman, has said that these
games teach young people to kill with all the precision of a mili-
tary-training program but none of the character training that goes
along with it."[12]

President Clinton cited Grossman to the nation as a viable
source who showed how dangerous violent video games can be for
children. These were welcome words but, really, only words. Nothing
has been done to curtail the violence in these games and in other
forms of entertainment that are readily available to kids. Grossman
presented the following case study:

Michael Carneal, the fourteen-year-old killer in
the Paducah, Kentucky school shootings, had
never fired a real pistol in his life. He stole a
.22 pistol, fired a few practice shots, and took it
to school. He fired eight shots at a high school

prayer group, hitting eight kids, five of them
head shots and the other three upper torso.[13]

Military and law-enforcement personnel around the world
were amazed at this feat of marksmanship. Grossman stated the fact,
"Where does a fourteen-year-old boy who never fired a gun before
get the skill and the will to kill? Video games and media violence."[14]
Unfortunately, parents can forget about using the courts to ban
the sale of violent video games to their children. In 2011, the US
Supreme Court struck down a 2005 California law aimed at protecting children from harmful videos unless they had parental permission to play them. In a 7–2 decision, the court ruled in *Brown
v. Entertainment Merchants Association* that video games enjoyed the
same First Amendment rights as books, plays, movies, and other
forms of protected art.[15] Regardless of whether the games are violent
or nonviolent, it would be hard to argue that they are healthy for
kids. Video games have proved to be highly addictive, and they also
take children away from other activities, such as reading and playing
outside.[16]

THE PORN PATH

Pornography is an epidemic in our culture. It affects both men
and women. It affects unbelievers and churchgoers alike and even a
significant percentage of pastors.[17] One study showed that 50 percent
of Christian men and 20 percent of Christian women admitted to
having a pornography addiction. Even more serious was the revelation that a majority of pastors are struggling with the same problem.
Below, Steve cites several cases in which pornography was cited as a
factor in violent crimes. I (Carol) recognize that correlation does not
imply causation. Far more men are viewing pornography than are
committing acts of violence. Nevertheless, we have every reason to be
concerned that the addiction has now ensnared many Christians who
give the appearance of being upright followers of Jesus Christ but
secretly indulge in porn. Parents are addicted, and so are teens—and

so are many of the authority figures they might seek out for advice. It is a dangerous symptom of our moral decay.

In 2002, I (Steve) became a filmmaker and produced a documentary on the problem of pornography as it is encountered by young men. It was titled *Every Young Man's Battle* and was based on the book of the same name by Steve Arterburn and Fred Stoeker. The film has won two awards, including the Crown Award for Best Youth Film of 2002. The video included a portion of a famous death row interview of serial killer Ted Bundy by Dr. James Dobson. In the interview, Bundy explains how pornography played a major role in his turn to violent crime. He admitted to sexually assaulting and killing more than twenty-eight women. The number may be much higher. He also said that every criminal he met in prison who had committed a violent crime also had, "without exception," a problem with pornography.[18]

In the culture championed by the New Morality, pornography is protected by the First Amendment. The same amendment is cited as the reason that Christianity is to have no part in civic affairs and especially in the public school systems. The so-called separation of church and state is diligently guarded. The names of Melissa Smith and Laura Aime are most likely not familiar to you. They have one thing in common; they both were seventeen when they became Ted Bundy victims. They were teenagers, still in high school, when this serial killer, his mind warped by legal pornography, stole their lives. Bundy voiced his regrets for what he did and gave a warning that other children are destined to be victims of Ted Bundys of the future, who will start down this path because of their addiction to pornography.[19] This warning, given in 1989, seems to have gone unheeded, as we have had to endure discussions on cable-news channels of case after case of children, teenagers, and college females who were abducted, sexually assaulted, and murdered. The New Morality gets its way; our beautiful, innocent children pay the price.

In February 2002, David Westerfield kidnapped seven-year-old Danielle van Dam, the daughter of one of his neighbors in San Diego. Westerfield was an engineer who made a salary of $170,000 a year. In this case that received much national publicity, Westerfield didn't fit the profile of a deranged criminal. He had a high-paying job and a nice house in a good neighborhood. What would make him want to kidnap, sexually assault, and murder a seven-year-old girl? The answer was found on his computer. It was loaded with child pornography.[20] Child pornography is against the law, but it is very hard to police when it is on the Internet.

The nation viewed Carlie Brucia's abduction, which was captured by a security camera. The Sarasota, Florida, sixth grader was returning home from a sleepover at a friend's house when Joseph Smith pulled her into his car. There was evidence that Smith was a consumer of child pornography when he was investigated. The video from the security camera made it easy to identify Smith. Nevertheless, he wasn't identified fast enough. Carlie's body was found in some brush behind a church a few days later. Smith was found guilty of the crime—one many believe he should have never been able to commit because he should have been in custody for parole violation, but a judge let him go free.[21] Over and over again, we see that pornography plays a role in the lives of violent criminals.

DANGEROUS AGENDA

There is a website that is deplorable in every sense of the word. Its very presence is a painful reminder of how far New Morality forces have advanced in the cultural war and how bold they are willing to be in their attempt to steal more of our kids. The site belongs to an organization known as the North America Man/Boy Love Association (NAMBLA). If you dare to visit this site, you might want to have one of those airline barf bags handy. This organization proudly proclaims its support and encouragement of sexual relations between adult men and underage boys, as long as both are consenting to the activity. Thus, we have a wing of the homosexual movement that dares to combat the statutory rape laws of our nation. You might think they will never succeed, but, remember, if the New Morality and its liberal cohorts and their activist judges gain power, it can only be a law away. NAMBLA is not shy about its mission. Its website proudly says its goal is "to end the extreme oppression of men and boys in mutually consensual relationships," which it aims to do by:

- Building understanding and support for such relationships
- Educating the general public on the benevolent nature of man/boy love
- Cooperating with lesbian, gay, feminist, and other liberation movements
- Supporting the liberation of persons of all ages from sexual prejudice and oppression.[22]

This organization wants to end the age restrictions placed on sex; in fact, it is calling for no restrictions on sex as long as both parties are consenting. Would it mean that adults could have heterosexual sex with children as long as there was consent by all? To avoid discrimination, it would have to include such relationships. Do we really want to say that our teens and even younger children are old enough to consent to sex with an adult? Do you see now why the cultural war is a war, which, if lost, could cost our nation all decency and virtue? The New Morality wants our kids, and we must do all we can to say, "You can't have them."

A teenager may hit puberty and be physically able to have sex, but that doesn't mean his or her judgment in the area of sexuality is fully developed. Teenagers lack the necessary life experience to weigh the consequences of their actions. Do you think the NAMBLA gang cares about that? No way. They are seeking their own goals for their own selfish reasons. They seek to exploit kids for their own pleasure while trying to frame the context as a loving relationship. They don't care what emotional scars will remain on a kid. They think that consent is the key and appear to nobly oppose all forced sexual encounters; but we know that you can sometimes bribe, manipulate, or intimidate a kid into doing almost anything.

When there is a dispute about this, how will our unpredictable courts rule? You might be saying that what NAMBLA wants to do will never happen in our country. I bet you would have said that about same-sex marriage twenty years ago. Some homosexuals are uncomfortable with NAMBLA and with gay men and women who seek child partners. Paula Marinac, a lesbian journalist, expresses her disapproval of such behavior:

> Some gay men still maintain that an adult who has same-sex relations with someone under the age of legal consent is on some level doing the kid a favor by helping to bring him or her "out."... Adult-youth sex is viewed as an important aspect of gay culture, with a history dating back to "Greek love" of ancient times. The romanticized vision of adult-youth sexual relations has been a staple of gay literature and has made appearances, too, in gay-themed films...Last summer, I attended a reading in which a gay poet read a long piece about being aroused by a flirtatious young boy in his charge. In response, the man went into the boy's bedroom and [sexually abused the boy as he] slept...Disturbingly, most of the gay audience gave the poet an appreciative round of applause.[23]

There is an effort under way to normalize pedophilia. Rutgers law professor Margo Kaplan argued in a *New York Times* op-ed titled "Pedophilia: A Disorder, Not a Crime" that pedophilia is a sexual attraction that should be treated like other mental illnesses and covered by the Americans with Disabilities Act:

> Without legal protection, a pedophile cannot risk seeking treatment or disclosing his status to anyone for support. He could lose his job, and future job prospects, if he is seen at a group-therapy session, asks for a reasonable accommodation to take medication or see a psychiatrist, or requests a limit in his interaction with children. Isolating individuals from appropriate employ-

ment and treatment only increases their risk of committing a crime.[24]

In September 2015, the online magazine *Salon* gave a forum to a pedophile, who explained his sexual attraction to children.[25]

The eventual normalization and protection of pedophilia is the next logical step in the decline of our culture. The slippery slope is captured in this statement by J. Budziszewski, professor of government at the University of Texas:

> The list of what we are required to approve is growing ever longer. Consider just the domain of sexual practice. First we were to approve sex before marriage, then without marriage, now against marriage. First with one, then with a series, now with a crowd. First with the other sex, then with the same. First between adults, then between children, then between adults and children. The last item has not been added yet, but will be soon: you can tell from the change in language.[26]

Budziszewski notes that instead of calling pedophilia what it actually is, its proponents now refer to it most commonly as intergenerational intimacy.

PERMANENT SOLUTION TO TEMPORARY PROBLEM

She was a pretty, fifteen-year-old junior-varsity cheerleader. I (Steve) met her when I was pulling lunch duty as a substitute teacher at a rural high school in my county. When I talked with her, I inquired about the basketball games and her interests in school. She had an outgoing personality and seemed like your typical fifteen-year-old teenager. I did note the fact that she had more piercings in her ears than I thought was the norm, but, all in all, she appeared to be coping successfully with those awkward early years of adolescence as well as could be expected. I guess that's why it was such a shock when I heard the news. She claimed to be sick one Thursday and stayed home to hang herself in her bedroom. Her cousin found her when he came home from school.

She had planned it all carefully. She left detailed instructions for her funeral and requested she be buried in her cheerleading uniform. Why did she do this? I asked her friends this question when I returned as a substitute teacher, and no one could give a clear answer. There were rumors of typical problems that might befall a young female teen but no single cause that anyone could say for sure was the reason. Whatever she was dealing with, it was something she wanted to escape so badly that she was willing to kill herself to do it.

It has been said that suicide is a permanent solution to a temporary problem. It is the third leading cause of death for teenagers, behind traffic accidents and unintentional injury.[27] Whenever a young person takes her own life, it is a great loss—one that could have been prevented. The story of the student I had met is similar to a thousand others like it in our nation. The rate of teen and child suicide has risen dramatically in recent years. Suicide among adolescents and young adults nearly tripled between 1952 and 1995.[28] This corresponds to the time when the New Morality made its big advance. In those decades, prayer was chased from school, and Christianity was pushed further out of the public sphere. Sex and violence are now served up in large portions in the media. Sexual experimentation is encouraged and accepted. Pornography is protected. Pedophilia is celebrated. And today our kids are killing themselves at a faster rate than ever before.

WALKING WOUNDED

Many teens have been stolen by today's culture even though they still walk among us. Their values have been changed and their behavior altered. They are physically alive but spiritually dead. They are the walking wounded of the culture war and nonetheless a casualty. In the early sixties, one in fifty people had an STD. Now it is one in three.[29]

The mainstream media provide a disservice to our young people when they don't report items that are relevant to their lives. When there is a conflict between protecting a valued, liberal, politically correct group or reporting something that benefits kids or the parents who care for those kids, the politically correct group wins over the kids. A profound example of this is what media commentator Bernard Goldberg calls "The Biggest Story the Media Won't Cover." That is a chapter title in his book *Arrogance*.[30] The story Goldberg makes reference to appeared on the PBS program *Frontline* in October 1999; it was called "The Lost Children of Rockdale County."[31] The program documented the problems that kids were having in this county near Atlanta because of so much unsupervised time at the end of the school day before a parent came home. The kids were gorging themselves on Internet and TV pornography and sexual experimentation. An article by Kay Hymowitz that appeared in the magazine *City Journal* reported that the reason for the program appearing on PBS was an outbreak of syphilis that resulted in two hundred teenagers being treated.[32] The following quote from Hymowitz's article describes how despicable the situation was:

> Kids would watch the Playboy cable TV channel and make a game of imitating everything they saw. They tried almost every permutation of sexual activity imaginable—vaginal, oral, anal, girl on girl, several boys with a single girl, or several girls with a boy…During some drunken parties, one girl might be "passed around" in a game. A number of the kids had upward of fifty partners.[33]

Goldberg points out that the only reason some mainstream media reporters would even consider the Rockdale County information as a story was the health problem involved. The fact that teenagers were getting together to have sex was not news to them; it was expected behavior.[34] Pointing out the risks that attend kids who are home alone is not good for the liberal agenda because it opposes feminism. Women are encouraged to seek careers and get out of the house. The liberal Left championed this behavior years ago, and many mothers have done just that.

In some cases, a family needs the extra income just to pay the taxes. But there are some liberals who want women in the workforce and out of the house because they disdain the "happy homemaker" image, thinking it belittles women. So the moms are gone from the home and our kids are lost, even while they still live in our houses. Funny, but we don't remember any of the *American Pie* teens—or, for that matter, any other teen character that was blazing a trail of sexual conquest in a movie—dealing with any STDs. Where's the reality, Hollywood?

I (Steve) went into a grocery store in my hometown and saw the front page of the *Columbus Dispatch*. The headline that caught my eye read "Students Allegedly Watched Assault."[35] Under the headline were the words, "Girl beaten, media glare feared, Mifflin sex-case statements say."[36] The incident involved a sixteen-year-old girl with a learning disability who was forced to have oral sex with two boys in the school auditorium while other students looked on.[37] The girl was also punched in the face. Ironically, the school's nickname is "The Punchers." I spent the first four years of my schooling in this school district.

The school took heat when the public learned that the assistant principals tried to discourage the girl's father from calling the police. It was surmised that the school wanted to avoid any negative publicity. Nevertheless, the dad called, and the publicity came. Did it ever! The incident became a national story. It was covered by Glenn Beck on his nationally syndicated radio talk show and on *Hannity and Colmes* on Fox News.

The assistant principals were reassigned to other schools, and an effort to terminate the principal from her position was soon under way. These educational professionals were worried about their careers, but what about the girl? She was another casualty of the cultural war. Those who violated this young girl might be punished, but that won't erase the emotional trauma that she will carry for the rest of her life. Why would boys do something like this during school hours and in the school? They did it because they believed they could get away with it. And if you are following the values of the New Morality, with its self-centered emphasis, you begin to see how a group of boys developed such a callous disregard for a vulnerable young girl.

There is another type of walking wounded in this cultural war whose numbers would shock many Americans: teen prostitutes, who are more appropriately described as sexual-trafficking victims. Ohio governor John Kasich estimates that there are 1,100 underage children in his state who are forced to work in the sex trade.[38] Some girls are runaways whom pimps prey on and then abuse to keep them in line. Some so-called "Romeo pimps" give affection and gifts to a girl and then turn her into a product to merchandise. Dr. Celia Williamson, professor of social work at the University of Toledo, says the average age of girls caught up in sexual trafficking is thirteen.[39]

Ohio's Franklin County, which includes Columbus, Ohio, runs a program call CATCH Court, which treats teens arrested for solicitation as victims. If the girl completes certain specified courses and becomes free of addiction, her criminal record is wiped clean. It is great to see a municipality develop a program for the walking wounded in the cultural war.

Teens are not only being victimized by sex trafficking; there also are legal sexual businesses that employ adolescents. If a girl is eighteen, she can legally be employed in the sex industry. Strip clubs, for instance, hire college-age girls to be live, onstage porn for their patrons. Pernicious forces in our culture work to sexualize our kids at younger and younger ages, feeding them into the tentacles of the sex industry, which never stops devouring them.

BRAIN GONE

Some of our young people have been stolen from us by the New Morality in more subtle ways that did not end in death or prostitution. These kids took a hit to the brain. These are young people who have been trained to believe that everything is relative, and there is no objective reality or standards of right and wrong that would apply to all people. As a consequence, many of them lack the tools to make decisions guided by the kinds of moral principles associated with a Judeo-Christian worldview that acknowledges the dignity of every human being. A movie called *Body Snatchers*, produced in 1993, was about aliens that took over people's identities. They would place a pod nearby that would grow a person or a clone of the person to be taken over. The pod person would look identical to the real person, who, upon being taken over, was gone forever—replaced by the alien lookalike. The unique feature of the alien "person" was that it showed no emotions. It had total desensitization. It sometimes seems as if the New Morality has accomplished this with our kids.

There are teens who are totally selfish. They are without regard for the needs of others. Their behavior amounts only to what benefits them. They have embraced situational ethics and are learning to seek their own advantage above all else. All the avenues that the New Morality has used to reach them have done their job. These kids have a worldview that is opposed to the traditional morality and the values held by their parents. If they are not confirmed atheists, they are at least practical atheists. They may say they believe God exists, but they live their lives as if He doesn't. They take their self-centered values and behavior into their career, family life, and relationships. And, in time, they grow up to be adults lacking real character because they were stolen by the New Morality when they were young.

Discipline and moral guidance from trusted authority figures is playing a decreasing role in the lives of some of America's children. In August 2015, the Obama administration's Department of Education issued new rules aimed at making it more difficult for schools to suspend unruly students who create safety issues while disrupting the educational learning environment for others.[40] Hoover Institution fellow Paul Sperry explains the reasoning behind the new policy that has already been adopted in some cities, saying the new policy emerged from a perception that "traditional discipline is racist because blacks are suspended at higher rates than whites" and that, as a result, "New York City's Department of Education has in all but the most serious and dangerous offenses replaced out-of-school suspension with a touchy-feely alternative punishment called 'restorative justice,' which isn't really punishment at all. It's therapy."[41]

Parents should have the right to discipline their children.[42] Government can never replace the work of parents, who have the responsibility to develop the character of their children. Children are like vineyards; they need pruning to be productive. Sometimes that pruning comes in the form of a proper spanking.

The Bible addresses corporal punishment—spanking as a means of disciplining children. Liberals disdain spanking, and the government has, in some cases, threatened to remove kids from the home should the parent raise a firm but sensible hand at them. This situation poses a dilemma for parents who believe a swat on the behind is an effective form of child discipline. Christian parents have cited a number of Scriptures to support their belief in corporal punishment:[43]

> Folly is bound in the heart of a child, but the rod of discipline will drive it far from him.
> —Proverbs 22:15

> Do not withhold discipline from a child, if you punish him with the rod, he will not die.
> —Proverbs 23:13, NIV

> Punish him with the rod, and save his soul from death.
> —Proverbs 23:14, NIV

We can credit best-selling author Dr. Benjamin Spock for the reluctance of some parents to spank their children. His best-selling book, *The Common Sense Book of Baby and Child Care*, turned parents away from spanking and toward a more permissive approach to child-rearing. Spock advised parents against strict discipline while counseling for more verbal interaction—and what some would consider indulgence. According to Spock, spanking teaches children "that might makes right…and most fundamentally, that to the degree that it results in good behavior it's because of the fear of pain. I have a strong belief that the best reason for behaving well is that you like people, want to get along with them, want them to like you."[44] In later years, Spock came to believe that spankings taught children how to bully others: "It teaches children that the larger, stronger person has the power to get his way, whether or not he is in the right. Some spanked children then feel quite justified in beating up on smaller ones."[45] Spock believed that a link existed between violent behavior in society and childhood spankings. Several generations of children have been raised using Spock's methods. An article in the *Wall Street Journal* reported,

> More than five decades after Dr. Spock sent corporal punishment to the woodshed, spanking is making a comeback. A growing number of parents—many of whom were never spanked themselves—are shunning the experts, defying disapproving friends and neighbors, and giving their kids a slap on the bottom, the hand or the leg. Web sites popular with parents, such as iVillage.com and Oxygen.com, are filled with chatroom buzz from pro-spankers. Just last year, both Oklahoma and Nevada passed laws explicitly giving parents the right to spank their children.[46]

I (Carol) was whipped as a child with small tree branches called switches. I remember the humiliation of having to select the object that would be used for my own correction. I survived the butt whippings as generations of Americans have done in the past. It is important to distinguish between child abuse (beating or injuring a child) and prudent physical discipline, which does no harm to a child but is, in fact, a method parents have used to correct children for thousands of years. Prudent parents understand that all worthwhile discipline is motivated by love. The aim of discipline is the child's well-being.

MAKING A DIFFERENCE:
HOMESCHOOLING PARENTS

We cannot be with our children at all times, and we cannot protect them from all dangers. Instead, we must take responsibility for teaching our children right from wrong, so that they make better choices when confronted with temptations that can come from any number of different sources. Homeschooling gives parents greater influence while their children are young. As a result, some Christian parents are educating their children at home and swapping skills with like-minded parents. In Texas, the number of parents choosing to homeschool their children for religious or moral reasons jumped from an estimated 120,000 to 300,000 in just five years.[47]

However, courts are now attempting to limit homeschooling parents. Judges in North Carolina and New Hampshire have ordered homeschooled students into public schools in divorce situations where one of the parents complained about the appropriateness of their children's education.[48] In both states, the children involved were at or above grade level in class and the objections raised were about the narrowness of a Christian-based education. It should not surprise you to learn that many liberals are skeptical or outright hostile toward homeschooling. After all, homeschooling goes a long way toward removing children from the control of liberal educators and policymakers. Homeschooling may not be an option for everyone, but for many families, it offers terrific moral and academic advantages. There may be no better way to prepare your children to stand against the evils of our present time.

TAKE ACTION

- Read and study the forty-two Bible verses that apply specifically to raising godly children, available at www.open-bible.info/topics/raising_children.

- Take responsibility for teaching your children right and wrong. No matter what kind of schooling you choose for your child, the education of your child is too important to be left completely to others.

- Gather and distribute informational materials to teachers, youth leaders, and parent groups about legal and illegal drugs; repeated exposure to violent movies, videos, and TV shows; and sexual exploitation. Mothers against Videogame Addiction and Violence (MAVAV) is an organization that sounds the alarm against violent video games and how children's behavior can worsen when they become addicted to video games. Learn more at www.mavav.org.

- Have regular, age-appropriate conversations with your children about sexual predators who can lurk in neighborhoods, churches, and educational settings.

CHAPTER 9

Higher Learning and Lower Values

The politically motivated scholar and teacher is engaged in a dishonest act: pretending that his conclusions are reached impartially when they are not. This is particularly pernicious when the modern liberal scholar speaks to the public as an expert.[1]

—Robert Bork

A thorough knowledge of the Bible is worth more than a college education.[2]

—Theodore Roosevelt

In the fall of 1990, I (Carol) started my academic career as an untenured professor at Princeton University. I eventually received early tenure and later moved on to Vanderbilt University, where I am professor of political science and professor of law. Over the years, I have watched as the university environment has changed significantly, even as I have undergone my own metamorphosis. As I reflect on the current state of academia, I speak from the perspective of someone with twenty-seven years of experience in the trenches, with the last sixteen years of my life spent as a public Christian. I have been blessed with the opportunity to have earned degrees from just about every kind of educational institution that America offers: a community college, a private Christian college (Lutheran), two big state universities, and an Ivy League institution. Life in academia has always been challenging. It is not a career path I consciously chose from the outset. Rather, it's clear to me that God steered me in a direction that would normally have been off-limits to a black child born and raised in rural poverty.

By God's grace, I was successful at Princeton University, where I earned tenure and several national prizes. During that time, I was spiritually dead. My Christianity came from the fact that I was born and raised in a black Southern family with roots in the Methodist Church. Although my great-grandfather had been a pastor who hailed from a long line of missionaries to Barbados, I grew up in a nonattending family, and it was only as an adult in my forties that I received Jesus Christ as my Lord and Savior. As a young adult, I was spiritual enough to know something much larger and much bigger than me was guiding my life, but I never truly acknowledged who it was. Like many New Age and liberal Christians, I believed in one God and many paths. My faith journey meandered down many paths that turned out to be dead ends, including a teen stint as a Jehovah's Witness. Repulsion at the cultic tactics sent me fleeing from all forms of organized religion for more than twenty years. Fortunately, God didn't abandon me. I found my way back.

I was oblivious to the moral decline happening around me while I focused almost solely on achievement. Politically, I was a pro-choice Democrat who was totally indifferent to homosexuality and the gay-rights movement. In fact, in my younger days, I had close relationships with gay men and women, and I viewed myself as quite tolerant. In those days, the homosexual rhetoric was about tolerance and protection against violence. Along the way, I kindly rebuffed the sexual advances of gay and bisexual women who approached me at several points in my life. It wasn't something that appealed to me. Nowadays, it seems to be a rite of passage (with even stronger demands within academia) to demonstrate your acceptance of alternative lifestyles if one is to advance in the academic world.

It was on a university campus that God got hold of me. While I was doing my thing at Princeton, I frequently encountered Christian students and staff people who reached out to me in various ways. In fact, years after I left Princeton and had become a believer, I met a young man from South Carolina who was about to be ordained as a pastor. This former student of mine shared with me how he prayed daily for my salvation and that of another Princeton professor. He noted that we both had found Jesus. Today, when I share my testimony, I see the hand of a providential God who credentialed me at a world-class university before setting in motion a series of events that led me to accept my current position at Vanderbilt. Life in academia has been a tumultuous experience for me, as a person who spent her early years in a two-room shack without indoor plumbing or running water. Many times I have wanted to leave academia, but my love for the students has kept me committed.

I have witnessed major changes in higher education in which campus administrators have actively sought to indoctrinate students with liberal cultural norms that run counter to the beliefs of orthodox Christians, Jews, and Muslims. Anyone who dares challenge the prevailing campus norms and their worship of political correctness will find himself or herself isolated and marginalized. Tolerance of immorality and deviant behavior seem to be among the highest values practiced on many campuses. Ostracism awaits anyone who defends traditional values or dares question the rampant political correctness and multiculturalism that rules the campus environment. Power revolves around racial differences, sexual orientation, and feminism.

In recent years, there has been an overt assault on conservative Christians that seems geared toward silencing anyone who holds a biblical worldview. This assault is occurring even while universities and campuses have proved themselves to be unsafe places because of the rampant incidents of drunkenness, rape, and vandalism. Unfortunately, campus administrators have been reluctant to take steps that would discourage student-initiated drag shows—"sex weeks" that bring porn stars and sex-toy experts to campus—and any effort to suggest that a young woman might bear some responsibility for what happens when she gets drunk and naked in a dating situation. When my coauthor, Steve, and his wife went to college, there were clear norms about right and wrong. Cultural relativism and moral indifference had not yet captured the campus environment.

When I started college in the early 1980s, there were a fair number of conservative-leaning professors on the faculty who adhered to traditional values and norms. There were also a larger number of known sexual harassers who recruited their second and third wives from the graduate and undergraduate pool. Race relations and feminist studies dominated campus discussions. Discussions now center on LBGT rights and the tamping down of any expressions of orthodox Christianity—all in the name of creating a so-called safe space for those who hate the Christian message.

In 2011, Vanderbilt University made national news because it gave special recognition to the Wiccan religion. A few months later, it adopted a policy that eventually resulted in half the Christian student groups making the difficult decision to forego campus registration, which resulted in a loss of rights, including use of the e-mail system and access to student fairs and bulletin boards. These Christian groups had to accept sporadic and limited access to meeting spaces. Under the new rules, the disfavored Christian groups could not cosponsor events with willing mainline Christian groups that remained on campus. The world on a modern college campus is quite different from when Steve was in college.

It was August 1963, and my mother and I (Steve) embarked on a shopping trip to downtown Columbus, Ohio. The reason for this activity was to make sure that her youngest son (me) had a decent wardrobe for college. I look back on that day as one of the positive memories of my life. I sensed the pride Mom and Dad had because they had a son going to college. Neither of them had had that chance, and my older brother had opted for the air force. We chose and purchased clothing for different occasions and some luggage to pack it in.

A few days later, I was off to a small, private Christian college in northeast Illinois, Olivet Nazarene College (now a university), from which I graduated four years later. The college I attended reaffirmed my faith and values. The academics were challenging and sometimes downright difficult. The social life was tame compared with life on campuses today, but it was still enjoyable; and it was a part of the positive experience that prepared my classmates and me for the real world. I encountered no coed dorms, no pressure for sexual experimentation, and no classes that sought to indoctrinate me in the liberal point of view. It was a safe place in which to learn, access, and evaluate information that would be the foundation upon which I would build my life to come.

Today, parents send their children off to halls of higher learning with the expectation that they will get an education that will provide career opportunities and financial independence. In 1963, when I went off to my small "safe" college, many others my age went off to state universities and prestigious private schools. For the most part, all these schools were safe too. They might not have had the strict requirements and rules we had on our church-supported campus; but they also didn't have the coed dorms, the open season of sexual exploits, or the overplay of liberal ideology. However, those changes were on the way. After all, it was the sixties, and the times were a-changin'.

I (Carol) can attest that some of the changes were good. Had doors not opened, someone from my background would never have been given an opportunity to attend and later to teach at some of the world's most elite institutions. Affirmative action, which opened doors, also served as a double-edged sword because it sent strong signals about the inferiority of minorities. In some cases, this encouraged students to adopt an entitlement mentality that resulted in their not putting forth the effort they might have needed for success. In today's universities, minority students raised in integrated middle-class neighborhoods often complain about being pushed into boxes and forced to make uncomfortable decisions about their choice of friends and whether they will identify primarily as racial or ethnic minorities. Despite the pressures, I believe I had more latitude to approach life as an individual rather than as a representative of an entire race or gender group.

STUDENTS OR TARGETS?

Today, things are taking place on college campuses that never would have been imagined back in the early sixties. Changes have come to colleges and universities across the nation in the last forty years that have not been good for the country or the future of the children we send to them. The negative cultural changes prevalent in the public school system are intensified at the college level; and this time, unlike during the high school years, Mom and Dad are not there.

When you send a kid to a state university or private college today, they become direct targets of the New Morality. It takes aim at them in the classroom, in the dorm, and in campus-life activities to persuade them to embrace the values and culture of the Left, with its relativism, situational ethics, and secular emphasis. These encounters are not by accident. The liberal Left and the New Morality crowd saw higher education as an opportunity to strike a devastating blow in the cultural war. At these institutions of higher learning, they have our kids all to themselves for four whole years, without parents being there to provide daily influence.

On April 25, 2005, I (Steve) went to hear David Horowitz speak at Kenyon College some five miles down the road from where I live. Horowitz was once a dedicated liberal and an activist for their cause. He has made a 180-degree turn politically and now is an outspoken conservative. He came to the college to speak on his project Students for Academic Freedom. This cause is described as a "national coalition of independent campus groups dedicated to restoring academic freedom and educational values to America's institutions of higher learning."[3] The words that jump out at me are "restoring academic freedom and educational values." It is a sad commentary on the state of higher education in our country when organizations have to be formed to restore academic freedom and educational values. It begs the question, "Why were these lost in the first place, and who was responsible?"

It is important to understand what Horowitz means by academic freedom. In his speech at Kenyon College, he explained it as bias-free education that allows for the fair hearing of diverse ideas with no one political ideology being favored over another. This does not exist on the majority of campuses today, since, as Horowitz pointed out, liberal professors outnumber conservative ones ten to one—and, in some cases, thirty to one.[4] The liberals have taken control of the academy, and as we send our sons and daughters to it, we subject them to indoctrination in liberal thought, some of which is extreme to the absurd.

These great intellectual bastions that call for diversity in gender, race, and sexual orientation don't want any part of diversity when it comes to ideology. The fact that liberals dominate the faculty does not alarm them in the least. That's the way they designed it, and that's the way they want it to be. It is a tragedy to see this happen when history provides evidence that many of our leading universities, such as Harvard, Yale, Princeton, William and Mary, the University of Southern California, Duke, and a host of others, all were founded with the aim to advance Christian values. Horowitz notes that the Left began its advance on academia in the mid-1960s, and as their influence has grown, "they've trampled free speech, virtually banished conservative professors, and turned our schools into little more than huge megaphones for anti-American rhetoric."[5]

Besides not making a place for conservative professors, colleges are not even welcoming conservative guest speakers. Conservative author and speaker Ann Coulter once had to dodge a thrown pie meant for her face. Former National Security Adviser Condoleezza Rice bowed out of giving the 2014 commencement address at Rutgers University when students protested her invitation because of her involvement in the George W. Bush administration.[6] Dr. Ben Carson met a similar fate at Johns Hopkins University in 2013. He was deemed unfit by students because he did not embrace the same-sex marriage cause.[7] More could be listed who were denied or asked to withdraw, all because they did not measure up to a liberal philosophy.

Ken Paulson, president of the First Amendment Center and dean of the College of Media and Entertainment at Middle Tennessee State University, issued a defense for colleges that he says end up in a difficult position when protests erupt: "A college campus is a place where ideas should be freely exchanged"—but on the other hand, no school wants a rite of passage overshadowed by "boycotts, chants, and disruptions."[8] It comes down to the fact that a small group of liberal students can rule the day, no doubt making many of their liberal professors proud.

I (Carol) became the victim of an administrator-encouraged student protest in January 2015 after I published an opinion piece in a local paper that was critical of Islam. The dean of students took the very unusual action of sending out a campus-wide e-mail encouraging the students to "fully exercise freedom of expression" and engage in dialogue. "Exercising freedom of expression" is code for "protest" when dialogue is mentioned separately. Counseling services were offered for anyone harmed by my "microaggresive" words. This may well be the first occurrence of university students on a liberal campus denouncing a black woman for bigotry and hatred.

STUDENTS UNDER ATTACK

Tammy Bruce documents an outrageous case of one young man who faced grading prejudice in his college experience. The school was Lakeland Community College near Cleveland, Ohio. He was taking a class in which the professor required the students to wear a pink triangle to symbolize homosexual pride. The student refused to comply on the grounds that it was contrary to his personal moral beliefs. He tried to work within the system and asked for an alternative assignment, but his request was rejected. This honor student received an F grade in the class for his refusal to participate, even though to do so would require him to set aside his own moral convictions. You can bet one thing: there was no day when students had to wear golden arrows for "straight" pride to celebrate heterosexuality. The student was even facing expulsion until the story was covered by local TV news and created such negative publicity that the college had to back off.[9]

This happened at a community college supported by citizens' tax dollars. Public money was used to promote a controversial agenda that goes contrary to the moral and religious views of many people who are paying the tab, to say nothing of the fact that the rights and convictions of the student were trampled upon. Professors who use their position and assignments to push their ideology are misusing their authority and exploiting their students.

Bernard Goldberg recounts a situation with a journalism student at Columbia University that brings both of these unscrupulous realities together. Stacey Pressman, who became a producer at ESPN, was given an assignment by a professor to do a story on sexism. She was willing to tackle the assignment but also sent a polite e-mail to the professor stating that she felt the assignment was "loaded." In Stacey's words, "The professor freaked." Stacey pointed out that being sent out to do stories on sexism and racism is biased from the start because a preconceived conclusion is expected. The professor sought to punish Stacey for her actions by demanding that she write a nine-hundred-word essay on what sexism is. Stacey refused. The professor brought the matter up at a faculty meeting, telling her fellow professors that she had an insubordinate student, thereby jeopardizing Stacy's relationships with other faculty members.[10]

Journalism is not supposed to be manipulation of facts or stories to achieve a desired outcome. It is meant to be a quest for truth. But Pressman's experience gives evidence that this is no longer the case at Columbia's J-school, regarded by many as the most prestigious journalism school in the nation. Stacey sums up her ordeal in words that reveal the deplorable circumstances of the journalism program at this Ivy League school:

> It's a school full of Stepford students. That's how they want it. God forbid you challenge them, or rock the boat—you're gonna get it. Supposedly, they believe in the Socratic method of give-and-take and free and open dialogue. But what they really practice is the *autocratic* method: If you

think you have a point, forget it; you don't. End of discussion.[11]

Pressman's experience at Columbia is repeated at colleges and universities in a variety of disciplines across the nation. The "autocratic method" she describes is alive and well in our academic institutions. These schools never stop talking about their commitment to diversity and how the university is a haven for the free exchange of ideas. They want to be perceived as centers of learning where young people go to pursue truth and equip their minds for future service. They want the public to think that any ideology a student emerges with is a result of self-directed critical thinking, when, in reality, they have a mission to crank out as many liberal-leaning alumni as possible.

Classrooms have become tools of distortion as professors lambaste traditional values and the historical heroes that established them. Tammy Bruce discovered this firsthand when she took a history class at the University of Southern California. Her account of the experience is alarming:

> As the professor described them, the signers of the Declaration of Independence ran the gamut from drunkards to morons to hypocritical slave-owning racists. One of the textbooks we were assigned actually equated the American expansion West with "ethnic cleansing" and described our wars with the Indians as "genocide." The in-class discussion, for the most part, took the same tone.[12]

This was not a course in American history but instead a course in anti-American thought. As liberal professors have increased in number, Bruce's experience is being repeated by countless other students. If you're writing checks for your son's or daughter's tuition bill for one of these classes, then you're paying for this.

RELIGIOUS INTOLERANCE

The dilemma of the modern Christian student is illustrated in a recent movie *God's Not Dead*. Freshman Josh Wheaton finds himself in a required course taught by Dr. Radisson, a philosophy professor known for his disdain of Christians and his rejection of the "primitive" belief that God exists.[13] Josh is the only student in Radisson's class who refuses to sign a statement agreeing with the professor that God is dead. For that reason, Josh has to prepare himself with scientific knowledge and apologetics to debate Radisson and defend the antithesis—that God isn't dead—with his fellow students acting as final arbiters. In the movie, Josh makes his case and defeats the professor.

In real life, though, the battles are not so easily won. Across America, more and more Christian students are entering institutions that seek to reshape them into the mold the institution finds most acceptable. Concerted efforts are made to silence their voices and quell the beliefs of any who insist there is a God who expects human beings to live by a set of moral absolutes.

The opening salvo against religious freedom on college and university campuses came in the form of the US Supreme Court's decision in *Christian Legal Society v. Martinez*, 130 S. Ct. 2971 (2010). In this pivotal case, a sharply divided Supreme Court (5–4) allowed the University of California's Hastings College of Law to impose an "all-comers policy" that required all student organizations to accept anyone who wanted membership in an organization, regardless of whether or not the student agreed with the core values and principles of the organization. At issue was the written policy of the Christian Legal Society (CLS) requiring all members to agree with the following belief statement:

> "I believe in: The Bible as the inspired word of God; The Deity of our Lord, Jesus Christ, God's son; The vicarious death of Jesus Christ for our sins; His bodily resurrection and His personal return; The presence and power of the Holy

Spirit in the work of regeneration; [and] Jesus
Christ, God's son, is Lord of my life."[14]

CLS sued the law school, citing an infringement of its First
Amendment rights. In response, the law school claimed to have a
hitherto unwritten policy requiring all registered student organizations to allow "any student to participate, become a member, or seek
leadership positions, regardless of their status or beliefs." After losing
at the district level, CLS lost in federal appellate court. In a 5–4 decision, the US Supreme Court upheld the district court and the Ninth
Circuit Court of Appeals by ruling that the Hastings Law School policy did not violate CLS's First Amendment rights. Nevertheless, the
court stipulated that the all-comers policy had to be applied equally
across the board to all student organizations on campus.[15] Although
it is difficult to think of greater discriminators than fraternities and
sororities, Vanderbilt University and others across the nation have
adopted policies to neuter Christian groups but have not applied
these same rules to the Greek system.

What could be more ironic than the fact that Vanderbilt
University, located in Nashville, Tennessee, in the middle of the Bible
Belt, became the first major university to gain national and international headlines for adopting a "nondiscrimination" policy *more
extreme* than the policy upheld in *Martinez*.[16] In applying its policy
to religious groups, Vanderbilt removed language from the student
handbook that had previously recognized the special mission of religious groups.

The school also imposed a policy that would require these religious organizations to accept anyone seeking leadership in such an
organization—with no provisions for removal should that person
actively begin to undermine the goals of the organization or engage
in an unbiblical lifestyle.[17] This action was freely chosen by the university; it was not required by the *Martinez* ruling.

In adopting its policy, the university ignored the religious freedom guarantees in the US Constitution, as well as the state nondiscrimination laws that would have allowed religious organizations
to use religious criteria in the selection of leaders. The school's new

policy also discounts the common-sense need for organizations to be led by knowledgeable individuals who can share a common set of beliefs and can help students grow in their faith.

CLS general counsel Kim Colby authored a special memorandum, distinguishing Vanderbilt's policy from the *Martinez* case, stating,

> Vanderbilt University does not have such an "all-comers policy" but instead applies a typical nondiscrimination policy to prevent only religious groups from requiring their leaders to share the groups' beliefs. *The University claims it is "religious discrimination" for a religious group to want leaders who share its faith.* With such a wooden interpretation, the University turns its nondiscrimination policy on its head by using a nondiscrimination policy—intended to *protect* religious students from discrimination—to *exclude* religious student groups from campus.[18]

Especially troubling, Vanderbilt administrators interpreted their nondiscrimination/all-comers policy to mean that Christian groups could no longer require their leaders to perform the basic responsibilities expected of leaders of Christian organizations. Leaders could not be required to lead Bible studies or worship services. In a shocking directive, a university official informed one group that its Christian organization was out of compliance because it required a belief in Jesus Christ as Lord and Savior.[19] Moreover, the university's new policy contained no provisions for addressing inevitable situations in which organizational leaders might change their beliefs, reject biblical lifestyles, or embrace atheism or non-Christian religions. An exchange by a student and a faculty administrator at a town hall meeting revealed the extreme nature of the university's policy in that it exempted Greek organizations and left Christian leaders with little recourse to deal with problems that might arise under the new policy.[20]

Political Correctness Magnified

Colleges and universities are controlled by the liberal Left. If they have their way, there will be no room for critical thinking. A new trend is appearing on campuses that reveals just how absurd things have become. The term used to describe it is microaggressions, which are defined as "small actions or word choices that seem on their face to have no malicious intent but that are thought of as a kind of violence nonetheless."[21]

What this means is that you can be guilty of violence just from the words you say, even when you have no intent to inflict violence. The only way one could avoid not being offensive is to know the life history of everyone he or she encounters.

A student goes to college with the intention to enhance his or her learning by being open-minded, only to encounter a culture that makes him or her hypersensitive and ready to be offended at a moment's notice. An example of how bad it can be is illustrated by the simple question that might be asked of a Latino student: "Where were you born?" The Latino student could feel that their American citizenship is being questioned, which could cause distress.[22]

Social status is in play when it comes to microaggressions. If you asked a girl, "Where did you get those jeans?" she may be reluctant to tell you that they were purchased at Walmart because that could make her feel like she was being perceived as being in a lower economic class. Her perception may have nothing to do with your intent. Perhaps you simply liked the jeans and wanted to know where you could buy a pair yourself.

To prevent the oversensitive from becoming offended, some colleges are telling professors they must provide "trigger warnings." Meaning, they must tell their students in advance what material in the course might cause "strong emotional response."[23] How could any professor know all the possible things in the course material or what he or she might say about it that would set off a student emotionally, when that student has been preprogrammed to be quickly offended? Microaggression on college campuses is basically political correctness on steroids. Things have gotten so bad that many big-name comedians will no longer perform on college campuses. Jerry Seinfeld and Bill Maher have publicly denounced this oversensitivity among college students, proclaiming that they "can't take a joke."[24]

The desire may be to make a campus a "safe space" for students, where no verbiage or ideas can make them uncomfortable.[25] As good as this intention may be, all it does is create "a culture in which everyone must think twice before speaking up, lest they face charges of insensitivity, aggression, or worse."[26] This overprotective climate on campus can hamper the educational experience of the students.

The college years are a time to prepare for a career and a time to adjust to independent living. The overprotective environment that creates hypersensitive students is not preparing them for the life they will encounter in the real world. The corporate world is not going to provide supervisors who safeguard their speech so they will not hurt the feelings of their entry-level employees. Nevertheless, many faculty members are concerned about what damage could be done to them by the hypersensitive student who complains to administrators or takes to social media to stir up an "online mob" against them.[27]

In the past, a college education prepared one for a career but also instilled a desire to give back to others through community involvement or financial donations to worthy causes. Creating hypersensitive students has the additional negative impact of multiplying the number of self-centered graduates. Our society is not improved by an increase of selfish people trained to use their emotions as evidence to manipulate and silence others or play the part of the victim. President Thomas Jefferson wrote a statement of purpose about the University of Virginia. It would do well for colleges and universities to adhere to it today:

> This institution will be based on the illimitable freedom of the human mind. For here we are not afraid to follow truth wherever it may lead, nor to tolerate any error so long as reason is left free to combat it.[28]

The words *truth* and *reason* are worthy of note because they seem to be strangers on today's campuses. These two essential factors of learning will always be unwelcome when liberal bias is the desire of a college or university.

ANTI-AMERICAN PROFS

Some professors are political radicals. They hold views that are not just biased but also so extreme that they border on treason. A group known as the American Council of Trustees and Alumni is a nonprofit organization that endorses academic freedom. It reported some unusual comments made by college professors after 9/11:

> Anybody who can blow up the Pentagon gets my vote.[29]
> > —A professor of history,
> > University of New Mexico

> [The American flag is] a symbol of terrorism and death and fear and destruction and oppression.[30]
> > —A professor of physics, University
> > of Massachusetts–Amherst

> Imagine the real suffering and grief of people in other countries. The best way to begin a war on terrorism might be to look in the mirror.[31]
> > —A professor of anthropology,
> > Massachusetts Institute of Technology

After you read these comments, you are inclined to ask, "Whose side are these professors on?" If you think that the American flag is a symbol for death, fear, destruction, and oppression, then you have no business teaching in an American college. The professor who made these comments draws part of his salary from the tax dollars of the citizens of Massachusetts. They are not getting their money's worth. And many of these radical professors are happy to disparage the same American political system that provides them the freedom of speech they take for granted.

After David Horowitz finished his speech at Kenyon College, the one I (Steve) referred to earlier, he allowed questions from the audience. One question prompted Horowitz to define what he meant by the word *radical*. He stated that the term is given to those in the extreme liberal Left who want to change the System—that's "System with a capital S," he noted. Radicals want to destroy what exists now and replace it with something else. In their mind, our form of democratic government as a representative republic, our capitalistic economy, and our culture based on our founding heritage all need to be dismantled and replaced by something else. Robert Bork echoed Horowitz's sentiment on radicalism:

> The Left is fundamentally hostile to American culture and the economy. It would like to overthrow basic institutions and remake the world. This Left has been that way since the Sixties. There is no comparable group on "the right."
>
> There are a few academic conservatives, but they do not propose any attack upon our culture, polity, and economy with the object of drastic restructuring.[32]

Bork's statement is enlightening. We read and hear in the mainstream media how bad the "extreme Right" is. The validity of this opinion is certainly debatable, if not downright ridiculous, but no matter how extreme some on the Right may appear, they do not call for the destruction of the present system. They are not the ones rooting for the Islamic militants against the United States, and they are not the ones calling for a rewrite of the Constitution. We have radicals on the Left who stand in total opposition to what the Founding

Fathers stood for when they founded this nation. It is a tragedy that many of them stand before our children as professors. They are more dedicated to forcing an agenda than expounding truth. They see truth as a necessary casualty when it competes with their New Morality agenda.

CHANGE COURSE BY CHANGING COURSES

One way to attack truth is to blatantly distort it by rewriting history. We discussed this in an earlier chapter. Another way is to just ignore it. Who will hear the lines of an actor who is never allowed on stage? Core requirements are often no longer demanded of students. Tammy Bruce provides one reason why this change has taken place, explaining that some scholars have admitted that Western civilization and American history courses are often eliminated because of the Left's belief that West—and Christianity in particular—are by nature oppressive.[33]

If you want to portray America as oppressive and bash Christianity, the last thing you want is some inquisitive college student studying American history or the Declaration of Independence, with its direct reference to God. You would not want a student examining the speeches of George Washington and Patrick Henry, which tie the founding of our nation to the help and blessings of God. You would not want a student looking at the early years of our nation and noting the decisions from the Supreme Court that harmonized with the Christian faith. All of this is high risk for the liberal Left and its New Morality.

The safest strategy for them is to omit the courses that would challenge the indoctrination process. Tammy Bruce has their game figured out when she writes, "The Left Elite knows that if the truth of history is unleashed, if morals, values, and character help make dreams come true, then their morally vacant world of victims, anger, and hatred will collapse like the house of cards it really is."[34]

For the biased professor, truth is subordinate to the New Morality agenda. The late Chuck Colson, who was an evangelical Christian leader and author, lamented this tragic fact:

> "We are left with a disturbing paradox. While higher education is better funded and more accessible than ever before, it has nothing left worth teaching. Our educational establishment seeks to instill a passion for intellectual curiosity and openness, but allows for the existence of no truth worth pursuing."[35]

Bork weighed in on the loss of core courses that once were part of a student's basic education at the college level. He said the loss of general education requirements has produced students "who have information about narrow corners of subjects but no conception of the larger context that alone can give the niches meaning."[36] Today, academia teaches students how to make a living but fails to show them how to make a life.

Many liberal professors have relished the opportunity to insert courses near and dear to their social, politically correct, misguided interests. There are always those few courses on a campus that are considered an easy opportunity for boosting a GPA. When I (Steve) was getting my MBA at Arizona State University in the late eighties, the course that fit this bill was Jazz in America. Students could pull down an easy A by going on field trips to jazz clubs in the evening, then writing about the experience.

Special courses on campuses today are a bit more politically loaded to the Left. The Young America's Foundation is a nonprofit conservative organization dedicated to teaching young people, especially college students, the conservative viewpoint on key issues. It points out college courses that are slanted toward the liberal, politically correct side. The following samples are quite revealing of how bad things have become. (The descriptions of the courses are those used in the college catalog.)[37]

ABDUCTION

Students at Brown University can take Seeing Queerly: Queer Theory, Film, and Video. This course asks, "While cinema has typically circumscribed vision along (hetro) [*sic*] sexually normative lines, can film also empower viewers to see 'queerly'?" The course endorses films that will inspire and reaffirm people on to homosexual lifestyles.

Students can take a Who Is Black? course at Harvard. This course addresses "the social processes through which identities are constructed and changed." The course also discusses "how struggles about who is black take place not only between blacks and whites, but blacks and other radicalized groups, and among blacks themselves." Are we to understand from this that some blacks get together to debate the question that some of them who are black may not be black? Someone's giving up American history for this?

Afro-American Studies at the University of California, Los Angeles, offers Cultural History of Rap. This course presents students with a discussion "on musical and verbal qualities, philosophical and political ideologies, gender representation, and influences on cinema and popular culture" in rap. Since American history is played down, it's nice to know that the students at UCLA can at least get some rap history in their educational experience.

Georgetown University students can "beam" into philosophy and *Star Trek*. Claiming that there is no better way to learn philosophy than to watch *Star Trek*, this course asks, "Is time travel possible?" "Could we go back and kill our grandmothers?" and "Is Data a person?" Parents get to pay private tuition prices for this. The only thing that comes to mind is, "May the Farce be with you." (Quote refers to the wrong movie, but it fits.)

Women's studies students at the University of Florida take ecofeminism. These students study "Western tradition's naturalization of women and feminization of nature, drawing the conclusion that the domination of women and the domination of nature are intimately connected and mutually reinforcing." What does this mean—if you drain a swamp, you're likely to be a wife beater?

University of Wisconsin students can study Daytime Serials: Family and Social Roles. In this course, students analyze "the themes and characters that populate television's daytime serials and investi-

217

gation of what impact these portrayals have on women's and men's roles in the family and in the work place." What an opportunity—you get to pay tuition to watch soaps. We all know what reality they bring our world.

Vassar College offers students Black Marxism. Students learn how "the growth of global racism suggests the symmetry of the expansion of capitalism." It's a two-for-one special: a course created to distort racism and capitalism at the same time. It seems liberal educators are becoming more efficient. Capitalism is seen as a problem for blacks, not an opportunity.

These course offerings reveal how bad the liberal Left's takeover of our colleges is and the biased message the Left is sending to our children. It is obviously clear that truth is not the main concern of the liberal Left professors in academia. They see college as a place to shape the minds of young people to think a certain way—their way. Education becomes secondary to indoctrination. How else can you explain why schools like the University of California, Berkeley; Mount Holyoke; and the University of Wisconsin have made courses in ethnic studies mandatory while not requiring students to take courses in Western civilization?[38] Tammy Bruce's words are on target when she writes that the growing moral confusion among college students isn't some cultural anomaly—it is being taught to them on university campuses.[39]

HOW FAR THE LEFT WILL GO

An incident at the University of North Carolina shows how far the Left will go to gain an advantage on campus. The school at one time required all incoming freshmen and transfer students to read a book titled *Approaching the Quran: The Early Revelations*. The book included excerpts from the Islamic Quran. The UNC website described the book as a volume of "enduring interest" that introduces the literature and culture of a "profound moral and spiritual tradition." Later, the website reported that the book would no longer be required but that students refusing to read it because they found it in conflict with their faith would have to write a one-page essay explaining why they chose not to read it.[40]

It is interesting that a public university would require students to read an Islamic book that features passages from the Quran. Do you think they would ever require students to read from the Bible?

Non-Christian religious literature seems to be welcomed in a way Christian literature no longer is. Surely, politics is part of the reason for this double standard. Maybe the temptation is just too great for the liberal brain trusts on campus to resist when they see an opportunity to prejudice students' thinking on issues that relate to national policy on the war on terrorism (specifically, terrorism that comes from militant Muslims).

Christianity lost out to Islam at UNC, and it lost out to homosexuality at DePauw University in Indiana. Janis Price, an education professor, placed issues of Dr. James Dobson's magazine *Teachers in Focus* on a table in the back of the room. She told the students that the magazines contained articles that were pro-Christian and were merely made available if they had an interest in reviewing them. Reading them was not required.

One article in Dobson's magazine dealt with how a teacher should approach the homosexual issue in a public school. One of the students in her class complained to the administration, and the war was on. Professor Price received a letter of reprimand from the vice president of academic affairs accusing her of providing students with "intolerant" material. This was said to create a "hostile environment," which was in violation of school policy. Price's salary was cut by 25 percent, and she was suspended from teaching responsibilities.[41]

Christianity must be tolerant of the views of the liberal Left, but intolerance of Christianity is acceptable to the Left. What really makes the Price case appalling is that DePauw is a private school. In fact, it was founded as a Methodist college.

In 1999, the play *Corpus Christi*, which portrays Jesus Christ as a homosexual, was scheduled to be performed at Temple University. A student named Michael Marcavage was offended by this. He decided to sponsor a counter-event that would show "who the real Jesus is." Gospel singers, speakers, and a play about Christ's life titled

Final Destiny would be featured at his event. Marcavage volunteered to pay the expenses for his event, but the university administration turned him down.[42]

The boldness that some liberal professors take in the classroom is irrational. Horowitz, in his Kenyon speech, told of how a biology professor at Penn State University showed Michael Moore's *Fahrenheit 911* on the eve of the presidential election. What did this piece of left-wing political propaganda have to do with biology? Not a thing. This professor overstepped his domain and misused the time of his students.

Academic left-wing bias reached a point of absurdity in March 2015 on the campus of the University of California, Irvine. Six undergraduates on the university's student legislative council voted to ban the American flag from the campus common areas. The reason for the action was said to be that national flags bear a range of cultural significances that could be interpreted negatively by some people and that the American flag has been "flown in instances of colonialism and imperialism."[43] Sixty professors on the campus supported the ban. Our sympathies go out to the taxpayers of California who partially pay the salaries of those professors. The Student Executive Council later rescinded the action of the lower council, but this does not erase the anti-American sentiment of the students and the professors who supported them.

DORMS OR BROTHELS?

The cultural war does not just take place in campus classrooms. It rages in the dorm rooms as well. In an earlier chapter, we looked at how the New Morality was influencing the sex education your kids are getting in the public schools. The sex education they get in college comes complete with lab partners that could be living right next door. The entertainment media and peer pressure all urge a young person to experiment sexually; and what do many colleges, both private and public, do? They operate a policy of coed dorms. Some have even gone further than just the dorm, according to Naomi Schaefer Riley, who wrote *God on the Quad*:

> And if you're crazy not to want to share a bathroom with a member of the opposite sex, why not a bedroom? Several schools, like Haverford College, have recently added the option of coed dorm rooms as a way of accommodating homosexual students who don't feel comfortable living with someone to whom they might be sexually attracted. Of course, since the schools involved would never question students about their sexual orientation, the policy gives a free pass for heterosexual couples to live together.[44]

This means students can practice cohabitation while they get an education.

The sexual norms are deplorable on college campuses. Many college administrations have little concern. Many are only too happy to provide opportunities for students to freely engage in sexual dalliances. What other conclusions can you reach when a school such as James Madison (named after the Founding Father called by many as "the father of our Constitution") holds a "Sex-Fest" at which one session deals with how to put on a condom while drunk?[45]

Dr. Vigen Guroian, professor of theology at Loyola College in Baltimore, wrote a revealing article on the subject of sex and the college campus. The article appeared in *Christianity Today* in February 2005. The title of the article itself was shocking: "Dorm Brothel." Maybe the word *brothel* was not accurate, because the sex described was not motivated by a financial transaction. Guroian believes that much of the illicit sex on campus has been aided and abetted by the colleges and universities:

> The sexual revolution, if that is an appropriate title, was not won with guns but with genital groping aided and abetted by colleges that

forfeited the responsibilities of *in loco parentis* and have gone into the pimping and brothel business.[46]

The administrations of colleges and universities have been willing to give in to the wishes of the New Morality. Parents can no longer rely on colleges to execute rules that seek to keep promiscuous sexual activity in check. In fact, parents have to worry about policies that actually create situations that encourage sexual activity.

We (the authors) are not so out of it that we think sex will not go on among college students. There were incidents of it even on Christian college campuses in the sixties. But back then, you never heard of college policies, Christian or secular, that made such activity so accessible.

We live in a time when STDs are afflicting young people at an alarming rate. These diseases are serious; some are even fatal. Rather than invoking policies that would curb risky sexual behavior, we have academic institutions promoting policies that encourage it. Guroian believes that schools cannot escape accountability:

The lure and availability of sexual adventure that our colleges afford is teaching young women also to pursue sexual pleasures aggressively. Yet, based on my conversations and observations, there is no doubt that young women today are far more vulnerable to sexual abuse and mistreatment by young men than when I was a college student, simply because the institutional arrangements that protected young women are gone and the new climate says everything goes.[47]

The new term on college campus related to student relationships is hooking up. In essence, it is merely pairing off for casual sex—no-strings-attached sex. One of Guroian's female students wrote a paper on what goes on at the college regarding sex. It provides a jolting description of hooking up:

Hooking up is basically dating without the romance. It has become customary for young adults to simply cut to the chase, the sexual… part of a relationship. A hook-up can be a one-time thing, as it most often is, or it can be a semi-regular thing, but not a full relationship.[48]

We send our children off to college to learn, but not all learning takes place in the classroom. Values and acceptable behavior can be learned from the community in which one lives. When a college kid regards sex as something entirely divorced from love or human intimacy, something of value is lost. The loss might not be apparent at the moment, but it can lurk inside a person, leaving an emotional scar, the pain of which may not be felt until years later. Hooking up is about using people, which is deplorable.

We are inclined to think that the modern sex scene on campus victimizes young women while the males are given a pass—as in, "Boys will be boys." Guroian realizes this is not true. He believes great damage is being done to many young men's characters by "deforming their attitudes toward the opposite sex." He states, "I am witnessing a perceptible dissipation of manly virtue in the young men I teach."[49]

You would think the feminists would take issue with this development. They work so hard to have women recognized as valuable people with real personhood who need to be taken seriously. While they are doing this, academia is creating an environment that runs counter to the efforts of feminists, and feminists do not voice a peep of a protest. A Midwest private college's student newspaper ran an article about a student committee on campus called the Beer and Sex Committee, which was approved by the administration. The committee's concern was that consensual sex would truly be consensual. If consent was present, the action was encouraged.

PORN 101

Sex is not just an extracurricular pursuit on campus. Sometimes it's an assignment. Pornography has been deemed an appropriate academic topic to explore at some colleges. One college offered a course titled Pornography: Writing of Prostitutes. Professor Hope Weissman gave an assignment in which the students were to produce a piece of pornography, and she stressed there were no constraints. Some of the projects were despicable: "One student produced a video, training the camera's lens on a man's eyes while he was masturbating. Another turned in pictures of herself engaged in oral sex with her boyfriend."[50]

Someone objected to this course, and the administration investigated it, only to receive outcries from students protesting that their academic freedom was being encroached upon. The college, in Middletown, Connecticut, is Wesleyan University, named after John Wesley, the founder of the Methodist Church. It is a tragedy when our colleges teach lust in that area of life where our children need to learn love.

SEX WEEK

Porn assignments in class fit right in with a new extracurricular event that many colleges across the country are now sponsoring each year. It is called Sex Week; and it features speakers, seminars, and workshops on a range of topics. Some of the topics, like "Help for Sexual Assault Victims" and "A Discussion of Abstinence," appear quite acceptable; but other topics, such as "Negotiating Successful Threesomes" or "How to be a Gentleman and Get Laid," have made it into some universities' Sex Weeks. One university even ventured a topic called "Slut Walk."[51] Sex-toy manufacturers are even invited on campus to market their products directly to students. Most parents are unaware of the aggressive sexual agenda their kids are being subjected to on today's college campuses.

Sex Week amounts to an intangible Trojan horse, where outlandish sexual acts and lifestyles can be introduced under the cover of a university-sponsored event that appears to be all-inclusive in addressing an interest of college students. There has been strong criticism from parents and alumni regarding Sex Week activities because mandatory student fees often support the event.

At the University of New Mexico, two members of Students for Life on the campus were supportive of the sex-education material presented at Sex Week but were offended by the vulgar elements presented.[52] We wonder if they would get any traction claiming micro-aggression due to the content of some of the seminars that presented perverted material. When it comes to sex for the liberal Left, one has to wonder if there is anything they regard as too perverted for the classroom.

For its first Sex Week, the University of Tennessee booked lesbian-bondage expert Sinclair Sexsmith as host. The cost of the week's events came to $20,000, covered in part by university grants. Your tax dollars at work for those of you living in the Volunteer State. What seminars and workshops did your tax dollars help pay for? Some of the topics covered: "Getting Laid," "Loud and Queer," and "How Many Licks Does It Take?"[53]

Ms. Sexsmith has "great" credentials, since she served on the board of the New York Lesbian Sex Mafia and runs the website "Sugarbutch Chronicles: Queer Sex, Kink, Gender, and Relationships by Sinclair Sexsmith."[54] Student Brianna Rader, one of the founders of Sex Week at UT, said university officials were "overwhelmingly supportive."[55] The UT Sex Week also included a sex talent show (your guess is as good as ours) and drag show.[56] Something tells us the drag show was not about car racing.

CHRISTIAN COLLEGES FIGHT THE BATTLE

The denomination I (Steve) belong to has eight liberal-arts colleges, and it takes great pride in them. I am an alumnus of one of them. I have served as a staff member at one, as well as an adjunct professor. I have firsthand experience observing happenings on the private Christian-college scene.

I was on staff at Mount Vernon Nazarene University when it hosted a conference for the seven sister colleges of the denomination. There were various discussion groups one could attend. I chose one focusing on history and a political theme. I was amazed as the professor began to talk and basically turned the session into a time of complaining that too many of the students on campus were conservative. A professor from Point Loma Nazarene University in the San

Diego area was especially distraught about this situation. He could not get over the fact that 80 percent of the student body considered themselves conservatives.

My first thought was, Doesn't this guy know he is teaching in an evangelical Christian college that belongs to a very conservative denomination? I realized that liberalism was gaining a foothold in one of the last bastions conservatives had in academia. The private evangelical Christian college is not without its problems, but it still represents a positive place where parents can send their children without fear that teachings will equate to nonstop liberal indoctrination. These schools play an important role in providing students with a place where they can be educated in a way that does not attack Christianity on every front. Yet a Christian heritage does not guarantee an unchallenged future. The money issue is always critical for a college, and even more so for a small evangelical school. There is the temptation to focus on the bottom line at the sacrifice of the spiritual mission.

The changes seem to come gradually and silently, like a boat slowly drifting out to sea until one day the shoreline is out of sight. Harvard, Yale, Princeton, the University of Southern California, Duke, Oberlin, William and Mary, DePauw, and many others have experienced this drift and in some cases are now hostile to the very principles that brought them into existence. Even today's Christian schools are vulnerable to the reach of the New Morality.

The student newspaper of a Midwest Christian university contained an article regarding the rules that students were expected to obey. The rules, now called community policy, were formerly referred to as lifestyle guidelines. For the article, students were surveyed to see how they were obeying the "rules." Nearly half admitted to violating the "no consumption of alcohol" restriction, and a little more than 20 percent were sexually active. The dean of students stated, "At the heart of our policy is a desire for our students to be making healthy choices focused upon their academic success and personal growth."[57] You might think that a school that regarded itself as a Christian university would link the heart of its behavior policy to Christian values or to biblical principles.

The Christian college, however, is on the front line of the cultural war. It walks a very thin line, on which it tries to balance academic excellence and religious morality while also making sure all the bills are paid. If a Christian school compromises its standards for financial security or acceptance in the eyes of modern academia, our children are the real losers and the New Morality gains more ground.

MAKING A DIFFERENCE: FOUNDATION FOR INDIVIDUAL RIGHTS IN EDUCATION AND YOUNG AMERICA'S FOUNDATION

Conservative faculty and students who find themselves in the crosshairs of liberal administrators can reach out to the Foundation for Individual Rights in Education (FIRE). Founded in 1999 by university professor Alan Charles Kors of the University of Pennsylvania and Boston attorney Harvey Silvergate, FIRE has as its mission "to defend and sustain individual rights at America's colleges and universities."[58] The rights defended include "freedom of speech, legal equality, due process, religious liberty, and sanctity of conscience—the essential qualities of individual liberty and dignity."[59] Its core mission is "to protect the unprotected and to educate the public and communities of concerned Americans about the threats to these rights on our campuses and about the means to preserve them."[60]

Before founding FIRE, the two men exposed the hypocrisies and double standards on university campuses in their widely acclaimed book *The Shadow University: The Betrayal of Liberty on America's Campuses.*[61] According to FIRE, the twelve worst colleges for academic freedom are the University of Cincinnati, Syracuse University, Widener University, Harvard University, Yale University, St. Augustine's College, Michigan State University, Colorado College, Johns Hopkins University, Tufts University, Bucknell University, and Brandeis University. They write, "Each of these schools earned its place on FIRE's list by severely violating the speech rights of students, faculty members, or both."[62]

Fortunately, there is help for faculty members and students at public and private secondary schools, as well as colleges and universities. Anyone who suspects he or she is a victim of ideological discrimination can reach out to a number of organizations for advice and, in some cases, legal representation. In addition to the Foundation for Individual Rights in Education, aggrieved individuals can contact Liberty Counsel (www.lc.org) and the Liberty Institute (www.libertyinstitute.org).

Young America's Foundation provides a list of what it believes are the top conservative colleges. Some of the schools are Catholic, some are evangelical Christian, and some have no religious affiliation but are strongly aligned with conservative principles and take no federal aid. These schools are Christendom College, College of the Ozarks, Colorado Christian University, Franciscan University, Grove City College, Harding University, Hillsdale College, The King's College, Liberty University, Ohio Christian University, Patrick Henry College, Regent University, Saint Vincent College, Thomas Aquinas College, Thomas More College, and Wisconsin Lutheran College.[63]

Some students are inclined to attend state schools for financial reasons or because of the specialized degree they wish to earn. Churches near these campuses can develop creative outreach ministries to these students and also support the ministries of groups like Cru (formerly Campus Crusade for Christ). We are aware of one church that provides a mentoring program for male students that emphasizes sexual purity.

Parents who are planning to send a child to college should do their due diligence in evaluating the colleges being considered. Visits should be made to the campuses when possible. Research needs to be done to find a school that both matches the academic goals of the student and maintains high moral standards. If the child is opting for a state school, parents should help connect their college student with a church support group near the college. The parents may want to take an active role in locating off-campus lodging for their child's physical and moral well-being.

TAKE ACTION

- Investigate campus environments before spending your tuition dollars at institutions that will destroy your child's faith.
- Contact trustees, organize protests, and withhold funds to universities that discriminate against conservative ideological positions.
- Use the power of the purse and withhold financial contributions to universities that engage in activities offensive to traditional values.

CHAPTER 10

Black Robes Bring Dark Days

Unique among the nations, America was founded at a particular time, by a particular people, on the basis of a particular idea.[1]
—Matthew Spalding, Heritage Foundation

At the establishment of our constitutions, the judiciary bodies were supposed to be the most helpless and harmless members of the government. [E]xperience however soon showed in what way they were to become the most dangerous: that the insufficiency of the means provided for their removal gave them a freehold and irresponsibility in office; that their decisions, seeming to concern individual suitors only, pass silent and unheeded by the public at large; that these decisions nevertheless become law by precedent, sapping by little and little the foundations of the Constitution.[2]
—Thomas Jefferson, October 31, 1823

As Thomas Jefferson noted in his 1823 letter to M. M. Coray, quoted above, what was supposed to be the least-powerful branch of government, the judiciary, had already begun to usurp power never intended by the men who founded our nation and ratified its Constitution in 1787. When it came to nation building, the brave men who founded our country drew heavily on the writings of English philosopher John Locke, who provided the intellectual foundation for the revolution that resulted in the birth of America. The consent of the people was necessary to establish political legitimacy and the rule of law. Governments owed a duty to the people to protect their "life, liberty, and property." People were justified in overthrowing governments that violated the "laws of nature" and "nature's God." These were part of the self-evident truths acknowledged in the Declaration of Independence.

To their credit, our Founding Fathers established a representative republic, meaning that power resided in the hands of the people. The preamble of the Constitution states,

> We the People of the United States, in Order to form a more perfect Union, establish Justice, insure domestic Tranquility, provide for the common defence, promote the general Welfare, and secure the Blessings of Liberty to ourselves and our Posterity, do ordain and establish this Constitution for the United States of America.

Clearly, the founders and the framers of the Constitution saw the need to establish a system in which power resided in the hands of the people. They had had enough of being ruled by tyranny, where the voice of the people was forsaken for the whim of a king. The founders would be shocked today if they could visit the nation they founded to see that "We the People" has been replaced by "Us the Judges."

AGENDA BEFORE CONSTITUTION

Under the Constitution, the role of the judicial branch is to interpret the law, settle disputes, and serve as a watchdog for balancing the separate branches of government. This was to ensure that the legislative branch did not encroach on the executive branch and vice versa. The judiciary was given the ability to ensure that the national government respected the autonomy granted state governments under the Tenth Amendment, or the "reserved powers" amendment, which states that powers not delegated to the federal government or prohibited by it are reserved for the states. This forms the constitutional basis for individuals in the various states to enact laws that reflect their value system.

Unfortunately, our country is now overrun with activist judges who seem more interested in advancing their own liberal, personal agendas and the New Morality embraced by cultural elites than in upholding the Constitution. Often it seems like these judges totally ignore the Constitution and past precedents when they issue a ruling, creating new rights the framers never imagined. It is unthinkable that the court would have invented a right to privacy to justify its abortion decision in *Roe v. Wade* or its decision to use the equal-protection clause of the Fourteenth Amendment to justify overturning marriage laws in the fifty states.

Increasingly, it looks like our judges are appointed to the bench with their ideologies fixed and minds made up about the values and principles they hope to advance. When the Supreme Court issues a decree, it usually explains its decision using some combination of past precedents and legal analysis. Judges differ in how they interpret the Constitution. Strict constructionists look to the text of the Constitution and try to infer the original intent of the framers, whereas judicial activists go beyond the text. Activist judges see the Constitution as a living document that changes with the times and the people. As a consequence, new rights can be invented for new groups and situations.

Federal judges are appointed to life terms, which means they are not accountable to the people. Many of these judges are activists with deep roots in political parties. Phyllis Schlafly calls the activist judges supremacists:

> A supremacist is one who believes in or advocates the supremacy of a particular group. The threat to America comes precisely from those who believe in and advocate the supremacy of one particular group—judges—over the lawful wishes of the people.[3]

The activist judges of today don't think they wear robes; they think they wear crowns. They don't hand down decisions; they issue decrees. By these decrees, judges have removed the Ten Commandments from public places, changed the definition of marriage, banned prayer in schools, imposed taxes, rewritten laws for criminal procedures, and outlawed term limits for members of Congress. They have created rights that are not stated in the Constitution, such as the right to abortion, the right to same-sex marriage, the right to publish pornography, and the right for illegal aliens to receive taxpayer-paid benefits.[4] This dark reality in our judiciary branch is insulting to the Founding Fathers and the Constitution they created. It is contemptuous to all citizens who value virtue and decency. The late Supreme Court Justice Antonin Scalia, who opposed judicial activism, summed up how many Americans feel regarding the decisions that have recently come down from the high court:

> What secret knowledge, one must wonder, is breathed into lawyers when they become Justices of this Court, that enables them to discern that a practice which the text of the Constitution does not clearly proscribe, and which our people have regarded as constitutional for two hundred years, is in fact unconstitutional?....Day by day, case by case, [the court] is busy designing a Constitution for a country I do not recognize.[5]

There was a day when liberals were calling for a new Constitutional Convention. With what they have going for them in the Supreme Court, they don't need one. Justice Scalia made reference to two hundred years, a time period beyond which many things that were considered in line with the Constitution are now deemed unconstitutional. Usually the Supreme Court applies the doctrine of *stare decisis* ("to stand by decided matters") as part of its decision-making process, whereby it looks at previous cases in search of legal rules and principles that can be applied to the case under consideration. The reliance on past precedents helps the justices gain valuable insight about what the framers of the Constitution originally intended. When you want to advance your own agenda that is tied to your political ideology and history does not favor it, then history is the last place you want to visit. Activist judges who embrace the New Morality may avoid history, but we will look at it to see what original intent and beliefs were regarded as acceptable and in harmony with the Constitution by those who once wore the robes of the high court.

HISTORY HAPPENS, AND JUDGES HATE IT

In 1844, a case came before the Supreme Court known as *Vidal v. Girard's Executors*. Stephen Girard was a wealthy Frenchman who settled in Philadelphia. He died in 1831 and left his estate, valued at more than $7 million, to the city. There was a condition for the gift. The city had to build an orphanage and a college according to Mr. Girard's stipulations that "no ecclesiastic, missionary, or minister of any sect whatsoever, shall ever hold or exercise any station or duty in the said college; nor shall any such person ever be admitted for any purpose or as a visitor."[6]

This requirement of excluding religious teachings from a school was unprecedented.[7] If Girard was living in our era, he would be a hero for the Left and the New Morality. Daniel Webster, a lawyer for the plaintiffs (family members), stated before the court, "No fault can be found with Girard for wishing a marble college to bear his name forever, but it is not valuable unless it has a fragrance of Christianity about it."[8] The lawyers for the city argued that the gift should come to the city with the "obnoxious" requirement removed, since they also felt the exclusion of the clergy was wrong.

Can you imagine anyone having a chance to win a case today by citing that a college has to have a "fragrance of Christianity"? We have judges today who make careers by taking Christianity out of schools. Mr. Webster could not conceive of a school in America back in his day that would be void of religious teachings. It should be noted that Webster was born six years after the Declaration of Independence was signed. His generation was the first generation to be raised under the Constitution, so how could he hold such an idea that is now considered unconstitutional?

The decision was a unanimous one that the estate be given to the city but that the clergy and anti-Christian clause be discarded, and the opinion was stated by Justice Joseph Story:

> Christianity...is not to be maliciously and openly reviled and blasphemed against to the annoyance of believers or the injury of the public...It is unnecessary for us, however, to consider...the establishment of a school or college for the propagation of Judaism or Deism or any other form of infidelity. Such a case is not to be presumed to exist in a Christian country.[9]

These are words from a Supreme Court justice as he writes the opinion for a unanimous majority who grew up in the years immediately following the ratification of the Constitution. And some incredible words they are. First, all the justices agreed that "Christianity is not to be maliciously and openly reviled and blasphemed against." This is evidence that the entire Supreme Court once believed it was wrong to attack Christianity. This is unlike the court of today, which has declared open season on Christianity.

Second, the justices did not want Christianity to be attacked because it might annoy Christians and do harm to the public. What a comparison this is to today. Our contemporary judges might make some effort to make sure atheists are not offended by Christian symbols and the like, but they are not very worried about Christians being annoyed by anti-Christian remarks. If the Story court were in office today, this decision would have restored prayer in schools, put a number of college professors out of work, and shut down more than half the entertainment industry. The country would likely be the better for it.

Finally, the words that stand out most are the last four: "in a Christian country." A Supreme Court justice, writing a unanimous opinion, describes the United States of America as a Christian nation. How can this be? How could the first generation raised under the Constitution come to power and believe that this nation was a Christian nation? The historical revisionists tell us otherwise. In truth, the country was regarded as a Christian nation because the laws and culture were based on Christian principles, and no one considered it to be out of line with the Constitution. Every decision Supreme Court justices have made adverse to Christianity could have been decided to the benefit of Christianity based on the precedence of this case. But when Christianity doesn't fit your agenda, why make the effort?

In 1885, the Supreme Court was called on to rule in a polygamy case, *Murphy v. Ramsey*. The court rendered a decision that was not in favor of polygamy, sanctioned by religion. The wording the court used is noteworthy, given the issues we face today:

> Certainly no legislation can be supposed more wholesome and necessary in the founding of a free, self-governing commonwealth...than that which seeks to establish it on the basis of the idea of the family, as consisting in and springing from the union for life of one man and one woman in the holy estate of matrimony; [the family is] the

sure foundation of all that is stable and noble in
our civilization; the best guarantee of that reverent morality which is the source of all beneficent
progress in social and political improvement.[10]

These words actually came from our Supreme Court. They
conclude that the nation benefits from the family and that a family
originates from the "union…of one man and one woman in the holy
estate of matrimony." This is not good news for those who favor
same-sex marriage, but it will make no difference. This case could
really save some time for the courts of today. All they have to do is
stroll down history lane and cite this case, saying that the Supreme
Court has already ruled on this issue of same-sex marriage. Today's
court chose otherwise.

The court of 1885 said the family was the "best guarantee of
that reverent morality which is the source of all beneficent progress in
social and political improvement." The court actually welcomed that
which provides the country with morality because it helps to bring
social and political improvement. In contrast, we have Supreme
Court justices and other judges who concoct ways to reduce morality's influence on the country.

There is a reference to our nation being a nation of "religious
people" as recently as 1952, in a case known as *Zorach v. Clauson*.
The decision of the court showed an attitude toward religion by justices that sadly does not exist today:

> The First Amendment, however, does not say
> that in every and all respects there shall be sepa-
> ration of Church and State…Otherwise the state
> and religion would be aliens to each other—hos-
> tile, suspicious, and even unfriendly. We are a
> religious people whose institutions presuppose
> a Supreme Being…When the State encourages
> religious instruction or cooperates with religious
> authorities by adjusting the schedule of public
> events to sectarian needs, it follows the best of

our traditions. For it then respects the religious nature of our people and accommodates the public service to their spiritual needs. To hold that it may not would be to find in the Constitution a requirement that the government show a callous indifference to religious groups. That would be preferring those who believe in no religion over those who do believe...We find no constitutional requirement which makes it necessary for government to be hostile to religion and to throw its weight against efforts to widen the effective scope of religious influence.[11]

These words are encouraging and disappointing at the same time. It is encouraging that our nation's Supreme Court justices once were positive toward religion; however, it is disappointing to realize how far current justices have strayed from those beliefs and how the nation has suffered for it.

The 1952 justices had no problem stating that we, as a nation, believed in a Supreme Being. They wanted to make sure that a decision rendered by them would not show preference for those with "no religion" over "those who do believe." Today that preference is exercised over and over again. The last line of the quote says that there is "no constitutional requirement which makes it necessary for government to be hostile to religion and to throw its weight against efforts to widen the effective scope of religious influence." If this is true, then why do the courts of today show hostility to religion? When it is unconstitutional for a kid to say grace before eating his meal in a school cafeteria, this is being hostile to religion.

The point simply is, there is enough historical evidence in prior Supreme Court decisions for present-day justices to maintain the religious heritage of our nation in decisions they render. Why doesn't it happen? It doesn't happen because they don't want it to happen. They wear the uniform of the liberal New Morality under their black robes and don't want the America of reverent morality of the Founding Fathers. They want an America where morality is relative, always in question, and free from any religious influence. They do not find the history of their predecessors to be a source of enlightenment. These judicial sojourners are attracted to another path that America should not tread in search of justice. That path is the international community.

THE OVERSEAS LOOK THAT IS TAKING US UNDER

We have judges who choose to defend their decisions based on what other countries are doing. If you can't use the history of your own Supreme Court of your own country because it does not agree with your agenda, then you have to go shopping elsewhere to try and justify your warped style of justice. The overseas market appears attractive to activist judges, even at the risk of undermining United States sovereignty.

On the issue of delays of execution, Justice Stephen Breyer said in the case of *Knight v. Florida* (1999) that it was "useful" to consider court decisions in the countries of India, Jamaica, and Zimbabwe.[12] When thinking of a nation that would be a role model to copy for establishing laws, especially those dealing with execution, Zimbabwe doesn't come to mind. Maybe Justice Breyer could pick up some pointers by watching *The Lion King*.

A case that sent shock waves through the country was *Lawrence v. Texas* (2003), which overturned Texas sodomy law and made homosexuality a constitutional right. Justice Anthony Kennedy was on the majority side that came down in favor of homosexuality as a constitutional right. He ignored a past case before the Supreme Court, *Bowers v. Hardwick* (1986). In that case, Michael Hardwick wanted the court to declare that it is a "fundamental constitutional right to engage in homosexual sodomy."[13] The Supreme Court ruled against him. Justice Byron White, a President Kennedy appointee, wrote the majority opinion, which is recounted by Mark Levin in his book *Men in Black*:

STEVEN FEAZEL AND DR. CAROL M. SWAIN

White noted that the rights announced in prior cases involving family, marriage, and procreation had no relationship with a right to engage in homosexual sodomy. Furthermore, he wrote, "Any claim that these cases nevertheless stand for the proposition that any kind of private sexual conduct between consenting adults is constitutionality insulated from state proscription is unsupportable."[14]

Notice the words "prior cases." This means that Justice White researched previous cases related to the topic of this case when making his decision and writing his opinion. Justice Kennedy could not find anything in *Bowers v. Hardwick* to support the decision he wanted rendered, so he had to look elsewhere. He found support for his out-of-this-world decision outside of our country. He cited a committee that advised the British Parliament, which recommended the repeal of 1957 laws that punished homosexual conduct. He further referred to the European Convention on Human Rights, which supported a homosexual in a case in Ireland who claimed the law he was confronted with was invalid.[15] Justice Kennedy's own words in his opinion are disturbing:

To the extent *Bowers* relied on values we share with a wider civilization, it should be noted that the reasoning and holding in *Bowers* have been rejected elsewhere. The European Court of Human Rights has followed not *Bowers* but its own decision in *Dudgeon v. United Kingdom*. Other nations, too, have taken action consistent with an affirmation of the protected right of homosexual adults to engage in intimate, consensual conduct. The right the petitioners seek in this case has been accepted as an integral part of human freedom in many other countries.[16]

Why would he refer to a law in the United Kingdom? It was some of their laws that inspired us centuries ago to start a revolution and draft a Declaration of Independence. If we have a Constitution and a history of law and court decisions, why do our Supreme Court justices have to seek guidance from the courts of other countries? How can a justice assume that the cultures and values of another country automatically fit our country and then dare to copy their decision? It doesn't make any sense.

It may not make any sense, but it is a way that a judge can advance the New Morality agenda and help his fellow social engineers reshape our culture. Justice Kennedy is not the only high-court judge to be enamored with the laws of other nations in order to justify his or her views. Justice Ruth Bader Ginsburg believes that we are moving from a "Lone Ranger mentality" and becoming more open to comparative and international law perspectives.[17]

Justice John Paul Stevens rewrote the Eighth Amendment by outlawing capital punishment for offenders who have a low IQ. Stevens cited laws from the European Union that disapprove of the death penalty for the mentally retarded as reason enough for his decision.[18] Justice Scalia stated, "The views of other nations...cannot be imposed upon Americans."[19] The reality is they have been imposed on us by five of the nine high-court justices.

We are an independent nation with a high, if not still the highest, level of morality of any nation, despite all the efforts from the liberal Left to diminish it. We do not need our justices to leave our shores to interpret law. Our Constitution and historical precedents will suffice.

TAKING SIDES IN THE CULTURAL WAR

You might wonder how this affects our children. Court decisions change things that touch the lives of our children. It was the courts that took prayer out of schools and forced the busing of kids all around town to achieve racial equality, an action opposed by all races concerned. It is the court that makes decisions that run contrary to the moral values held by the majority in a community.

It seems the courts have little concern for our kids and are willing to put them at risk while they methodically rid the land of virtue. The court's treatment of pornography is a prime example. They apply the First Amendment free-speech clause to this subject and how they deal with it is not good news for our children or our country. Justice Scalia stated, "The Court has taken sides in the culture war, departing from its role of assuring, as neutral observer, that the democratic rules of engagement are observed."[20] Bork echoes Justice Scalia when he writes, "Americans are force-fed a new culture and new definitions of virtue, all in the name of a Constitution that neither commands nor permits such results."[21]

This bias in the cultural war is evident in the way the courts have treated pornography in the environment of the First Amendment. Congress passed a law requiring cable-television networks that presented sexually oriented programming to limit the transmission of the programs to hours when children would not be likely to view it. This law was tested in the case of *United States v. Playboy Entertainment Group, Inc* (2000). The court found the law to be a restriction on the content of speech. Their reasoning was that other less-restrictive methods of protecting children were available.[22]

The justices on the majority side were, in essence, equating sex and speech, something that certainly was never the original intent of the Founding Fathers.[23] Justice Scalia, in his dissent, gives us an idea of what the majority justices were willing to consider as "speech" (which actually were visual images the cable channels were putting forth). He described this visual speech as "female masturbation/external," "girl/girl sex," and "oral sex/cunnilingus."[24] Regarding to the decision of this case, Robert Bork states, "The Court's discussion centered upon the pleasures of adults. No weight was given to the interest of society in preserving some vestige of moral tone."[25]

The court didn't argue that the sexually oriented material is appropriate for children, only that parents should bear the responsibility to protect their eyes. By this decision, the court was saying that the financial welfare of the pornographers was more important than the welfare of children as a whole in society.

On the topic of pornography, the modern-day court has applied the same blind eye to history as it has to other topics. In *Roth v. United States* (1957), the Supreme Court made the following ruling:

> Implicit in the history of the First Amendment is the rejection of obscenity as utterly without redeeming social importance…We hold that obscenity is not within the area of constitutionally protected speech or press.[26]

We once had a Supreme Court that believed obscenity had no "redeeming social importance" and therefore was not protected by the First Amendment. The New Morality would not accept this ruling and would seek to change it when it had the chance. Nine years later, the New Morality had its opportunity in the case known as *A Book Named "John Cleland's Memoirs of a Woman of Pleasure" v. Massachusetts* (1966). The case was nicknamed the *Fanny Hill* case. Charles Rembar, the lawyer for the pro-obscenity side, convinced the court to make two subtle changes in the language of the *Roth* case.

The first was to change "social importance" to "social value." The second was to transpose the word *utterly* to another part of the sentence so that something would be considered to be obscene only if it was found to be "utterly without social value." What the lawyer did was give the New Morality what it really prizes: a loophole in a law they don't like so that it will, in effect, be rendered useless.[27] The absurdity of this judicial folly is noted in the words of Phyllis Schlafly:

> "Social value" quickly became a password to pornography; all a smut peddler had to do was to insert a few social or literary passages, and his obscenity was clothed with the Constitution. The obscene Swedish movie *I Am Curious (Yellow)*

was defended on the ground that although it pictured intercourse explicitly and in public, it was protected by the First Amendment because the couple did their act on the balustrade of the royal palace in Stockholm as a protest against social institutions.[28]

The two changes have radically affected how our society tries to cope with obscenity and pornography. With these changes, there is no clear standard upon which localities can determine what is over the line, as Robert Bork attested to in his remarks regarding *Miller v. California* (1973), which was to place some restraints on pornography but did little good:

> Communities now find it impossible to control the torrent of pornography loosed upon them. Juries can no longer agree, as *Miller* requires, that any depiction of sexual conduct is "patently offensive" or that "the work, taken as a whole, lacks serious literary, artistic, political, or scientific value."[29]

One thing that can be said about the court is that when it comes to decisions on pornography, it has been consistent. It has ruled in favor of the pornographers in case after case after case. In the period from 1966 to 1970, the Warren court made thirty-four decisions that devastated obscenity laws. In many of those cases, they just printed their decision without documenting the debate. All thirty-four decisions were anonymous, meaning that no judge would put his name on it. This was great news for Hollywood, which ended its production code and started pushing the envelope with more violence and explicit sex scenes.[30]

REWRITING THE FIRST AMENDMENT

The Child Pornography Prevention Act of 1996 passed overwhelmingly in Congress and was signed into law by President Clinton. In the case of *Ashcroft v. Free Speech Coalition* (2002), the court rendered half of this law invalid. The ban on computer-generated child pornographic images was removed.[31] How does this help our kids? We watch the news and see stories of some weirdo who abducts a child, sexually assaults her, and more often than not kills her. When his background is investigated, pornography, and in many cases child pornography, is involved.

Schlafly accurately sums up the damage the court has done to the First Amendment and to Americans with their ridiculous decisions regarding the subject of pornography:

> The courts are not *interpreting* the First Amendment; they are rewriting it to guarantee the profits of pornographers. The judicial supremacists have made the First Amendment a traffic signal that flashes green to pornographers but red or yellow to religious and political speech. From Hollywood movies, to primetime and cable television, to dirty books and songs, "the suffocating vulgarity of popular culture" is all around us.[32]

Pornography is not the only topic that the court appears confused about when it comes to the First Amendment. You can add political speech to the list. The court was set up by the founders to be a nonpolitical branch of the government, but that has not stopped the court from acting in political ways and becoming active in shaping the rules of political debate.

Congress passed the McCain-Feingold Act in 2002 to rid corruption from political campaigns. It was to take money out of politics. This law, along with complicated regulations on the raising and spending of money by candidates, was restrictive of advertising. Designated organizations and individuals were prevented from running advertisements for a candidate sixty days before Election Day.[33] In the past, the expenditure of money to promote a candidate, whether spent personally or as a donation to a campaign, was seen as a lawful exercise of one's free speech. Money was seen as one's voice.

The McCain-Feingold Act was to change this. It was regarded as a highly controversial and unconstitutional piece of legislation. Many legal experts and politicians predicted that the law would be declared unconstitutional by the Supreme Court. President George W. Bush thought this and signed the bill into law. A case related to this law made it before the Supreme Court. But guess what? The court upheld McCain-Feingold as constitutional. A lesson was learned. You can't trust the Supreme Court. As Mark Levin writes, "The Court, these days, is no reliable guardian of the Constitution."[34] The law did not restrict the media or limit their right to print and broadcast what they wanted, right up to Election Day. We have already seen that the mainstream media tilts a little—Okay, a lot—to the liberal side. The act gave the advantage to the media, incumbents, and those individuals who are wealthy enough to finance their own political campaign. The law did not really take money out of politics; it just forced it to creatively move around. What went out of politics with this law was a portion of free speech that the Founding Fathers designed for us to have, especially when it came to politics. We have a Supreme Court that creates more avenues of influence for pornographers but restricts political speech. Jefferson, Adams, Madison, and their colleagues would not recognize this as the same nation they helped to establish if they were to personally observe this insanity.

BATTLING THE BALLOT BOX

The federal judges are appointed and not elected, but this has not stopped them from getting their hands into the ballot box when it comes to other people's elections. Liberals and the New Morality don't like elections when they can't win them. When they haven't been able to win them by the people's choice, they have sought to win them by judges' decrees. This is articulated profoundly by Robert Bork:

> The New Class's problem in most nations is that its attitudes command only a political minority. It is able to exercise influence in many ways, but when cultural and social issues become sufficiently clear, the intellectual class loses elections. It is, therefore, essential that the cultural left find a way to avoid the verdict of the ballot box. Constitutional courts provide the necessary means to outflank majorities and nullify their votes. The judiciary is the liberals' weapon of choice. Democracy and the rule of law are undermined while the culture is altered in ways the electorate would never choose.[35]

The most famous example of the court system overstepping its jurisdiction regarding election law is the 2000 presidential election results in the state of Florida. After vote tabulation, George W. Bush had won Florida over Al Gore by seventeen hundred votes. According to Florida law, this required a machine recount, which, when done, gave Bush a victory margin of 327 votes. Gore now had the option to ask for a manual recount in any county. How this recount was to be done in the county was clearly spelled out in Florida law:

> When such a request is made, the county's canvassing board could then, in its discretion, conduct a manual recount of one percent of the county's total votes in at least three precincts. If that one percent sampling dictated "an error in vote tabulation which could affect the outcome of the election," the board was required to correct the error and recount the other precincts with the vote tabulation system, request the Department

of State to verify the tabulation software, or conduct a full manual recount.[36]

A full manual recount could only be enacted if the initial selective recount revealed an error. Nobody claimed there were any machine errors, and that included anyone on the Gore team. There was no basis, according to Florida election law, for a full manual recount to take place in the selected counties.[37] The election was legally over, and Bush was the winner of Florida's electoral vote. Gore then called for a manual recount of four counties that were overwhelmingly Democrat in voter registration. The Gore team prevailed on the Democrat-laden Florida Supreme Court to allow for this outside-the-law manual recount of the selected four counties. This recount was not within the realm of Florida law. What's a liberal to do when the law gets in the way? What any good liberal would do: go to the courts and get a judgment to override the law. That is what happened, and that's why we had the election mess in Florida.

Florida also has a law that states election results have to be in the secretary of state's office for certification by 5:00 p.m. seven days after the election.[38] Some counties had difficulty conducting their illegal recount fast enough to meet this deadline. The Gore team then asked for the Florida Supreme Court to extend this deadline, which it did, even though it had no state constitutional authority to do so.[39]

The whole issue, as we all know, ended when the Supreme Court ruled that the Florida Supreme Court was wrong in allowing for the manual recount. The decision was 5–4, which reveals that even four Supreme Court justices were okay with courts getting involved in election results. Liberals bemoan this decision as ill-conceived and partisan. Given the limbo of the nation at the time, it is not clear what would have happened had the court not stepped in to resolve what was certainly a political question.

Liberals were again to use a state high court to thwart election law. The state was New Jersey, and the issue was the resignation of Senator Robert Torricelli, who withdrew as a candidate for reelection to the Senate in light of a scandal. State law stated that a political party could not replace one candidate with another within fifty-one days of the election. Torricelli made his withdrawal thirty-six days before the election. He had won the party's nomination by winning the primary but was seen as a political liability because of the scandal.

The Democrats wished to replace him on the ballot with a scandal-free candidate who would likely win easily in the predominantly Democrat state. However, there was a problem regarding the replacement: the law. Liberals know that when the law's in the way, let the courts have their say. Off to the New Jersey Supreme Court went the Democrats, and what a surprise: the court ignored the law and let the Democrats have their way in replacing Torricelli.[40]

The disturbing thing about what happened in Florida and New Jersey was that the courts had no problem discarding laws—laws that were enacted by the representatives of the people elected by the people. The courts were, in effect, saying to the people and their representatives, "You don't count. We know better than you what should be done." These were efforts to have government by the judges and not by the people.

We hear on the news that we are a nation of law, as long as that law does not block the advancement of the New Morality agenda. If it does, then we become a nation of judicial tyranny, and law becomes relative. This is evident by how the courts have dealt with law that was created directly by the people through ballot initiatives.

POWER TO THE PEOPLE? THINK AGAIN

The people of California passed what was known as Proposition 187, which prohibited tax dollars being used for benefits for illegal aliens. Five million citizens voted for this proposition, but it took only one judge to strike it down and make it inoperative. One judge made it possible for people to enter the country illegally and then get in line at the welfare office. California citizens, against their will, had to let people who broke our national law to get into our country get into their wallets.[41]

Californians were victimized by one judge again when Proposition 209 was nullified. This was the California Civil Rights Initiative, which aimed to end state racial preferences. The United States Court of Appeals for the Ninth Circuit overturned this ruling, saying that Prop 209 was indeed constitutional, stating, "A system which permits one judge to block with the stroke of a pen what 4,736,180 state residents voted to enact as law tests the integrity of our constitutional democracy."[42]

Continuing the long trend of ignoring the people of California, courts struck down two voter-passed propositions pertaining to the institution of marriage. In 2000, voters passed Proposition 22, which changed the Family Code to define marriage as an arrangement between a man and a woman. Eight years later, this law was struck down in a 4–3 decision. Voters quickly passed Proposition 8, defining marriage as a union between one man and one woman. Activist judges struck down this law in the August 2010 case of *Perry v. Schwarzenegger*.[43] Vaughn Walker, chief judge of the US District Court for the Northern District of California and a noncloseted homosexual, argued that Proposition 8 unconstitutionally burdened gays and lesbians by placing the "the force of law behind stigmas against gays and lesbians."[44] Despite Walker's obvious conflict of interest, he was not required to recuse himself.

We watched a similar situation unfold on the US Supreme Court when Justice Ginsburg and Justice Elena Kagan both officiated at gay weddings and violated federal laws by indicating how they would vote on a matter pending before the court. Judicial activism was in full display when the court issued its 5–4 ruling in *Obergefell v. Hodges*[45]—a case the court used to redefine marriage to include same-sex relationships. And it did so without any reliance on traditional methods of judicial interpretation: textual, structural, or original intent. Instead, the court developed a new jurisprudence based on identity rather than traditional methods of analysis. In doing so, the court essentially imposed its New Morality on the American people, and it did so without providing them with a compelling reason to justify the trashing of the Constitution.

KILLING COURTS

It is bad news when courts kill, especially when it's the innocent who are killed. In Florida, a thirty-seven-year-old man named Joseph Smith told police where to find the body of Carlie Brucia, an eleven-year-old girl he had murdered on February 1, 2004. This girl should not have been killed because Smith should not have been free to do the killing. He was a drug addict who had been arrested thirteen times in Florida since 1993. He was released from prison on New Year's Day and arrested ten days later for possession of cocaine, a violation of his parole. He had additional violations, but Judge Harry Rapkin refused to send him back to prison, as the law required. The result was he murdered Carlie Brucia.

Another case in Florida that captured the nation's attention involved the courts and a young woman named Terri Schiavo. Terri suffered a cardiac arrest on February 25, 1990, causing her brain to be deprived of oxygen and putting her into what doctors termed a "persistent vegetative state." Her husband, Michael Schiavo, sued a doctor who treated her before her cardiac arrest. In 1992, a jury awarded the couple $1 million, with $700,000 of it designated for her perpetual care.[46]

Michael Schiavo filed to have Terri's feeding tube removed in 1998, some eight years after her heart attack. His reason for this action was that he remembered Terri once saying she did not want to live in this condition should she ever have the misfortune to experience it. He didn't remember this when he was in the trial for the medical malpractice suit, but now it had all come back to him. The law in Florida designates the spouse as the legal guardian of the incapacitated spouse.

The issue in this matter was Terri's wishes. She was unable to speak for herself, and her husband could produce no written documents wherein she specifically stated what he claimed to be her wishes. The courts granted Mr. Schiavo's request to remove Terri's feeding tube, an action that would bring death by dehydration and starvation. Years of legal battles ensued as the husband, seeking his wife's death, was opposed by Terri's parents, who wanted her to live.

The thing that is most troubling is that we had only the word of the husband that Terri would choose death over living in her brain-damaged condition. It is always presumed that a court will take into consideration the character of the witnesses. Michael Schiavo doesn't pass the character test. He only "remembered" that his wife preferred death over living in a so-called persistent vegetative state, and his recollection came years after she was stricken and after the million-dollar award.

Also during this time, Michael became a confirmed adulterer. He played house with another woman, even announcing his engagement to her and having two children by her, but still the law claimed him as Terri's legal spouse with the right to remove her feeding tube and cause her death. If television personality Mr. Rogers was still with us, he would be saying, "Can you say, 'Conflict of interest'?"

Congress passed a law and President George W. Bush signed it, asking the court in Florida to take another look at the case and review all the facts again to be sure it was making the right ruling in regard to ending the life support treatment for Terri. The court told the Congress and the president to butt out. It is amazing that a court system in Florida will ignore state constitutional law when it wants to elect a liberal president (2000 election), but will be so concerned about exercising the law when a young woman's "will to die" is based on the hearsay evidence proclaimed by her adulterous husband. There is only one way this could happen in our country, and that is because virtue and decency are no longer held in high esteem.

A NEW ALLY FOR TERRORISTS

The high court even has become an ally to terrorists. President Bush sent troops into Afghanistan to hit the stronghold of the terrorists responsible for the 9/11 attack on our nation. Captured enemy combatants were taken to our military base in Guantanamo Bay, Cuba. One such combatant, Yaser Esam Hamdi, was an American citizen, born in the US in 1980. He moved with his family to Saudi Arabia when he was a child. He was captured as a fighter with the

Taliban and, after an interview process, was declared an enemy combatant, so he was sent off to Cuba. He was later sent to a brig in Virginia, where it was learned he was a US citizen, but this still did not change his status as an enemy combatant.

Hamdi protested his detention, and his protest made it to the Supreme Court. This gave Mr. Hamdi the right to bring arguments regarding his detention and to challenge his classification in our legal system.[47] The court, in essence, was allowing a POW to become an ordinary defendant. In dissent, Justice Clarence Thomas pointed out a significant danger in this decision:

> It also does seem quite likely that, under the process envisioned by the [Court], various military officials will have to take time to litigate this matter. And though the [Court] does not say so, a meaningful ability to challenge the Government's factual allegation will probably require the Government to divulge highly classified information to the purported enemy combatant, who might then upon release return to the fight armed with our most closely held secrets.[48]

The court's decision was putting our war intelligence at risk and, with that, our national security. The court's ruling opened the door for detainees at Guantanamo Bay to contest their detentions in American courts.[49] Who needs enemies when you have the Supreme Court? Given what can sometimes happen in our court system, that's the last place you would want a terrorist enemy combatant.

AMERICA'S FIRST PROPHET

Thomas Jefferson was the third president of our country, but he may have also been its first prophet in his assessment of our judiciary when he wrote to a friend:

> You seem...to consider the judges as the ulti-
> mate arbiters of all constitutional questions; a
> very dangerous doctrine indeed, and one which
> would place us under the despotism of an oligar-
> chy. Our judges are as honest as other men and
> not more so. They have, with others, the same
> passions for party, for power, and the privilege
> of their corps...And their power is the more
> dangerous as they are in office for life and not
> responsible, as the other functionaries are, to the
> elective control. The Constitution has erected no
> such single tribunal.[50]

It is obvious from Jefferson's words that the Founding Fathers never wanted judges to ascend to a level of power whereby they, in fact, ruled as royalty with disregard for the people, who are the electorate. He understood that the Constitution "erected no such single tribunal." It is amazing how quickly the New Morality quotes Mr. Jefferson, or misquotes him, on the separation of church and state issue while at the same time ignoring his wisdom on judges. Jefferson's beliefs on the judiciary were very strong, and he was not shy in voicing them. He wrote on the subject again, stating,

> Our Constitution...intending to establish three
> departments, co-ordinate and independent that
> they each might check and balance one another,
> it has given, according to this opinion, to one
> of them alone the right to prescribe rules for
> the government of the others; and to that one,
> too, which is unelected by and independent of a
> nation...The Constitution, on this hypothesis, is
> a mere thing of wax in the hands of the judiciary,
> which they may twist and shape into any form
> they please.[51]

Jefferson again takes a hard shot at judges in a letter to John Adams's wife, Abigail:

> The opinion which gives to the judges the right to decide what laws are constitutional and what are not, not only for themselves in their own sphere of action, but for the Legislative and Executive also in their spheres, would make the Judiciary a despotic branch.[52]

Sadly, his words are now true, to the delight of the New Morality. It rejoices that in order to get its way in advancing its virtue-free and indecent agenda, it doesn't have to convince millions in the electorate—just a handful of justices on the Supreme Court. This is a much easier way to alter the culture and put our kids and our nation at risk.

MAKING A DIFFERENCE: THE BALLOT BOX

When it comes to activist, liberal federal judges, there is very little you can do except for the recourse given you by the political process. If you want to stop the influence of liberal judges, the best way is to elect conservative presidents and senators who share your values. The president appoints federal judges, and the Senate confirms them. It sometimes takes years to reverse the direction of the judiciary since they have lifetime terms. Very few voters ask the question, "What kind of people will the president appoint as judges to the federal courts?" It should always be a major issue you consider when you vote for a presidential candidate. But you can also do more than vote. You can become actively involved in campaigning for a president who will not appoint liberal judges.

TAKE ACTION

- Keep informed about potential nominees to the federal bench. Make sure you know their qualifications and as much as possible about their previous decisions.

- Get on the mailing lists of organizations such as Eagle Forum, the Family Research Council, the Heritage Foundation, American Center for Law and Justice, and American Values. These organizations will keep you informed about what is happening in Congress and in other relevant areas of American life that pertain to traditional values and individual liberty.

- Be prepared to write letters, make phone calls, write op-eds, and organize protests against candidates and nominees who stand for principles that run contrary to traditional values and principles.

CHAPTER 11

Fighting Back

Politics and religion are different enterprises, and it is understandable that many people would like to keep them as separate as possible. But they are constantly coupling and getting mixed up with one another. There is nothing new about this... What is relatively new is the naked public square. The naked public square is the result of political doctrine and practice that would exclude religion and religiously grounded values from the conduct of public business.

The doctrine is that America is a secular society...[that] doctrine is demonstrably false and exceedingly dangerous.[1]
—Richard John Neuhaus, Christian Cleric

It has been decades since Richard Neuhaus warned us of the dangers of a public square stripped of religiously grounded moral arguments and principles. Today we are increasingly witnessing what happens when a secular worldview gains the upper hand in the culture war. We have leaders who are indifferent to the Judeo-Christian principles that have undergirded our nation in times past. We have too many federal judges who reject the authority of the Constitution and instead advance their own personal and political agendas. The New Morality affects every sphere of our lives, including churches and seminaries, where we find religious scholars and leaders who reject the authority of Scripture while sending the message that divorce, fornication, and homosexual lifestyles can be reconciled with a Christian way of life. No wonder we have lost, dying, and stolen children. We are raising them in a culture that rejects God and any notion of absolute right and wrong.

Indeed, the culture war is real, and the New Morality and the liberal Left have made great advances since the 1960s, when prayer and Bible reading were ousted from public schools. One reason for the successes of the New Morality is a lack of any effective opposition from the institutions, organizations, and people who oppose the agenda of the New Morality. For far too long, Christians have stood on the sidelines, doing nothing, while those who oppose the gospel run away with the culture.

Rabbi Daniel Lapin, in his book *America's Real War*, correctly sums up the situation of the cultural war:

> I suspect that most of our cultural institutions are now firmly in the hands of those who reject the Almighty. Those who run our entertainment and news media are consistently shown by polls to attend worship services far less, and to be less likely to have a religious affiliation, than the nation's population as a whole. Those who run our schools, universities, and courts are constantly implementing anti-God doctrines no matter how often they might invoke His name. I am not even too certain of many of our churches and synagogues. It is time for the rest of us to recognize that there is a war being waged and to fight back.[2]

His words "fight back" need to be taken seriously. Yes, the other side has gained much ground and appears to be rolling along, but that does not mean that we on the other side just give up. We can fight back. There are ways to do this. The fight will be long and at times frustrating, but it is a fight worth waging because what is at stake is of vital importance: our kids and, we fear, our nation itself. However, it is not a fight that can be fought using solely political means. For decades now, conservatives have fought with little success to end abortion on demand, to preserve traditional marriage, and to shield children from inappropriate media content and exploitation. Yet our cultural corruption reaches into the churches and middle-class and upper-class families of all races and ethnicities. In this cultural war, African Americans suffer greatly because of their acceptance of the New Morality, which has weakened their family structures and has undermined their religious tradition's support for marriage and morality.

(Carol): Many young parents with traditional moral or Christian perspectives feel isolated and rejected by the culture—a culture they would like to belong to and contribute to, if it were not so ungodly. The New Morality consists of friends, coworkers, family members, and others considered "cool," and many young people would like to be accepted by them. While older people such as Steve and I might wish for a return to traditional morality and an openly Judeo-Christian society, young adults steeped in political correctness and multiculturalism are reluctant to oppose contemporary trends. To them, righteous culture is not about going back to the "good old days" that many of them are convinced never existed.

If we want to reach and protect our youth, then we must lead by example and be righteous and relevant to our times. We must rebuild the moral foundations by standing on sound ethical and moral truths related to biblical principles and the natural law. We also need to broaden the base of allies, so that it is not always us against them. Remember what Jesus told His disciples in Luke 9:50, after they challenged a man who was not a part of their group: "Do not forbid him, for he who is not against you is for you" (MEV). In the battle for the culture, we need like-minded people from every religious denomination to stand together against the evil.

Often older people in the Christian world do not realize they need to actively resist the cultural influences around them. Whether we like it or not, we are profoundly influenced by the people around us and their values. Our culture is not merely a matter of philosophical ideas; it's about the practical choices we make each day. For instance, a family with traditional moral values teaches kids to put the needs of others above their own, but the New Morality teaches kids that their self-esteem and status is of the highest value. The truth is that you must make a choice about whom you will serve and which moral code of behavior you will obey. To select one means to reject the other.

WHICH MORALITY?

In the Old Testament, we read,

> If My people, who are called by My name, will humble themselves and pray, and seek My face and turn from their wicked ways, then I will hear from heaven, and will forgive their sin and will heal their land.
> —2 Chronicles 7:14, NIV

The cultural war is a battle for the moral soul of the nation. The liberal Left will loudly proclaim that you cannot legislate morality. That is nonsense. If you cannot legislate morality in a nation, then you have a nation predisposed to anarchy. *The real issue is whose morality will be legislated.* Will it be a morality based on right and wrong, as conveyed in Judeo-Christian principles and values? Or will it be the morality fashioned from the decrees of liberal judges who are steeped in cultural Marxism? The alternative to a traditional morality is a dangerous worldview that emerges out of cultural relativism. Societies function more efficiently when there is structure; relativism, which is the heart and soul of the New Morality, claims that there is no such thing as an absolute right and wrong. Relativism wants movable boundaries—"my truth" versus "your truth," which leads people to justify all kinds of destructive and selfish behavior. We are living in an age of moral chaos.

Theologian Erwin Lutzer clearly describes the purpose of the Left when it proclaims morality cannot be legislated:

> But all laws are an imposition of someone's morality. That is why the statement "You cannot legislate morality," as it stands, is absurd. Secular humanism is imposing its own morality on the American public. It does so through the media, the schools, and the courts. There is a clear intent to keep Christian thinking out of the mainstream of media and the nation's political life.[3]

Many Christians seem to be clueless about what is going on in our country regarding the moral struggle we face. They have the attitude that they are powerless to take on the giants of politics, education, and entertainment. They are content to take care of their own and to try to live above the fray. They will bemoan the disturbing trends in society and voice disapproval of actions and events that are adverse to traditional morality, but they will take little or no personal action to combat them. When the liberal cohorts of the New Morality made their advance in the sixties, they were not large in numbers or strong in power. But, little by little, using many of the strategies outlined by Saul Alinsky in *Rules for Radicals*, they gained ground; until today they dominate the culture.

Those of us who have chosen to fight back do so for a number of reasons. One is scriptural. If we fear God, we have an obligation to warn the wicked rather than compromise with them. In Ezekiel 33:8, God warns the people through his prophet,

> When I say to the wicked, 'O wicked man, you shall surely die,' and you do not speak to warn the wicked from his way, that wicked man shall

die in his iniquity. But his blood I will require from your hand (MEV).

We fight back because we love God, country, and children. We fight back not because we have victory guaranteed but because it is the right thing to do for our nation and its people.

THE LIBERAL LEGACY

The New Morality plays for keeps. It takes no prisoners. It wants the idea of absolute right and wrong to be eliminated. It does not want the restraints that such a belief brings to society. Author and conservative commentator Tammy Bruce effectively alerts us to this fact when she writes, "Moral relativism *is* the death of right and wrong…Think about it. If everything is relative, then there simply can be no judgment. Without judgment there is no right and wrong."[4]

Do we really want our children to live in a country that is confused about what is right and wrong? Do we want them to live with the idea that you are not accountable to anyone but yourself? We have countless laws designed to keep kids safe physically. We have to strap them in car seats. We have to be careful not to spank them too hard in the supermarket, or we'll have a government agency breathing down our necks. If there is no law in place, we take personal action to ensure their physical safety. The helmet goes on the head before they go on the bike. What do you think the boys back in the fifties would have said to me if I (Steve) showed up for the bike ride wearing a helmet? We are so concerned about the physical well-being of our children, but we take a haphazard attitude toward their moral safety. Rebecca Hagelin is on the mark when she writes, "It's time we ask ourselves: *while we're strapping on our kids' helmets to protect their brains, what are we doing to protect their minds?*"[5]

The liberals and the New Morality have gained the upper hand in our educational system and media. The term many liberals like to use to describe themselves is *progressive*. It seems that *liberal* has developed a negative connotation. In time, progressive is likely to do the same. Let's first review the report card of the New Morality as it has touched the lives of our children:

- From 1960 to 1995, teenage suicides tripled.
- From 1965 to 1995, juvenile arrests for violent crime tripled.
- From 1992 to 1995, marijuana use nearly doubled among eighth and tenth graders; the University of Michigan's Institute for Social Research found that 50 percent of twelfth graders and 40 percent of tenth graders have tried an illicit drug.

Today, 52 percent of girls and 67 percent of boys have sex before the age of eighteen, compared with the early 1970s, when it was 35 percent for girls and 55 percent for boys.[6]

Wow! This is the liberal legacy. This is the culture that the New Morality has been fighting for. Does it really look like progress? It is a national tragedy that we have a large segment of influential people and special-interest groups that assault the morality of our national heritage and then expect the public to refer to them as progressives. I (Steve) am a political junkie. I stay current with what is happening on the political scene in our country. I have friends who pay little attention to it. Some people pay little attention to politics because it is regarded as an unsavory side of life that wholesome people of virtue avoid. If you are one who values traditional morality, that is exactly the attitude the New Morality wants you to have. Whether you like it or not, politics affects your quality of life. It even affects the moral tone of the nation as it applies to national security.

This wasn't always the case. In 1960, I was a sophomore in high school and was aware of the Kennedy-Nixon election. Four years later, I was a sophomore in college and was taking a closer look at the political process when Johnson and Goldwater ran against each other. In those two elections, you never heard anything derogatory about Christianity. There was no talk about Christian groups being too influential in public affairs. Abortion was not an issue.

Both parties campaigned with an attitude of respect toward the Christian faith and the traditional values of America. There were different views expressed on the economy, nuclear weapons, the threat of Communism, civil rights, and some social programs; but neither party displayed any anti-American feelings.

Times have changed, because one party now has a large portion of supporters bent on the destruction of America's capitalistic economic system, many of its institutions that are linked to traditional moral values, and morality based on Judeo-Christian principles. The Democrat Party is a different party now because left-wing extremists have seized control of a large part of it. The Left desires to reshape the culture of our nation and make moral relativism the norm. Liberals will choose vice over virtue for votes.

Democrats who care about their party and its future should resist and speak out against the extreme, radical, liberal Left groups that desire to hijack the party. They should distance the party from the likes of the Reverend Al Sharpton, filmmaker Michael Moore, billionaire George Soros, and others who push a radical liberal agenda. They should demand that their party maintain integrity in discourse, and they should admonish people such as Illinois senator Dick Durbin, who, on the Senate floor, compared our troops who guard Islamic detainees to Nazi storm troopers and our military detention centers to Communist gulags. Instead, the liberal politicians with their mainstream-media comrades assault us with misleading information, which they think we, the public, are too stupid to discern as pure propaganda.

I (Carol) recognize that there is no perfect political party or a political solution for the moral decline of the nation, because we are dealing with a spiritual problem that affects members of both parties to varying degrees. What Republicans have over Democrats is a political platform at the national level that recognizes the sanctity of human life and the need to honor and respect the Constitution and our Judeo-Christian heritage.

In recent years, the differences between the two parties have been so stark that some politicians and millions of Americans, including myself, have found it expedient to switch parties to align ourselves with individuals who are more likely to espouse and defend the values and principles we hold dear. As Christians, we have made some mistakes by thinking that either sitting out elections or getting too heavily involved is going to bring about the changes we desire. Engaging in the political process is important. But doing so will not solve our problems by itself. Theologian Vern Poythress has written,

> Bible-believing Christians have not achieved much in politics because they have not devoted themselves to the larger arena of cultural conflict. Politics mostly follows culture rather than leading it...A temporary victory in the voting booth does not reverse a downward moral trend driven by cultural gatekeepers in news media, entertainment, art, and education. Politics is not a cure-all.[7]

Although politics is important and every Christian should vote for politicians whose views line up with biblical values and principles, voting, by itself, will not change the culture or the environment that has resulted in the loss of so many of our young people. We need to do more to teach our young people moral values and principles before they enter the environments designed to transform them into atheists, material naturalists, and secular humanists.

TAKING THE LION'S SHARE

In April 2013, Dr. Kermit Gosnell went on trial in Philadelphia for murder. He was an abortion doctor who allowed babies that survived an abortion to die. He was also tried for the death of a patient who was aborting a baby at his clinic. The courtroom had reserved pews for news reporters, but as the trial started, the media seats remained empty. Kirsten Powers, a liberal writer for *The Daily Beast* and a Fox News contributor, was appalled at this obviously biased coverage and called out the mainstream media on it—and made an impact. It is rare that liberals take on other liberals in this way, but to her credit, Ms. Powers stood up for what was right even on the controversial issue of abortion.[8]

The mainstream media is so used to carrying the water for liberal politicians that it was easy for them to ignore the Gosnell trail. Why take a chance that the public might see the horrible reality inside an abortion clinic? The mainstream media followed the same course in the summer of 2015, when the nation was hit with the story that Planned Parenthood was selling body parts of fetuses, which is against the law. The evidence of this atrocity was provided by the Center for Medical Progress, which produced a number of undercover videos showing a Planned Parenthood officer clearly describing the process. As the story of the Planned Parenthood chop shop broke, another story emerged. A lion named Cecil that lived comfortably with his pride on an African game preserve was allegedly lured from his safety only to be killed by a dentist from Minnesota. Reporters were outraged and did their best to vilify the dentist. The news of the dead lion became a higher-priority story than the illegal sale of baby parts by Planned Parenthood.

While broadcast news shows covered Cecil the lion more in one day than they spent on the Planned Parenthood videos in two weeks, CBS and NBC did cover Planned Parenthood after the release of the fourth undercover video.

Here's the breakdown of network coverage of Cecil the lion:
ABC: 12 minutes, 14 seconds
NBC: 16 minutes, 54 seconds
CBS: 13 minutes, 51 seconds

Here's the breakdown of time by network on the Planned Parenthood videos:
ABC: 46 seconds
NBC: 5 minutes, 12 seconds
CBS: 12 minutes, 4 seconds

In all, the networks spent 42 minutes, 59 seconds on Cecil the lion and 18 minutes, 2 seconds on the Planned Parenthood videos.[9]

The priorities of the Left are clear. How far will the New Morality go to advance its agenda? The above comparison reveals to what diabolical extreme it will go. The dirty secret of abortion is that it pays financial dividends. Planned Parenthood gets close to $500 million a year in taxpayer dollars from the federal government. What is not reported is that Planned Parenthood has a political action committee that can make contributions to political campaigns. You can bet that they have ways to make sure that money goes into liberal politicians' campaign coffers. If you pay taxes, you support Planned Parenthood and, albeit indirectly, liberal politicians running for office, whether you like it or not.

BALLOTS CAN BE OUR BULLETS

Casting a vote will not change the culture or the New Morality, but it can make a difference if we elect the right politicians. And, truly, it is our responsibility to do so. When you go to the ballot box, your vote matters. Make sure you do your homework and vote for politicians who reflect your values and principles, and not just your political party. The New Morality will not hesitate to use the political system to advance its cause. It is a force to take seriously. Robert Bork astutely pointed out that beginning in the sixties, the Left has stood adverse and hateful to America's institutions and traditions, which they would only be too happy to destroy if given the chance.[10] In America, we say we value truth. Now we have those among us who seek to make us a republic of relative morality, where there is no absolute truth. One of the ways we can fight back is to realize that votes have moral implications and vote for candidates who still hold to biblical morality. If a candidate buys into the New Morality, with its relativism and situational ethics, where the end justifies the means, how can you believe what he or she says? If a person has an "end justifies the means" philosophy, then telling a lie to get a vote is a justifiable strategy. A broken campaign promise is nothing for them to worry about. If the promise got you elected, it did its job. In 1988, George H. W. Bush said, "Read my lips: no new taxes."

Bill Clinton promised a middle-class tax cut when he ran in 1992. It may have gotten him your vote, but you never got that tax cut. Obama told us we could keep our health-care plan and our doctors. How did those promises work out for you?

The 2004 election baffled the experts and irritated the liberal crowd. George W. Bush won reelection, and moral values played a key role in the campaign. Many states included same-sex marriage amendments to their state constitutions on the ballots, which brought out a large number of voters who overwhelming voted against same-sex marriage—and while they were there, they voted for Bush. It was apparent that the secularization of America hadn't gone as far as the liberal Left thought. Traditional morality had won a battle in the cultural war in the national election of 2004—although many more battles were to follow. Bork tells us how important such victories are:

> Campaigns and elections are crucial, nevertheless, precisely because our parties have, by and large, lined up on opposite sides of the cultural divide. Elections are important not only because of the policies adopted and laws enacted but as symbolic victories for one set of values or the other.[11]

We must remember that as good as election wins are, they are not the main theater of battle in the cultural war. Bork points out that the forces of the New Morality have obtained their lead in the cultural war by capturing the culture itself. They reign in the entertainment and mainstream media, they control the public school systems, and they dominate the college classrooms and influence the courts. Bork has the courage to state the reality we must acknowledge when he says, "Conservative political victories will always be tenuous and fragile unless conservatives recapture the culture."[12] He noted a hopeful sign among the religious camp in the rise of an energetic, optimistic, politically sophisticated religious conservatism. This group, he said, might prove more powerful than economic or political conservatism because its ambitions were also cultural and moral.[13]

A REENERGIZED AND MORAL CHURCH FOR CULTURAL CHANGE

An army of God-fearing pastors and energized congregants has the potential to land some deathblows on the New Morality and its misguided adherents in the mainline churches. Yes, even some who claim to be Christians have compromised biblical morality and joined with radical liberals to promote a form of social justice that often runs contrary to biblical teachings on any number of political issues.

I (Steve) consider myself an evangelical Christian and believe evangelicals are in a good position to do much good in the restoration of traditional morality. Some individual churches are making great strides in taking back ground in the cultural war; others are struggling for survival as they hold on to unproductive methods of the past to placate their older donors while becoming culturally irrelevant to the unchurched around them.

I have mentioned that I became a filmmaker and made a documentary on the problem of pornography as it relates to young men. I did so because I am aware that kids watch screens instead of reading books. This project was my personal contribution to the broader cultural war. It was exciting to hear a caller on the Glenn Beck Radio Program credit this video as one of the things that helped save his life regarding his addiction to pornography. Sadly, evangelical institutions often lag far behind the times when it comes to creating media that might effectively reach teenagers with content geared toward teaching and reinforcing Christian morality.

Research shows that 75 percent of those who commit to the Christian faith are between the ages of twelve and twenty-one.[14] This age group watches more than it reads. My hat is off to Sherwood Baptist Church in Albany, Georgia, which has a full film-production company that cranks out feature films and markets them nationally. This church is leading the way in fighting back to regain ground lost to the entertainment media. Christians need to do more of this— much more.

Teenagers might not be avid readers, but some adults are. Religious book sales increased at a rate far beyond secular books in 2004. Rick Warren's book *The Purpose Driven Life* enjoys sales in the millions. It is changing the lives of people who have the potential to be foot soldiers for traditional morality in the cultural war. The need for Christians to become personally involved in some way in the cultural war is critical. Words by conservative commentator David Limbaugh affirm this:

> If they [Christians] remain silent, especially about the moral foundations behind their policy prefer-ences, they can expect those policies to crumble under their own weight, and if not, certainly by the onslaught of secular forces opposed to such measures. Christians must champion unfet-tered religious freedom, oppose those forces that threaten it, and strengthen their own churches, without which any hope to influence the political system and our culture will be futile.[15]

Christians need to get involved in the culture in numerous ways that go beyond voting. Some need to run for office, some need to volunteer, some need to write columns, and some need to support candidates via social media. Christians need to make financial contri-butions to candidates that embrace traditional values and principles. A lot can be accomplished at the local level, as Bork attests: "Because it is a grass roots movement, the new religious conservatism can alter culture both by electing local officials and school boards (which have greater effects on culture than do national politicians), and by setting a moral tone in opposition to today's liberal relativism."[16]

Some Christian leaders advise against getting involved in the political arena because it is a way of wallowing in the mud of life.

The founders did not feel this way. Their hope was that Christians would aspire to leadership and allow their moral beliefs to define their leadership. Author Larry Schweikart, who teaches history at the University of Dayton in Dayton, Ohio, says that if Christians avoid getting involved in politics, then "there will soon be no mud left for us to roll around in," since the Left will dominate over all.

Increasingly, the cultural wars have placed us into distinct political camps, where the choice is between liberal Democrats and Republicans who purport to be conservative. Most of us hold our noses and vote for the lesser of the two evils. Clearly, there is a stark political reality that needs to be noted. Eighteen states and the District of Columbia have voted for the Democratic candidate in the last six presidential elections. This means that a Democratic presidential candidate can count on 242 electoral votes, which means that only twenty-eight more are needed to win the election. Those states that have voted only for a Republican candidate in the last six elections deliver only 102 electoral votes.

It's easy to do the math. It is more of an uphill battle for a Republican to win the White House, and it is often a tough battle for a true conservative to win the Republican nomination. Nevertheless, we need to be involved at all levels of government and make our voice heard when it comes to holding politicians accountable after the election. Republicans who campaign as conservatives and vote like Democrats need to be held accountable, just as Democrats themselves need to be held accountable if they are violating our values and principles. There must be consequences if we are to successfully combat the New Morality and its influence on our children and our culture.

In the midterm election of 2014, there was a sweeping landslide victory for Republicans, and many conservatives led the charge. This resulted in the Republicans holding the governorships of thirty states in which the electoral votes for a presidential election would total 310. Unfortunately, not much changed in Washington because conservatives did not control the White House and many of the Republicans who purported to be conservatives easily caved to Democrats.

If more Christians will take the challenge to push back against the New Morality and liberal Left for the sake of our children, then what appears insurmountable can be overcome. We cannot just surrender our nation and the political process to the liberal Left and its New Morality cohorts. We must find creative ways to make our voices heard, to increase the number of like-minded registered voters, and then to make those votes count. As Christians, we have to be willing to do more than warm the pews on Sunday morning. We need to be willing to get our hands dirty by taking on the battle for the soul of our nation.

A WAY BACK

The now-deceased Robert Bork was discussing with some friends what would have to happen to bring America back to the traditional morality of its heritage. The group came up with the following four events that could produce a moral and spiritual regeneration:

- Religious revival
- The revival of public discourse about morality
- A cataclysmic war
- A deep economic depression[17]

Bork wrote those words in 1996, five years before 9/11—an event that did temporarily unite our country and for a while made more people sensitive to spiritual values. Time and the robust efforts of the mainstream media and liberal politicians have helped to curb the enthusiasm for spiritual renewal in the wake of the 9/11 tragedy. The liberal Left fears the military success of America in the war on terror, regardless of what you might hear them say, because they know that such success will give their opponents credibility and help them win support from the public.

A religious revival in America is still possible because with God all things are possible. Indeed, revival is the last best hope for our

nation. It is clear that our nation cannot continue to thumb its col-
lective nose at God and expect to prosper. We do not know what
catastrophic event it will take to awaken a majority of Americans to
see the folly of the New Morality and the havoc it has wreaked on
our once-prosperous nation. If revival happens, it could take a variety
of forms. We cannot rule out God's use of new technology, whether
it will be social media, Christian movies and films that can reach
and galvanize millions, or some other medium. I (Steve) believe it
could come through films that buck the Hollywood trend, such as
The Passion of the Christ. Mel Gibson's blockbuster film impacted
the culture far more than any religiously themed film in history and
confronted millions of moviegoers with a powerful spiritual message.

I (Carol) agree with Steve that movies can inspire and galvanize
millions of Americans who relate to the characters and the storylines.
Fortunately for our culture, Christian movies and films have been
doing extremely well at the box office. However, we need to continu-
ously be vigilant to ensure that the ones we support adhere to sound
biblical principles.

One such movie that has inspired me is *War Room.* It features
a family of young, professional parents with one child. They live in
what seems to be the perfect home in the perfect neighborhood, but
their lives aren't what they appear. We learn that the parents' marriage
is falling apart and that their child feels neglected and only partially
loved.

The turning point comes after the wife meets and establishes a
relationship with a real-estate client named Miss Clara. Miss Clara
is an elderly black woman who shares with her young mentee the
necessity of having a dedicated prayer room, where one develops a
prayer-based battle plan. Miss Clara's room is called the "war room,"
a place where battle plans are launched. Taking the family's issues
into the prayer closet changes the family dynamics and eventually
saves the marriage. The movie inspired me and countless others to
clean out basements and closets to set up our own dedicated prayer
spaces.[18]

TERMS TO TERMINATE

We are rightfully concerned about expressions of racism and violence toward groups that are politically unpopular for religious or other reasons. Unfortunately, there seems to be no concern about the growing anti-Semitism and anti-Christian sentiments in our society. Bork reveals the position of the liberal New Morality concerning Christianity and introduces a concept that is worth examining. Modern liberals, as Bork analyzed it, are open enemies to religious conservatism regardless of the denomination. People of faith and the message they convey are a threat to the liberal agenda. This is why it benefits Liberals to use the phrase "religious right." These two words are used in a disparaging way to tie any conservative ideology to extremism. Bork felt that no conservative, whether religious or secular, should tolerate this degrading label.[19]

Bork makes a valid point regarding the term religious Right. It is a term the Left uses to cast Christians in a disparaging light. The word Right just entices one to add the words *wing extremists*, which is how the liberal Left wants the public to think of Christians. In comparison, you don't hear George Soros, Michael Moore, or any of Hollywood's political hacks being described as members of the atheist Left, the pagan Left, or the humanistic Left. The mainstream media loves to attach the word Right to any conservative group to cast that extremist cloud over it. If those who were once known as black can demand to be referred to as African Americans, then we who are Christians can demand that we not be referred to as the religious Right. If they want to call us evangelical Christians, conservative Christians, or traditional moralists, we'll accept any of those tags, but don't call us right-wing extremists. Our position is not extreme.

We advocate a way of life that was lived by the majority of those who founded this country, and it is woven into the heritage of our nation. I (Carol) have no problem with the name-calling that the political Left uses to silence people. If we spend our time quibbling over what we are called, it takes us off message. Instead of complaining about the names, I prefer to focus on the issues at hand. Calling conservatives racists, homophobes, nativists, or xenophobes is merely a method to change the subject by shifting the discussion away from substantive issues that conservatives can win if they focus on facts and logic.

MAKING NOISE IN THE MARKETPLACE

Those who treasure traditional morality can fight back in the marketplace. The American Family Association often alerts people to companies that support events and TV shows that are contrary to traditional moral values and urges boycotts of these companies. Such actions are legitimate and are employed by the liberal Left also. Companies do fear loss of revenue through boycotts. Pepsi went into major damage control on its website when its female CEO made the gaffe of referring to America as the "middle finger" in a commencement address.[20]

We don't have to watch the junk delivered to us on TV. When the ratings go down, the show goes off the air. The same is true with movies. Movies that do poorly at the box office send a message to Hollywood that says, "Stop making this stuff." When it comes to entertainment and the media, we can vote with our wallets.

EMBRACING NEW NEWS ALTERNATIVES (SORRY, MAINSTREAM MEDIA)

The cultural war is being fought in many areas, as Bork notes, "We are well along the road to the moral chaos that is the end of radical individualism and the tyranny that is the goal of radical egalitarianism. Modern liberalism has corrupted our culture across the board."[21] Wherever the culture war is being waged, we need to be in that area making a difference.

We need to discard the bunker mentality that has encompassed many traditional moralists and evangelicals. The odds were against Christianity being successful in the culture of the Roman Empire, but it beat the odds. The character of those who won the day back then needs to be recaptured today. The situation does look bad at times as we view the evening news, but the perspective of Rabbi Lapin is helpful:

Not that long ago, when Americans said something was right or wrong, they meant right or wrong in the eyes of God as revealed in the Bible. In advocating a return to those days, I am not suggesting anything new; I am recommending something old and proven. I am not suggesting further exploration and experimentation down a dark and unknown alley; I am suggesting we turn around and retrace our steps until we once again find ourselves in familiar territory.[22]

We can take actions that will help us turn around as a nation. Movements are alive and well that provide opportunities for us to fight back. None is more welcome than what is taking place in the news media. The biased mainstream media has competition, and that competition is succeeding big-time. Conservative talk radio has given traditional morality and conservatives a megaphone to the nation that is successfully influencing people's attitudes and political ideology. Conservative television networks, as well as Internet news and publishing companies, have also made a huge impact. If conservatives did as much to influence the entertainment media as they do the news media, we would be well on our way to cultural renewal.

MATRICULATION WITHOUT LIBERAL INDOCTRINATION

The alternatives in higher education are available to our children. The liberals hold control of most colleges and universities, but there are places where your child can get a college education without getting a liberal indoctrination. There are many conservative liberal arts colleges that are good alternatives. You must do your homework when considering them. Some are slowly starting down the Harvard Road (our term for colleges that leave their original spiritual mission).

Two things colleges highly value are financial solvency and academic acceptance. Some evangelical schools are going heavily into the accelerated adult-study programs, in which nontraditional students attend classes one night a week to finish the last two years needed to earn a degree. There is nothing wrong with this, except when different standards of conduct are required from traditional students than from nontraditional students. If the main reason for an adult-study program is financial, then even some Christian colleges may be putting money before mission. They are taking steps down Harvard Road.

Most of the Ivy League colleges were started with strong religious affiliations. And although they abandoned that path long ago, Christians have not given up on these influential institutions. For example, the *New York Times* wrote of an organization, Christian Union (now University Christian Union), that is establishing evangelical groups on Ivy League campuses. Its efforts were proving effective, as roughly 450 students, alumni, and supporters met in April 2005 for the Ivy League Congress on Faith and Action at Princeton.[23] Like the individuals involved in these efforts on Ivy League campuses, we must do all we can to proclaim the truth—even more so in places where it is not always welcomed.

MAKING SCHOOL DAYS GOOD DAYS

We are not powerless when it comes to public education. Something is seriously wrong when some school systems cannot graduate half the kids who enter their high schools and when some of those who do graduate are functionally illiterate. You can make your concerns known to school board members, and you can support candidates for the school board who believe in traditional morality.

You do not have to vote for a school tax levy. If you have the opportunity and the means, you can send your kids to a private school that agrees with your values. If you have time and flexibility to do so, you can homeschool your children. As discussed at the end of chapter 8, the homeschool movement has become a viable alternative because the public schools are failing our society academically and morally.

CHANGING THE COURTS

We can fight in the cultural war by making known our desire for needed reform in the judicial branch of our government. This fight will be long and hard. Some of us who begin it most likely will not be around to see victory, but this should not discourage us from the effort. On the very day that these words were written, the Supreme Court decided on a case regarding private-property rights. The decision was reported as follows:

> A divided Supreme Court ruled that local governments may seize people's homes and businesses against their will for private development in a decision anxiously awaited in communities where economic growth conflicts with individual property rights.[24]

This ruling is in conflict with the Fifth Amendment of the Constitution. This amendment contains the words "nor shall private property be taken for public use, without just compensation."

What this ruling means is that cities can take a person's private property for "shopping malls and hotel complexes."[25] This is not the property use of eminent domain. The property seized in this ruling is not earmarked for a courthouse, city hall, or any public building—it's not even for a highway that all citizens could use. The ruling give cities the right to take property and resell it to developers, knowing that the new taxes a city will get on the commercial property will be more than it got when the property was privately owned. The Supreme Court violated the Constitution that they are supposed to uphold.

The Congress was given a check on presidential decision-making with the override provision of the Constitution, which limits the president's power. On the other hand, there is no limit on the Supreme Court's power. Congress is supposed to be the representatives of the people. It is strange that the peoples' representatives can possess a check on presidential power but not on the power of the

Supreme Court. Amen to the suggestion of an amendment to give Congress the power to reverse Supreme Court decisions.

A mandatory retirement age for justices would not be a bad idea either. The federal government requires airline pilots to retire at sixty because aging may cause problems in judgment and put passengers at risk. Some of the recent judgments from the high court put our whole nation at risk because of bad judgment.

HOLDING THE LINE AT HOME

The most important place where we can vigorously fight in the cultural war is the home. The home is our domain. As parents, we are the official gatekeepers of what comes into the home. We can control the computer use, the TV time, what videos are brought in, and what behavioral rules are to be observed. The home is a place of teaching. We teach by how we live. We teach by what we prioritize. Parents are either a force against the New Morality or an asset to it, depending on what attitudes and actions they display in front of their kids.

Some parents put up little resistance to the inroads made by the New Morality, and, little by little, they lose their kids. Other parents are very diligent in trying to combat the force of the New Morality but find that the prevailing culture of the day still touches and influences their children. The late Chuck Colson, an author and the founder of Prison Fellowship, informed us just how important this all is when he wrote, "We've no time to lose. All the evidence shows that we're already losing our kids. With only 9 percent of born-again teens believing in absolute truth, can we rescue this generation? Can we afford not to try?"[26]

A homeschooling parent wrote us to say,

> It is extremely difficult to parent in the era of the New Morality. Most parents of young children, even liberal parents, want their kids to uphold traditional virtue—sharing, being thoughtful,

acting justly. They want their kids to be loving and diligent, to share and help a friend in need. But the selfish and godless trend in our culture makes it difficult for parents.[27]

This parent is one of millions of young Christians who are trying to raise godly children in an environment that is hostile to anyone who publicly shares their faith.

Children today cannot remember a time when our nation and culture were supportive of and amiable toward the Christian faith. There has to be a checklist for young parents. Ask yourself this question, Are you putting too much focus on their momentary happiness and not enough on their long-term character? Today, parents face all kinds of pressure to give their children everything and to make life as easy as possible for them. The risk is that this can give rise to the kind of self-centered mind-set of the New Morality. We must be careful to set proper boundaries for our kids and to teach them not to be overly materialistic—and not to view their own happiness as the most important thing in the world.

We would be wise to be mindful of the words of Charles Carroll, the last signer of the Declaration of Independence to pass away, who wrote in a letter to James McHenry on November 4, 1800:

> Without morals a republic cannot subsist any length of time; they therefore, who are decrying the Christian religion, whose morality is so sublime [and] pure, which denounces against the wicked eternal misery, [and] insures to the good eternal happiness are undermining the solid foundation of morals, the best security for the duration of free government.[28]

He notes that a republic cannot stand when it loses its moral footing. He warns that those who work ill on the Christian faith weaken the moral foundation of our nation and put its liberty in jeopardy. The liberal Left, with its New Morality, is busy working this ill and doing its best to undermine the moral foundation that made this nation the best the world has seen. Their diabolical efforts put our children at risk.

We don't know what the near future holds in the cultural war, but the end of the Good Book says that our side wins. It may take the second coming of Christ to finalize that victory, but if that's the plan, so be it. It does not change the fact that we have a responsibility, and so do you, to fight against the advance of the New Morality—relativism, humanism, and secularism—that seeks to steal our kids and render them void of any real character, decency, and virtue. We have to fight back. Our kids are worth it.

MAKING A DIFFERENCE: YOU

We, the authors, believe it is important to remind you of two organizations that are positive alternatives to the conventional scouting program. It is appropriate to single them out here because they were founded by ordinary people who dared to fight back, take a risk, and do extraordinary things. They are examples to follow, and we recommend a visit to their websites: American Heritage Girls (www.americanheritagegirls.org) and Trail Life USA (www.traillife-usa.com).

We conclude this book by issuing a call to action to our readers. What actions will you take to help protect our nation's most valuable resource, its children? None of us should idly sit on the sidelines of a raging war. In this battle, you get to decide whether you will surrender or go down fighting. We have decided to fight. One day, we would like to hear our Master say, "Well done, you good and faithful servant[s]. You have been faithful over a few things. I will make you ruler over many things" (Matt. 25:21, MEV). Now is the time to gird your loins for the battle.

TAKE ACTION

- Encourage your church and Sunday school superintendent to offer classes in apologetics for teens and middle-school children so they will be equipped to respond to the secularists who would mock their faith and corrupt their values.
- Refuse to send your children to private and public schools that push the New Morality and radical secularism.
- Invest in businesses, institutions, and people who support the values and principles that you would like to see inculcated in our children.

NOTES

Introduction

1. Beatrice Dupuy, "Parents Call on School's Chief to Resign After Smitten Kitten Field Trip," *Star Tribune*, June 5, 2015, accessed December 22, 2015, http://www.startribune.com/school-s-sex-store-field-trip-brings-calls-for-new-leader/306215651/.
2. James Vaznis, "At Boston Public Schools, Condom Wrappers Raise Ruckus," *Boston Globe*, March 6, 2014, accessed January 27, 2016, https://www.bostonglobe.com/metro/2014/03/06/boston-schools-replacing-condoms-amid-concerns-about-messages-wrappers/9KGlIvcesOMTMOjy 49EVWI/story.html.
3. Carla Castano, "Does Sex Ed Conference for Students Go Too Far?" KOIN 6, November 18, 2014, accessed February 10, 2016, http://koin.com/2014/11/18/does-sex-ed-conference-for-students-go-too-far/.
4. Daily Mail reporter and Snejana Farberov, "'What Young Man Would Not Jump on That Candy?': Judge Under Fire for 'Outrageous' Comments as He Let Married Female Teacher off with Just House Arrest for Having Sex with Student," *DailyMail.com*, April 5, 2015, accessed February 10, 2016, http://www.dailymail.co.uk/news/article-3027031/Outrage-judge-compares-teacher-Erica-Ginneti-dangling-candy-15-year-old-student-couldn-t-resist.htm.
5. "Five Myths about Young Adult Church Dropouts," Barna Group, November 15, 2011, accessed December 22, 2015, https://barna.org/millennials/534-five-myths-about-young-adult-church-dropouts#.Vnli 6BUrLx5.

6. Tammy Bruce, *The Death of Right and Wrong: Exposing the Left's Assault on Our Culture and Values* (Roseville, CA: Prima Forum, 2003), 58.

7. Sarah Pulliam, "Atheists Bond During 'De-Baptism'" *Columbus Dispatch*, August 3, 2008, accessed, June 4, 2015, http://www.dispatch.com/content/stories/local/2008/08/03/ baptism. ART_ART_08-03-08_B4_61AU3UV.html.

8. Bruce, *The Death of Right and Wrong*, 37.

9. Carol M. Swain, *Be the People: A Call to Reclaim America's Faith and Promise* (Nashville, TN: Thomas Nelson, 2011), 2.

Chapter 1: The Enemy Revealed

1. John F. Kennedy, "Commencement Address at Yale University," June 11, 1962, as quoted by the American Presidency Project, accessed July 30, 2015, http://www.presidency.ucsb.edu/ws/?pid= 29661

2. Mary Poplin, *Is Reality Secular? Testing the Assumptions of Four Global Worldviews* (Downers Grove, IL: InterVarsity Press, 2014), 14.

3. Ebenezer Hazard, ed., *Historical Collections; Consisting of State Papers, and Other Authentic Documents; Intended as Materials for a History of the United States of America*, vol. 1 (Philadelphia: T. Dobson, 1792), 72; David Barton, *Original Intent: The Courts, the Constitution, and Religion* (Aledo, TX: Wall Builders' Press, 2008), 76–78.

4. Hazard, *Historical Collections*, vol. 1, 252; Barton, *Original Intent*, 76–78.

5. Ebenezer Hazard, ed., *Historical Collections; Consisting of State Papers, and Other Authentic Documents; Intended as Materials for an History of the United States of America, vol. 2* (Philadelphia: T. Dobson, 1792), 612; Barton, *Original Intent*, 76–78.

6. *The Code of 1650, Being a Compilation of the Earliest Laws and Orders of the General Court of Connecticut* (Hartford, CT: Silus Andrus, 1822), 11.

7. Hazard, *Historical Collections, vol. 2*, 1; Barton, *Original Intent*, 76–78.

8. George Marsden, as quoted in Swain, *Be the People*, 29; George Marsden, *Religion and American Culture* (Boston: Houghton Mifflin, Harcourt, 1990), 15–16.

9. Isaac Kramnick and R. Laurence Moore, *The Godless Constitution*, as referenced and discussed in Swain, *Be the People*, 31.

10. Benjamin Pierce, *A History of Harvard University* (Cambridge, MA: Brown, Shattuck, and Company, 1833), appendix, 5; Barton, Original Intent, 81.

11. *The Laws of Harvard College* (Boston: Samuel Hall, 1790), 7–8.

12. Georgia Purdom, "Harvard: No Longer 'Truth for Christ and the Church,'" October 11, 2011, accessed January 26, 2016, http://answeringenesis.org/blogs/georgia-purdom/2011/10/11/har-vard -no-longer-truth-for-christ-and-the-church/; Harvard Graduate School of Arts and Sciences Christian Community, "Shield and 'Veritas' History," accessed January 26, 2016, http://www.hcs.harvard.edu/~gsascf/shield-and-veritas-history/.

13. Stacy Waite, "Harvard Magazine to Offer Nude Student Photos," *Badger Herald*, February 13, 2004, accessed February 10, 2016, https://badger herald.com/news/2004/02/13/harvard-magazine-to/.

14. *The Charter and Statutes of the College of William and Mary in Virginia* (Williamsburg, VA: Williams Parks, 1736), 3: accessed February 12, 2016, http://scdb.swem.wm.edu/wiki/index.php/Royal_Charter#The_Charter.2C_and_Statutes.2C_of_the_College_of_William_and_Mary.2C_in_Virginia.2C_1736.

15. *William & Mary Rules* (Richmond, VA: Augustine Davis, 1792), 6; Barton, *Original Intent*, 82.

16. *The Laws of Yale-College, in New Haven, in Connecticut, Enacted by the President and Fellows*, chapter 2, article 1, 4 (New Haven, CT: Josiah Meigs, 1787), 5–6; Barton, *Original Intent*, 82–83.

17. *The Charter of Dartmouth College* (Dresden: Isaiah Thomas, 1779), 1, 4; Barton, *Original Intent*, 83–84.

18. *Columbia Rules* (New York: Samuel London, 1785), 5–8; Barton,

19. *Original Intent*, 84.

20. Poplin, *Is Reality Secular?*, 35.

21. Robert Forbes and Ward Platt, eds., *The Christian Republic*, 2, no. 2 (February 1908), 22.

22. John Dickinson, *The Political Writings of John Dickinson, vol. 1* (Wilmington, NC: Bonsal and Niles, 1801), 111.

23. John Quincy Adams, *An Address, Delivered at the Request of the Committee of Arrangements for the Celebrating the Anniversary of Independence at the City of Washington on the Fourth of July 1821 Upon the Occasion of Reading the Declaration of Independence* (Cambridge, MA: Hilliard and Metcalf, 1821), 28.

24. Hezekiah Niles, *Principles and Acts of the Revolution in America* (Baltimore, MD: William Ogden Niles, 1822), 198.

25. William Wirt, *Sketches of the Life and Character of Patrick Henry* (Philadelphia, PA: James Webster, 1817), 121–123.

26. Bruce Feiler, *America's Prophet: Moses and the American Story* (New York: HarperCollins, 2009), 4, 60.

27. *Journals of the House of Representatives of Massachusetts: 1775, April 29, 1776* (Watertown, MA: 1776), 196–197; George Henry Preble, *Our Flag: Origin and Progress of the Flag of the United States of America* (Albany, NY: Joel Munsell, 1872), 142.

28. "Aitken's Bible Endorsed by Congress," Library of Congress, Religion and the Founding of the American Republic exhibitions, accessed January 26, 2016, https://www.loc.gov/exhibits/religion/rel04.html#obj115.

29. *Journals of the Continental Congress: 1774–1789*, vol. 12 (Washington, DC: Government Printing Office, 1908), 1001; Benjamin Franklin Morris, Christian Life and Character of the Civil Institutions of the United States (Philadelphia, PA: George W. Childs, 1864), 220.

30. Library of Congress, "Thanksgiving Proclamation," accessed February 15, 2016, http://lcweb2.loc.gov/ammem/GW/gw004.html.

31. Memorial of Robert Aitken to Congress, January 21, 1781, from the National Archives, Washington, DC., Library of Congress, Religion and the Founding of the American Republic

exhibition, "Aitken's Bible Endorsed by Congress," accessed January 26, 2016, https://www.loc.gov/exhibits/religion/rel04.html#obj115

32. Ibid.

33. Ibid.

34. Immanuel Kant, *The Critique of Practical Reason*, trans. Thomas Kingsmill Abbott, as quoted by ProjectGutenberg,accessedJanuary26,2016, http://www.gutenberg.org/cache/epub/5683/pg5683.txt.

35. Poplin, *Is Reality Secular?*, 45–49.

36. *The Humanist Religion, The Humanist Manifestos I and II* (New York: Prometheus Books, 1973), 8, as quoted in Francis A. Schaeffer, *A Christian Manifesto* (Wheaton, IL: Crossway Books, 1981), 53.

37. Michael Brendan Dougherty, "How Belgium Went Down the Slippery Slope of Assisted Suicide, *The Week*, June 18, 2015, accessed February 10, 2016, http://theweek.com/articles/561172/how-belgium-went-down-slippery-slope-assisted-suicide; Winston Ross, "Dying Dutch: Euthanasia Spreads Across Europe," *Newsweek*, February 12, 2015, accessed February 10, 2016, http://www.newsweek.com/2015/02/20/choosing-die-netherlands-euthanasia-debate-306223.html ().

38. Samuel Adams, to the legislature of Massachusetts on January 17, 1794, as quoted in *The Writings of Samuel Adams*, ed. Harry Alonzo Crushing, vol. 4 (New York: G. P. Putnam's Sons, 1908), 356.

39. John Quincy Adams, *The Jubilee of the Constitution* (New York: Samuel Colman, 1839), 13–14.

40. Alexander Hamilton, *The Papers of Alexander Hamilton*, vol. 1, ed. Harold C. Syrett (New York: Columbia University Press, 1961), 87.

41. James Wilson, *The Works of the Honourable James Wilson, LLD*, vol. 1 (Philadelphia, PA: Bronson and Chauncey, 1804), 137–138.

42. Schaeffer, *A Christian Manifesto*, 41.

43. Sarah Pulliam Bailey, "Is Polygamy Next in the Marriage Debate?", *Washington Post,* July 10, 2015, accessedFebruary10,2016,http://www.washingtonpost.com/news/acts-of-faith/wp/2015/07/10/heres-why-people-are-arguing-over-whether-polygamy-is-the-next-gay-marriage-debate/.

44. *Congressional Record, first session of the Eighty-Eighth Congress, January 9–May 7, 1963,* text-fiche reel 12, A!–2842.

45. W. Cleon Skousen, *The Naked Communist* (Salt Lake City, UT: Izzard Ink, 1958). Reprinted with permission. "W. Cleon Skousen: Modern-Day Founding Father," February 16, 2010, accessed February 10, 2016, https://wcskousen.wordpress.com/category/bio/.

46. Saul D. Alinsky, *Rules for Radicals: A Pragmatic Primer for Realistic Radicals* (New York City: Random House, 1971).

47. Schaeffer, *A Christian Manifesto,* 29.

48. Ibid., 41.

49. William Barclay, *Ethics in a Permissive Society* (New York: Harper & Row, 1971), 69.

50. Bruce, *The Death of Right and Wrong,* 60.

51. See "Howard Dean's Scream," YouTube video excerpt from 2004 Iowa campaign speech, accessed January 26, 2016, https://www.youtube.com/watch?v=D5FzCeV0ZFc.

52. *Annals of Congress,* vol. 1 (Washington, DC: Gales and Seaton, 1834), 27–28, April 30, 1789.

53. Ibid., 29.

54. George Washington, *Address of George Washington, President of the United States… Preparatory to His Declination* (Baltimore, MD: George and Henry S. Keating, 1796), 22–23.

55. *Annals of Congress,* vol. 1, 949.

56. Jared Sparks, ed., *The Writings of George Washington, Being His Correspondence, Addresses, Messages, and Other Papers Official and Private,* vol. 12 (Boston, MA: American Stationers' Company, 1838), 119.

57. Richard Peters, ed., *The Public Statutes at Large of the United States of America,* vol. 7 (Boston: Charles C. Little and James Brown, 1846), 78–79, accessed February 12, 2016, https://

memory.loc.gov/cgi-bin/ampage?collId=llsl&fileName=007/
llsl007.db&recNum=89.

58. Adolf Hitler, as quoted in *Nazi Conspiracy and Aggression*, vol. 1 (Washington, DC: United States Government Printing Office, 1946), 320, accessed February 10, 2016, http://www.loc.gov/rr/frd/Military_Law/pdf/NT_Nazi_Vol-I.pdf.

59. Joseph Stalin, interview with H. G. Wells, "Marxism Versus Liberalism," July 23, 1934, as quoted at the Marxists Internet Archive, accessed January 23, 2016, https://www.marxists.org/reference/archive/stalin/works/1934/07/23.htm.

60. Anne Graham Lotz, *The Early Show*, CBS Network, September 13, 2001, accessed December 22, 2015, http://www.cbsnews.com/videos/finding-a-healthy-obsession/.

Chapter 2: Exposing the Myth

1. Samuel Adams, letter to James Warren, February 12, 1779.

2. Swain, *Be the People*, 32.

3. Charles A. Fecher, *Mencken: A Study of His Thought* (New York: Alfred A. Knopf, 1978), 113–114.

4. Alinsky, *Rules for Radicals*, 36.

5. Joseph Story, *Commentaries on the Constitution*, vol. 3, paragraph 1871, as quoted by The Founders' Constitution, "Amendment I (Religion)," document 69, accessed February 10, 2016, http://press-pubs.uchicago.edu/founders/documents/amendI_religions69.html.

6. Swain, *Be the People*, 33.

7. Alexis de Tocqueville, *Democracy in America*, introduction to book 1, trans. Henry Reeve, as quoted by the Gutenberg Project, accessed February 10, 2106, https://www.gutenberg.org/files/815/815-h/815-h.htm.

8. Letter from the Danbury, Connecticut, Baptist Association to Thomas Jefferson, October 7, 1801, housed in the Thomas Jefferson Papers Manuscript Division, Library of Congress, Washington, DC.

9. Thomas Jefferson, *The Writings of Thomas Jefferson*, vol. 16 (Washington, DC: Thomas Jefferson Memorial Association of the United States, 1903), 281–282.

10. Ibid.

11. Thomas Jefferson, *The Writings of Thomas Jefferson*, vol. 19 (Washington, DC: Thomas Jefferson Memorial Association of the United States, 1903), 449–450.

12. Ibid.

13. Thomas Jefferson, *Memoirs, Correspondence, and Private Papers of Thomas Jefferson*, vol. 4 (London: Colburn and Bentley, 1829), 367.

14. Jefferson, *The Writings of Thomas Jefferson*, vol. 16, 291.

15. "An Ordinance for the Government of the Territory of the United States North-West of the River Ohio." Article 3, accessed February 10, 2016. http://www.ourdocuments.gov/doc.php?flash=true&doc=8#.

16. Story, *Commentaries on the Constitution*.

17. Conservapedia.com, "Joseph Story," accessed January 23, 2016, http:// www.conservapedia.com /Joseph_Story.

18. Thomas Jefferson, *Memoirs, Correspondence, and Private Papers of Thomas Jefferson*, vol. 3 (London: Coburn and Bentley, 1829), 441.

19. Kate Mason Rowland, *The Life of George Mason*, vol. 1 (New York: G. P. Putnam's Sons, 1892), 244.

20. Thomas Jefferson, *The Works of Thomas Jefferson*, vol. 11, ed. Paul Leicester Ford (New York: G. P. Putnam's Sons, 1905), as quoted by The Founders' Constitution, "Amendment I (Religion)," document 60, accessed January 23, 2016, http://press-pubs.uchicago.edu/founders/ documents/ amend I_religions60.html.

21. *A Constitution or Frame of Government Agreed upon by the Delegates of the People of the State of Massachusetts Bay in Convention* (Boston, MA: Benjamin Edes and Sons, 1780), 7–8.

22. House Judiciary Committee report, March 27, 1854, as quoted by Bill Bailey, "Religion and Government, Are We a Christian Nation?," The Federalist Papers Project, accessed February

10, 2016, http://www.thefederalist papers.org/history/religion-and-government-are-we-a-christian-nation.
23. *Engel v. Vitale*, 370 US 421 (1962).
24. *Abington School District v. Schempp*, 374 US 203 (1963).
25. *Reed v. Van Hoven*, 237 F. Supp. 48 (Dist. Court, WD Michigan, 1965).
26. *Lowe v. City of Eugene*, 451 P.2d 117 (1969).
27. *Warsaw v. Tehachapi* CV F-90-404 EDP (USDC, ED Ca. 1990).
28. *Wallace v. Jaffree*, 472 US at 103 (1985).
29. *Roberts v. Madigan*, 921 F. 2d 1047 (10th Circuit, 1990).
30. *Washegesic v. Bloomingdale Public Schools*, 33 F. 3d 679 (6th Circuit, 1994).
31. *Florey v. Sioux Falls School District*. 49-5, 464 F. Supp. 911 (Dist. Court, D South Dakota, 1980).
32. *Wallace v. Jaffree*, 472 US at 103 (1985), Rehnquist (dissenting).
33. Thomas Jefferson, *The Writings of Thomas Jefferson*, vol. 15 (Washington, DC: Thomas Jefferson Memorial Association of the United States, 1903), 277.
34. You can find Lisa Abler's curriculum and planning guide at http://www.amazon.com/Vacation-Liberty-School-Curriculum-Planning/dp/14564 20127. See also Billy Hallowell, "Vacation Liberty School Teaches Kids about America's Faith, Politics, and Founding Values," *TheBlaze*, August 8, 2011, accessed December 23, 2015, http://www.theblaze.com/stories/2011/08/08/tea-party-summer-school.

Chapter 3: Public Schools: Ground Zero

1. Noah Webster, "On the Education of Youth in America," *American Magazine*, December 1787.
2. Jeanette Rundquist, "Ban on School Christmas Carol Upheld,"
3. Beliefnet, 2010, accessed February 10, 2016, http://www.beliefnet.com/columnists/news/ 2010/10/ban-on-school-christmas-carols.php.

4. See "CAIR Rep Debates Religious Accommodation in Schools," YouTube video, accessed February 10, 2016, https://www.youtube.com/watch?v=sKy2H0yR4g4&feature=youtu.be.

5. Nancy Wurtzel, "Seinfeld Remembered: Festivus, for the Rest of Us," *Huffington Post*, December 23, 2012, accessed September 18, 2015, http:// www.huffingtonpost.com/nancy-wurtzel/festivus-seinfeld-episode_b_2300 875.html.

6. "Praying Ex-Coach Files Libel Lawsuit," *Bryan Times*, July 24, 2001, accessed January 23, 2016, https://news.google.com/newspapers?id=38k0AAAAIBAJ&sjid=mUkDAAAAIBAJ&pg=4563%2C2804653; ACLU.org,

7. "ACLU Declares Victory in Ohio School Where Football Coach Led Prayers, Read Scripture," October 19, 1999, accessed January 23, 2016, https://www.aclu.org/news/aclu-declares-victory-ohio-school-where-football-coach-led-prayers-read-scripture?redirect=religion-belief/aclu-declares-victory-ohio-school-where-football-coach-led-prayers-read-scripture.

8. *Everson v. Board of Education of the Township of Ewing*, 330 U.S. 1 (1947) accessed February 12, 2016, https://supreme.justia.com/cases/federal/us/330/1/case.html.

9. "People and Ideas: God and the Constitution," PBS.org, accessed February 10, 2016, http://www.pbs.org/godinamerica/people/god-and-the-constitution.html.

10. *McCollum v. Board of Education*, Supreme Court of the United States, 333 US (1948).

11. *Engel v. Vitale*, 370 US 421 (1962).

12. Ibid.

13. *Reed v. Van Hoven*, 237 F. Supp. 48 (WD Michigan, 1965).

14. Joseph Farah, "The First Homosexual School," *WND*, July 29, 2003, accessed February 10, 2016, http://www.wnd.com/2003/07/20005/.

15. "Yes to 'The Vagina Monologues' but No to 'West Side Story,'" FoxNews.com, partial transcript for *The O'Reilly Factor*, January 14, 2003, accessed February 10, 2016, http://www.foxnews.com/ story/2004/01/15/yes-to-vagina-monologues-but-no-to-west-side-story.html.

16. "Banned From Showing Students the Declaration of Independence," FoxNews.com, partial transcript for Hannity & Colmes, November 29, 2004, accessed January 23, 2016, http://www.foxnews.com/story/2004/11/30/banned-from-showing-students-declaration-independence.html.

17. Ibid.

18. Heather D. Koerner, "Documented Thanksgiving," *Focus*, 1999.

19. Library of Congress, "Thanksgiving Proclamation," October 3, 1789, http://lcweb2.loc.gov/ ammem/GW/gw004.html.

20. Abraham Lincoln, "Proclamation of Thanksgiving," October 3, 1863, as quoted by Abraham Lincoln Online, accessed February 10, 2016, http://www.abrahamlincolnonline.org/Lincoln / speeches/thanks.htm.

21. "The NEA Proves Itself Extremist Again," *The Phyllis Schlafly Report*, vol. 29, no. 1, August 1995, accessed February 10, 2016, http://www.eagle forum.org/psr/1995/psraug95.html.

22. Noah Webster, as quoted by April Shenandoah, "History of America's Education, Part II: Noah Webster and Early America," *The Progressive Conservative 4*, no. 34 (April 3, 2002).

23. Paul Vitz, *Censorship: Evidence of Bias in Our Children's Textbooks* (Ann Arbor, MI: Servant Books, 1986), 14.

24. Ibid., 80.

25. David Limbaugh, *Persecution: How Liberals Are Waging War Against Christianity* (Washington, DC: Regnery, 2003), 76.

26. Ibid.

27. Samuel Blumenfeld, "Death Education at Columbine High," *WND*, May 27, 1999, accessed February 10, 2016, http://www.wnd.com/1999/05/2771.

28. Ibid.; Eagle Forum, "Tragedy at Columbine: The Curriculum Connection," *Education Reporter*, July 1999, accessed February 12, 2016, http://www.eagleforum.org/educate/1999/july99 / columbine.html.

29. Peter Roff, "Obama Wrong on DC School Vouchers and Hypocritical, Just Like Congress," *US News & World Report*, April 22, 2009, accessed February 10, 2016, http://www.

usnews.com/opinion /blogs/peter-roff/2009/04/22/obama-wrong-on-dc-school-vouchers-and-hypocritical-just-like-congress.

30. "Milton Friedman on Vouchers," CNBC, interview, March 24, 2003, as quoted on the Friedman Foundation website, accessed February 10, 2106, http://www.edchoice.org/who-we-are/our-founders/the-friedmans-on-school-choice/article/milton-friedman-on-vouchers/.

31. Ben Waldron, "Home Schooling German Family Fights Deportation," March 31, 2013, accessed February 10, 2016, http://abcnews.go.com/US/home-schooling-german-family-fights-deportation /story?id=18842383.

32. Ibid.

33. Learn more about IndoctriNation at www.indoctrinationmovie.com.

34. Ibid.

35. Dagobert D. Runes, ed., The Selected Writings of Benjamin Rush (New York: Philosophical Library, 1947), as quoted by The Founders' Constitution, "Epilogue Securing the Republic," document 30, accessed February 10, 2016, http://press-pubs.uchicago.edu/founders/ documents/v1ch18s30.html.

36. Billy Hallowell, "Is There a 'Dramatic Increase' in Hostility and Harassment Directed at Christian Students in Public Schools?" *TheBlaze*, January 28, 2014, accessed February 10, 2016, http://www.theblaze.com/stories/2014/01/28/is-there-a-dramatic-increase-in-hostility-and-harassment-directed-at-christian-students-in-public-schools/.

37. Ibid.

38. David Limbaugh, "Enemies, Not Guardians of Religious Freedom," TownHall.com, September 14, 2002, accessed February 10, 2106, http://townhall.com/columnists/davidlimbaugh /2002 /09/14/ enemies,_not_guardians_of_religious_freedom.

39. See www.corestandards.org.

40. Alex Newman, "Opposition to Obama-Backed National Education Scheme Grows," *New American*, March

12, 2013, accessed January 23, 2016, http://www.the-newamerican.com/culture/ education/item/14756-opposition-to-obama-backed-national-education-scheme-grows.

41. Grae Stafford, "More Core: Homeschool Advocate Sharply Criticizes 'Common Core,'" *Daily Caller*, April 16, 2013, accessed February 10, 2016, http://dailycaller.com/2013/04/16/common-core-educational-program-sharply-criticized-by-home-school-advocate.

42. Phyllis Schlafly, "Let's Stop Judge-Ordered Tax Increases," *Eagle Forum*, September 22, 2004, accessed February 10, 2016, http://www.eagle forum.org/column/2004/sept04/04-09-22.html.

43. "Valedictorian, Roy Costner IV, Tears Up Speech on Stage, Recites the Lord's Prayer at Graduation," FoxNews, June 6, 2013, accessed February 10, 2016, https://www.youtube.com/watch? v=SofwwWkWkC4.

44. Mary C. Tillotson, "Wisconsin to Expand Voucher Program," The Heartland Institute, June 26, 2013, accessed December 23, 2015, accessed February 10, 2016, http://news.heartland.org/ newspaper-article/2013/06/26/wisconsin-expand-voucher-program.

45. Ibid.

Chapter 4: Sexy Kids

1. James Wilson, *The Works of the Honourable James Wilson, LLD*, vol. 2, 486.

2. See www.glsen.org.

3. Bruce, *The Death of Right and Wrong*, 103.

4. Kari Hudnell, "GLSEN Statement on Start of LGBT History Month," Gay, Lesbian & Straight Education Network, October 1, 2015, accessed February 12, 2016, http://www.glsen.org/article/ glsen-statement-start-lgbt-history-month.

5. Gary J. Gates, "How Many People Are Lesbian, Gay, Bisexual and Transgender?", The Williams Institute, April 2011, accessed February 10, 2016, http://williamsinstitute.

law.ucla.edu/research/ census-lgbt-demographics-studies/how-many-people-are-lesbian-gay-bisexual-and-transgender/.

6. Bruce, *The Death of Right and Wrong*, 104.

7. Ibid., 104–105.

8. Ibid., 105.

9. Ibid., 105.

10. bid., 207.

11. Ibid.

12. SIECUS, *Guidelines for Comprehensive Sexuality Education: Kindergarten–12th Grade*, 3rd Edition, 20, accessed January 23, 2016, http://www.siecus.org/_data/global/images/guidelines.pdf.

13. SEICUS, "Abstinence Only Until Marriage Programs," accessed February 15, 2016, http://www.siecus.org/index.cfm?fuseaction=page.viewPage &pageId=523&parentID=477.

14. SIECUS, *Guidelines for Comprehensive Sexuality Education: Kindergarten–12th Grade*, 2nd Edition.

15. SIECUS, *Guidelines for Comprehensive Sexuality Education: Kindergarten–12th Grade*, 3rd Edition, 25–26, 29-30, 32, 46, 51–52, 55–56, 74.

16. Douglas Kennedy, "ACLU Sues Louisiana Over Abstinence Ed," FoxNews.com, May 16, 2002, accessed February 10, 2016, http://www.fox news.com/story/2002/05/16/aclu-sues-louisiana-over-abstinence-ed.html.

17. Gabe Wildau, "O'Reilly: ACLU Is America's 'Most Dangerous Organization...Second to Al Qaeda,'" Media Matters for America, June 8, 2004, accessed February 10, 2016, http://mediamatters.org/research/2004/06/08/oreilly-aclu-is-americas-most-dangerous-organiz/131240.

18. P. J. McRae, "Sexual Abstinence From a Non-Religious Perspective," *Examiner.com*, June 6, 2011, accessed February 10, 2016, http://www.examiner.com/article/sexual-abstinence-from-a-non-religious-perspective.

19. S. Nobal, "Common Core Has a Porn-Sex Education Curricula for Middle School," *Independent Sentinel*, January 20, 2014, accessed February 10, 2016, http://www.independentsentinel.

com/ common-core-has-a-porn-sex-education-curricula-for-middle-school/.

20. Eric Metaxas, "The 'Saturation Process': Hooking Kids on Sex," *Breakpoint*, April 17, 2013, accessed February 10, 2016, https://www.break point.org/bpcommentaries/entry/13/21967.

21. Ibid.

22. American Life League, "Hooking Kids on Sex II," accessed February 10, 2016, https://www.youtube.com/watch?v=j7XR9yH2ETk.

23. Jason Pierce, "'Female Liberalism' Pervades Girl Scouts, Says ExScout," http://dev. cnsnews.com/news/article/female-liberalism-pervades-girl-scouts-says-ex-scout, as cited in Swain, *Be the People*, 110.

24. Nancy Manahan and Lynn Tuft, *On My Honor: Lesbians Reflect on Their Scouting Experience.* (Northboro, MA: Madwoman Press, 1998).

25. Kathryn Jean Lopez, "The Cookie Crumbles: The Girl Scouts Go PC," *The National Review*, October 23, 2000, accessed January 23, 2016, http://www.lifeissues.org/connector/2010/oct_10/3_girl_scouts_cookie_crumbles.pdf.

26. Swain, *Be the People*, 110.

27. "Principles," American Heritage Girls, accessed March 7, 2016, http://www. americanheritagegirls. org /about/principles/.

28. "Who We Are," Trail of Life USA, accessed March 7, 2016, http://www.traillifeusa.com /whoweare/.

29. "Core Values," Trail of Life USA, accessed March 7, 2016, http://www.traillifeusa.com/ corevalues/.

30. Amanda Covarrubias and Kim Christensen, "Settlement in Sex Abuse Case Keeps Scouts' 'Perversion Files' Closed," *Los Angeles Times*, January 29, 2015, accessed February 10, 2016, http://www.latimes.com/local/ california/la-me-boy-scouts-20150130-story.html.

31. Chris McGreal, "Sexual Abuse Scandal Rocks Boy Scouts of America After $18.5m Payout," *The Guardian*, April 29, 2010, accessed February 10, 2016, http://www.guardian.co.uk/world /2010 /apr/29/boy-scouts-sexual-abuse-dykes.

32. David Thorstad, "Harry Hay on Man/Boy Love," NAMBLA, accessed February 10, 2016, http://nambla.org/hayonmanboy-love.html.

33. William F. Jasper, "Obama's 'Safe Schools Czar' Kevin Jennings," *The New American*, November 24, 2009, accessed February 10, 2016, http://www.the-newamerican.com/culture/education/ item/158-obama%25E2%2580%2599s-%25E2%2580%259Csafe-schools-czar%25E2%2580%259D-kevin-jennings; Michael O'Brien, "Fifty-Three Republicans Demand Firing of 'Safe Schools Czar' Kevin Jennings," *The Hill*, October 15, 2009, accessed February 10, 2016, http://thehill.com/blogs/blog-briefing-room/news/63249-53-republicans-demand-firing-of-safe-schools-czar; this material was also included in Swain, Be the People, 112–113.

34. Meg Meeker, *Epidemic: How Teen Sex Is Killing Our Kids* (Washington, DC: Lifeline Press, 2002), 11–18.

35. Ibid.

36. See http://www.rebekkaarmstrong.com/#about.

37. See http://www.rebekkaarmstrong.com/#media.

38. Dave McKinney, "State Giving Away Flavored Condoms; Some Lawmakers Say They're Surprised at Purchase of 360,000," *Chicago Sun-Times*, November 1, 2004, accessed February 10, 2016, https://www.highbeam.com/doc/1P2-1553859.html.

39. Limbaugh, *Persecution*, 94.

40. M. Pollak, "Male Homosexuality," in *Western Sexuality: Practice and Precept in Past and Present Times*, edited by P. Aries and A. Bejin (New York: Blackwell, 1985), 40–61, cited in Joseph Nicolosi, *Reparative Therapy of Male Homosexuality* (Northvale, NJ: Jason Aronson, 1991), 124–125.

41. Linda P. Harvey, "'Gay' Groups Join Planned Parenthood to Attack Abstinence Funding," *Mission America*, Feb. 22, 2003.

42. Ibid.

43. Frank Newport, "Americans Greatly Overestimate Percent Gay, Lesbian in US," Gallup poll, May 21, 2015, accessed February

10, 2016, http:// www.gallup.com/poll/183383/ameri-cans-greatly-overestimate-percent-gay-lesbian.aspx.

44. Ian Sample, "Male sexual orientation influenced by genes, study shows," *The Guardian* February 13, 2014, https://www.theguardian.com/science/2014/feb/14/genes-influ-ence-male-sexual-orientation-study. Also see http://www.sciencemag.org/news/2014/11/study-gay-brothers-may-con-firm-x-chromosome-link-homosexuality

45. Alan P. Bell, Martin S. Weinberg, and Sue Kiefer Hammersmith, *Sexual Preference* (Bloomington, IN: Indiana University Press, 1981).

46. Alice Park, *Time*, "HIV Continues to Spread among Gay Men, Studies Show," July 20, 2012, accessed February 10, 2016, http://healthland.time.com/2012/07/20/hiv-contin-ues-to-spread-among-gay-men-studies-show; "US Statistics," AIDS.gov, accessed February 10, 2016, https://www.aids.gov/hiv-aids-basics/hiv-aids-101/statistics/.

47. Alan P. Bell and Martin S. Weinberg, *Homosexualities: A Study of Diversity Among Men and Women* (New York: Simon and Schuster, 1978), 308–309.

48. See www.focusonthefamily.com/socialissues.

49. David Bohon, "Psychiatric Group Backtracks on Pedophilia Classification," *New American*, November 12, 2013, accessed February 10, 2016, http://www.thenewamerican.com/culture/family item/16925-psychiatric-group-backtracks-on-pedo-philia-classification.

50. Ibid.

51. Bruce, *Death of Right and Wrong*, 46.

52. Debra W. Haffner, "The Really Good News: What the Bible Can Teach You About Sex," *SIECUS Report 26*, no. 1 (October/November 1997).

53. Ibid.

54. Ibid.

55. Ibid.

56. *Obergefell v. Hodges*, 135 S. Ct. 2584 (2015).

57. Jan Omega, "California High School Students Publicly Shamed for Opposing LGBT Agenda," *Inquisitr*, February 10, 2015, accessed February 10, 2016, http://www.inquisitr.com/1831614/california-high-school-students-publicly-shamed-opposing-lgbt-agenda.

58. "California Law Allows Transgender Students to Pick Bathrooms, Sports Teams They Identify With," CBS News, August 12, 2013, accessed February 10, 2016, http://www.cbsnews.com/news/ california-law-allows-transgender-students-to-pick-bathrooms-sports-teams-they-identify-with.

59. World Health Organization, "Gender and Genetics," accessed February 12, 2016, http://www.who.int/genomics/gender/en/index1.html.

60. "Sex Change Treatments for Children is on the Rise," *Daily News*, February 29, 2012). http://www.nydailynews.com/life-style/health/sex-change-treatment-children-rise-article-1.1025598

61. Walt Heyer, "What Parents Should Know About Giving Hormones to Trans Kids), February 2, 2015. http://thefederalist.com/2015/02/02/what-parents-should-know-about-giving-hormones-to-trans-kids/.

62. http://www.acpeds.org/the-college-speaks/position-statements/gender-ideology-harms-children), March 21, 2016.

63. Catherine Wood is a personal friend of coauthor Steve Feazel's, and he has firsthand knowledge of her work. For more information, visit http:// www.relationshipsunderconstruction.com/about-ruc.

64. For more information, visit http://www.exodusglobalalliance.org/ and http://www.pfox.org/.

65. Russell Moore, "What if your Child is Gay?" accessed February 12, 2016, https://www.russellmoore.com/2014/06/06/what-if-your-child-is-gay/.

Chapter 5: Music Hits a Sour Note

1. Baker Brownell, *Art Is Action: A Discussion of Nine Arts in a Modern World* (N.p.: Kennikat Press, 1972); "Music Quotes,"

NotableQuotes, accessed February 15, 2016, http://www.nota-ble-quotes.com/m/music_quotes.html.

2. Luke Leung, "Billy Ray Cyrus Regrets Bringing Miley to Hollywood: 'I'd Take It Back in a Second,'" *Gospel Herald*, September 17, 2013, accessed February 10, 2016, http://www.gospelherald.com/articles/48892/20130917/billy-ray-cyrus-regrets-bringing-miley-to-hollywood-id-take-it-back-in-a-second.htm.

3. As quoted in Kourosh Dini, "Aristotle on Music Education," February 14, 2011, accessed February 10, 2016http://www.kouroshdini.com/2011/02/14/aristotle-on-music-education/.

4. As quoted in Phil Chambers, *Music to Die For* (Atlanta: Falcon Video Productions, 2004); Plato, *The Dialogues of Plato*, vol. 1 (New York: Random House, 1937), 687.

5. Robert H. Bork, *Slouching Towards Gomorrah* (New York: Regan Books, 2003), 148.

6. Danny Goldberg, *Dispatches From the Culture War: How the Left Lost Teen Spirit* (New York: Miramax Books, 2003), 229.

7. Ibid., 241.

8. Chambers, *Music to Die For*.

9. Ibid.

10. Ibid.

11. Ibid.

12. Ibid.

13. *Commonwealth v. Jesse Sharpless and Others*, 2 Serg.&R. 91, 92 (sup. Ct. Penn., 1815).

14. Barton, *Original Intent*, 63.

15. Ibid.

16. Jesse Sharpless, at 97, 101, and 104.

17. Bork, *Slouching Towards Gomorrah*, 130–131.

18. Ibid., 124.

19. Ibid., 131.

20. Ibid.

21. Estelle Thurtle, "Ten Attempts to Blame Murder on Music," *Listverse*, June 24, 2014, accessed February 10, 2016,

http://listverse.com/2014/06/24/10-attempts-to-blame-mur-der-on-music.

22. "Gruesome Details Revealed in 'Syko Sam' Killings," NBC Bay Area, September 22, 2009, accessed February 10, 2016, http://www.nbcbayarea.com/news/local/Gruesome-Details-Revealed-in-Virigina-Killings-60278252.html.

23. Ibid.

24. Ibid.

25. Ibid.

26. Kia Makarechi, "Jay-Z's Obama Ad Demonstrates Rapper and President's Mutual Appreciation," *Huffpost Entertainment*, October 16, 2012, accessed February 10, 2016, http://www.huffingtonpost.com/2012/10/16/jay-z-obama-ad-video_n_1969699.html.

27. Ibid.

28. Ibid.

29. Chambers, *Music to Die For*.

30. Ibid.

31. Ibid.

32. "Dec. 9, 2004: Five Killed in Concert Chaos," *Columbus Dispatch*, December 14, 2009, accessed February 10, 2016, http://www.dispatch.com/content/stories/local/2009/12/07/alrosa-villa-original-story.html.

33. Lorraine Ali, "The Glorious Rise of Christian Pop," *Newsweek*, July 15, 2001, 40, accessed February 10, 2106, http://www.newsweek.com/glorious-rise-christian-pop-154551.

34. Ibid., 41.

35. Ibid.

36. Bork, *Slouching Towards Gomorrah*, 141. 37. Ibid., 142.

37. "Black College Women Take Aim at Rappers," *USA Today*, April 23, 2004, accessed February 10, 2016, http://usatoday30.usatoday.com/life/music/news/2004-04-23-spelman-protest-rappers _x.htm.

38. See Parental Advisory Scheme, "What Is the Parental Advisory Logo?," accessed February 10, 2016, http://parental-advisory.co.uk/advice-for-parents/what-is-the-parental-advisory-logo.

Chapter 6: Big Screen, Little Value

1. Diane Disney Miller and Pete Martin, *The Disney Story* (New York: Holt, 1957).
2. Michael Medved, *Hollywood vs. America* (New York: HarperCollins, 1992), 22.
3. Ibid., 19.
4. Ibid.
5. Ibid., 21.
6. Ibid., 222.
7. Ibid., 225–226.
8. Ibid., 228.
9. See www.americanpiemovie.com.
10. *American Pie*, directed by Paul and Chris Weitz, written by Adam Herz (Universal City, CA: Universal Pictures, 1999).
11. Information provided by www.boxofficemojo.com.
12. Ibid.
13. Moviefone, "Fifty Shades of Grey (2015)," accessed February 10, 2016, shades-of-grey /62570 / main.
14. "Pa. Middle School Students Given 'Fifty Shades of Grey' Puzzles," CBS Philly, February 11, 2015, accessed February 10, 2016, http://philadelphia.cbslocal.com/2015/02/11/pa-middle-school-students-given-fifty-shades-of-grey-puzzles/.
15. Karen Sternheimer, *It's Not the Media: The Truth About Pop Culture's Influence on Children* (Boulder, CO: Westview Press, 2003), 4.
16. Ibid., 5.
17. Ibid., 183.
18. Medved, Hollywood vs. America, 292.
19. Ibid., 289.
20. Ibid., 291.
21. Limbaugh, *Persecution*, 285–286.
22. Ibid., 289.

Chapter 7: Invader in a Box

1. Prince Frederick, "Mind Matters," *The Hindu*, June 11, 2011, accessed February 10, 2016, www.thehindu.com/todays-paper/ tp-features/tp-metro plus/mind-matters/article2094593.ece.
2. Donald E. Wildmon, *The Home Invaders* (Wheaton, IL: Victor Books, 1885), 76.
3. Ibid.
4. Ibid.
5. Ibid., 77.
6. Jean Tepperman, "Toxic Lessons: What Do Children Learn from Media Violence?", *Children's Advocate*, January/February 1997.
7. Wildmon, *The Home Invaders*, 78.
8. Ibid., 79
9. Ibid.
10. Ibid., 80.
11. James Poniewozik, "The Decency Police," *Time*, March 20, 2005, accessed December 23, 2015http://content.time. com/time/magazine/article/0,9171,1039700,00.html; "CBS Escapes Fine for Janet Jackson 'Wardrobe Malfunction,'" *USA Today*, June 29, 2012, accessed February 10, 2016, http://usa-today30.usatoday.com/money/media/story/2012-06-29/jan-et-jackson-wardrobe-malfunction-supreme-court/55913802/1.
12. Poniewozik, "Decency Police," 29.
13. Bernard Goldberg, *Arrogance: Rescuing America From the Media Elite* (New York: Warner Books, 2003), 237.
14. Poniewozik, "Decency Police," 29.
15. Ibid., 28.
16. Bork, *Slouching Towards Gomorrah*, 128.
17. Bryan Kemper, "MTV in Bed With Planned Parenthood." This article originally appeared in *Special Reports*, an official period-ical of Life Decisions International (LDI), but it is no longer available. Kemper's comments were confirmed in an interview with author Steve Feazel on December 28, 2015.
18. Ibid.

19. Ibid.
20. *Sex and the City*, synopsis of season 1, episode 1, accessed February 10, 2016, http://www.hbo.com/sex-and-the-city/episodes/1/01-sex-and-the-city/synopsis.html.
21. ClassicTVHits.com, "Will and Grace," accessed January 23, 2016, http://www.classictvhits.com /show. php?id=681.
22. Bork, *Slouching Towards Gomorrah*, 127; S. Robert Lichter, Linda S. Lichter, and Stanley Rothman, *Prime Time: How TV Portrays American Culture* (Washington, DC: Regnery Publishing, 1994), 416, 404–405.
23. Ben Domenech, "The West Wing: Big-Hearted and Wrongheaded," *Boundless* (webzine), www.boundless.org/2000/ (link no longer active); "Liberal Drama," *Washington Times*, accessed March 8, 2016, http://www.washingtontimes.com/news/2000/dec/29/20001229-013640-3967r/.
24. Ibid.
25. Medved, *Hollywood vs. America*, 331.
26. Susan Carney, "Advertising to Teens," *Suite*, February 23, 2007, accessed February 10, 2016, https://suite.io/susan-carney/59v2bc.
27. Ben Tinker, "TV Ads May Be Driving Children to Drink," *The Chart*, January 29, 2013, accessed February 10, 2016, http://thechart.blogs.cnn.com/2013/01/29/tv-ads-may-be-driving-children-to-drink.
28. Allison Kasic, "Planned Parenthood's Racy New TV Ad," *Human Events*, April 26, 2006, accessed February 10, 2016, http://humanevents.com/2006/04/26/planned-parenthoods-racy-new-tv-ad/.
29. "Planned Parenthood of the St. Louis Region and Southwest Missouri TV Commercial," Planned Parenthood of the St. Louis Region and Southwest Missouri, YouTube video uploaded March 15, 2013, accessed February 10, 2016, https://www.youtube.com/watch?v=f0A12YpJK6I.
30. "Birth Control," PlannedParenthood.org, accessed February 10, 2016, https://www.plannedparenthood.org/teens/going-to-the-doctor/birth-control.

31. Sally Robinson and Keith Bly, "Protecting Your Child From TV," *NewsforParents.org*, accessed February 10, 2016, http://www. newsforparents.org/expert_protecting_child_from_tv.html.

32. "The V-Chip: Putting Restrictions on What Your Children Watch," Federal Communications Commission, accessed February 10, 2016, https:// www.fcc.gov/ guides/v-chip-putting-restrictions-what-your-children-watch.

33. "Psychologists Study Media Violence for Harmful Effects," American Psychological Association, November 2013, accessed February 10, 2016, http://www.apa.org/action/resources/ research-in-action/protect.aspx.

Chapter 8: Children, Stolen and Gone

1. "Another Mass Shooting, Another Psychiatric Drug? Federal Investigation Long Overdue," CCHR International, accessed February 10, 2016, http://www.cchrint. org/2012/07/20/the-aurora-colorado-tragedy-another -senseless-shooting-another-psychotropic-drug.

2. Alison Leigh Cowan, "Adam Lanza's Mental Problems 'Completely Untreated' Before Newtown Shootings, Report Says," *New York Times*, November 21, 2014, accessed February 10, 2016, http://www.nytimes.com/2014/11/22/nyre-gion/before-newtown-shootings-adam-lanzas-mental-prob-lems-completely-untreated-report-says.html.

3. Thomas Insel, "Director's Blog: Are Children Overmedicated?" National Institute of Mental Health, June 6, 2014, accessed February 10, 2016, http://www.nimh.nih.gov/about/direc-tor /2014/are-children-overmedicated.shtml; Alan Schwarz, "Thousands of Toddlers Are Medicated for ADHD, Report Finds, Raising Worries" *New York Times*, May 16, 2014, accessed February 10, 2016, http://www.nytimes.com/2014/05/17/us/ among-experts-scrutiny-of-attention-disorder-diagnoses-in-2-and-3-year-olds.html.

4. Insel, "Director's Blog."

5. Ibid.

6.   Matt Philbin, "After Oregon Shooting: Top 10 Movies Show 121 Acts of Gun Violence," *NewsBusters*, October 7, 2015, accessed February 10, 2016, http://newsbusters.org/blogs/ culture/matt-philbin/2015/10/07/after-oregon-shooting-top-10-movies-show-121-acts-gun-violence.

7.   Brad J. Bushman et al., "Gun Violence Trends in Movies," *Pediatrics* 132, no. 6 (December 1, 2013): 1014–1018.

8.   Maria Konnikova, "Why Gamers Can't Stop Playing First-Person Shooters," *New Yorker*, November 25, 2013, accessed February 10, 2016, http://www.newyorker.com/tech/elements/ why-gamers-cant-stop-playing-first-person-shooters.

9.   See, for example, Christopher L. Heffner and Aimee Tompkins, "The Psychological Effects of Violent Media on Children," *AllPsych*, December 14, 2003, accessed February 10, 2016, http://allpsych.com/journal/violentmedia/; Tom A. Hummer, "Media Violence Effects on Brain Development: What Neuroimaging Has Revealed and What Lies Ahead," *American Behavioral Scientist*, July 22, 2015, accessed February 10, 2016.

10. http://abs.sagepub.com/content/early/2015/07/22/000276421 5596553.abstract; and Haejung Paik and George Comstock, "The Effects of Television Violence on Antisocial Behavior: A MetaAnalysis," *Communication Research 21*, no. 4 (August 1994): 516–546.

11. Dave Grossman, "Teaching Kids to Kill," Killology Research Group, accessed February 10, 2016, http://www.killology.com/ print/print_teachkid.htm.

12. Ibid.

13. Ibid.

14. Ibid.

15. Ibid.

16. *Brown v. Entertainment Merchants Association*, 564 U.S. 08-1448 (2011).

17. "Video Game Addiction: 81 Percent of American Youth Play; 8.5 Percent Are Addicted," *Metrics 2.0*, January 2007, accessed February 10, 2016, http://www.metrics2.com/

blog/2007/04/04/ video_game_addiction_81_of_american_
youth_play_85.html.

18. "Pornography Statistics," *Covenant Eyes*, 2014 edition, accessed
February 10, 2016, http://www.rescuefreedom.org/wp-con-
tent/uploads/2015/01/covenant_eyes_pornography _statis-
tics_2014.pdf; "Christian Porn Stats," *Proven Men Ministries*,
accessed February 10, 2016, http:// www.provenmen.
org/2014pornsurvey/christian-porn-stats.

19. "Fatal Addiction: Ted Bundy's Final Interview," Focus on the Family,
accessed February 10, 2016, http://www.focusonthefamily.com/
media/social-issues/fatal-addiction-ted-bundys-final-interview.

20. Ibid.

21. David Gotfredson, "David Westerfield Files Supplemental
Appeal Asking for New Trial," *CBS8.com*, May 13, 2013, accessed
January 23, 2016, http://www.cbs8.com/story/22240195/
david-westerfield-files-supplemental-appeal-asking-for-new-
trial.

22. "No Bond for Suspect in Carlie Case," *CNN.com*, February 7,
2004, accessed January 23, 2016, http://www.cnn.com/2004/
LAW/02/07/brucia.case/; "Joseph Peter Smith," Murderpedia,
accessed January 23, 2016, http:// murderpedia.org/male.S/s/
smith-joseph-peter.htm.

23. "Who We Are," North America Man/Boy Love Association,
accessed January 27, 2016, http://www.nambla.org/welcome.
html.

24. Paula Martinac, "Do We Condone Pedophilia," *PlanetOut.
com*, February 27, 2002, as cited in Peter Sprigg, "The Top Ten
Myths about Homosexuality," Family Research Council, 2010,
accessed December 23, 2015, http://www.frc.org/brochure/
the-top-ten-myths-of-homosexuality. See also Swain, *Be the
People*, 111.

25. Margo Kaplan, "Pedophilia: A Disorder, Not a Crime," *New
York Times*, October 5, 2014, accessed February 10, 2016,
http://www.nytimes.com/2014/10/06/opinion/pedophilia-a-
disorder-not-a-crime.html.

26. Todd Nickerson, "I'm a Pedophile, but Not a Monster," *Salon*, September 21, 2015, accessed February 10, 2016, http://www.salon.com/2015/09/21/im_a_pedophile_but_not_a_monster/.

27. J. Budziszewski, *The Revenge of Conscience: Politics and the Fall of Man* (Eugene, OR: Wipf and Stock, 2010), 20.

28. "Teen Suicide," *Menstuff*, accessed February 10, 2016, http://www.menstuff.org/issues/ byissue/teensuicide.html.

29. Ibid.

30. Peter Bronson, "STD Scourge an Epidemic among Teens," *The Cincinnati Enquirer*, June 22, 2004, accessed February 10, 2016, http://www.enquirer.com/editions/2004/06/22/loc_col 1bronson.html.

31. Goldberg, *Arrogance*, 237. 31. Ibid., 241.

32. Ibid., 241.

33. Ibid., 242.

34. Ibid., 243.

35. Bill Bush, "Students Allegedly Watched Assault," *Columbus Dispatch*, April 12, 2005, A1; Bill Bush, Kevin Mayhood, Alayna DeMartini, "Mifflin Teens Charged With Rape," *Columbus Dispatch*, accessed January 23, 2016, http://www.dispatch.com/content/stories/local/2008/02/25/060205 _story.html; "Two Students Charged in School Sexual Assault Case," *USA Today*, June 1, 2005, accessed January 23, 2016, http://usatoday30.usatoday.com/news/nation/2005-06-01-students-assault_x.htm.

36. Bush, "Students Allegedly Watched Assault."

37. Ibid.

38. Steve Feazel and Gunther Meisee II, *Shadow on the Heartland* (2015). See www.shadow ontheheartland.com.

39. Ibid.

40. "Rethinking Discipline," US Department of Education, last modified December 2015, accessed February 10, 2016, http://www2.ed.gov/policy/gen/guid/school-discipline/index.html.

41. Paul Sperry, "How Liberal Discipline Policies are Making Schools Less Safe," *New York Post*, March 14, 2015, accessed February

10, 2016, http://nypost.com/2015/03/14/politicians-are-making-schools-less-safe-and-ruining-education-for-everyone.

42. See "Parental Authority, Spanking, and the Role of the State," in Swain, *Be the People*, 118–119.

43. Albert Mohler, "Should Spanking Be Banned? Parental Authority Under Assault," *Christianity.com*, accessed October 12, 2010, accessed February 10, 2016, http://www.christianity.com /christian-life/marriage-and-family/resources-for-parents/should-spanking-be-banned-parental-authority-under-assault-1269621.html.

44. Benjamin Spock, *Dr. Spock on Parenting* (New York: Pocket Books, 1988), 172.

45. Benjamin Spock, *Dr. Spock's Baby and Childcare: 9ᵗʰ Edition* (New York: Pocket Books, 2012), 687.

46. Daniel Costello, "Spanking Makes a Comeback: Tired of Spoiling the Child, Parents Stop Sparing the Rod; Dr. Dobson vs. Dr. Spock," *Wall Street Journal*, June 9, 2000, W1.

47. "More Texas Parents Opt for Home Schooling," *WFAA.com*, August 23, 2010, accessed September 27, 2010, http://www.wfaa.com/news/texas-news/More-Texas-parents-opt-for-home-schooling-101292714.html.

48. Valonda Calloway, "Wake Judge Orders Home Schoolers Into Public Schools," March 12, 2009, accessed February 15, 2016, http://www.wral.com/news/local/story/4727161; Julia Duin, "Home-Schooler Ordered to Attend Public School," *Washington Times*, September 4, 2009, accessed September 27, 2010, http://www.washingtontimes.com/news/2009/sep/04/home-schooled-christian-girl-ordered-to-join-publi/print/.

Chapter 9: Higher Learning and Lower Values

1. Bork, *Slouching Towards Gomorrah*, 261.

2. As quoted in William J. Federer, *America's God and Country: Encyclopedia of Quotations* (Virginia Beach, VA: Amerisearch, 2000), 539–540.

3. *Mission and Strategy Handbook, Students for Academic Freedom,* accessed February 12, 2016, http://www.studentsforacademic-freedom.org/documents/1917/pamphlet.html.

4. David Horowitz, speech at Kenyon College, Gambier, Ohio, April 25, 2005.

5. As quoted in Bruce, *The Death of Right and Wrong,* 166.

6. Aliyah Frumin, "Latest Campus Trend? Tossing Out Graduation Speakers," MSNBC.com, May 14, 2014, accessed February 10, 2016, http:// www.msnbc.com/msnbc/college-commencement-speakers-backing-out-trend.

7. Aaron Blake, "Ben Carson Withdraws as Johns Hopkins Graduation Speaker," *Washington Post,* April 10, 2013, accessed February 10, 2016, https://www.washing-tonpost.com/news/post-politics/wp/2013/04/10/ben-carson-withdraws-as-johns-hopkins-graduation-speaker/.

8. Frumin, "Latest Campus Trend?"

9. Bruce, *The Death of Right and Wrong,* 162–163.

10. Goldberg, *Arrogance,* 213–214.

11. Ibid., 214.

12. Bruce, *The Death of Right and Wrong,* 182.

13. *God's Not Dead* directed by Harold Cronk, Pure Flix Entertainment, 2014.

14. "Statement of Faith," Christian Legal Society, accessed February 10, 2016, http://www.clsnet.org/page.aspx?pid=367.

15. *Christian Legal Society v. Martinez,* The Oyez Project at IIT ChicagoKent College of Law, accessed February 10, 2016, http://www.oyez.org/cases/2000-2009/2009/2009_08_1371.

16. *Christian Legal Society v. Martinez,* 130 S. Ct. at 2995.

17. "Equal Opportunity Policies: Nondiscrimination, Equal Opportunity, and Disability Policies," Vanderbilt University, accessed February 10, 2016, http://www.van-derbilt.edu/studentorgs-anchorlink/registering-your-org/equal-opportunity-policies.

18. Kim Colby, in communication with Carol Swain, March 3, 2016.

19. "Vanderbilt to Christian Student Organization: Drop Commitment to Jesus Christ for Leaders," The Christian Legal Society, April 20, 2012, accessed February 10, 2016, http://www.clsnet.org/page.aspx?pid=791.

20. See a short video summary of the related Vanderbilt town-hall meeting, "Exiled From Vanderbilt: How Colleges Are Driving Religious Groups Off Campus," accessed January 23, 2016, https://www.youtube.com/watch?v=dGPZQKpzYac; Katherine Weber, "Vanderbilt University's Religious Groups Lose Recognition," *Christian Post*, April 24, 2012, accessed January 23, 2016, http://www.christianpost.com/news/vander-bilt-universitys-religious-groups-lose-recognition-73807/.

21. Greg Lukianoff and Jonthan Haidt, "The Coddling of the American Mind," *The Atlantic*, September 2015, accessed February 10, 2016, http://www.theatlantic.com/magazine/archive/2015/09/the-coddling-of-the-american-mind/399356.

22. Ibid.

23. Ibid

24. Ibid.

25. Ibid.

26. Ibid.

27. Ibid.

28. As quoted in Lukianoff and Haidt, "The Coddling of the American Mind."

29. Diana Jean Schemo, "A Nation Challenged: The Campuses," *New York Times*, November 25, 2001, accessed February 10, 2016, http://www.nytimes.com/2001/11/25/us/a-nation-chal-lenged-the-campuses-new-battles-in-old-war-over-freedom-of-speech.html?pagewanted=all.

30. Jerry Martin and Anne D. Neal, Defending Civilization: *How Our Universities Are Failing America and What Can Be Done About It* (Washington, DC: American Council of Trustees and Alumni, 2002).

31. Ibid; see also Bruce, *The Death of Right and Wrong*, 160.

32. Bork, *Slouching Towards Gomorrah*, 266.

33. Bruce, *The Death of Right and Wrong*, 176.

34. Ibid., 185.

35. Charles Colson, *Against the Night: Living in the New Dark Ages* (Ann Arbor, MI: Vine Books, 1989), 85.

36. Bork, *Slouching Towards Gomorrah*, 257.

37. Coeur de Lion, "The Dirty Dozen: Twelve College Courses You Are Paying For," Young America's Foundation, August 30, 2002, accessed January 23, 2016, http://www.freerepublic.com/focus/news/745350/posts.

38. Don Closson, "The Power of Political Correctness," Probe Ministries, June 18, 2008, accessed December 23, 2015, https://www.probe.org/politically-correct-education/; Tait Trussell, "Universities Abandon Western Civilization," *Frontpage Mag*, January 22, 2012, accessed February 10, 2016, http://www.frontpagemag.com/fpm/120063/universities-abandon-western-civilization-tait-trussell.

39. Bruce, *The Death of Right and Wrong*, 169.

40. "Court Allows College to Use Koran Book," *Chicago Tribune*, August 20, 2002, accessed February 10, 2016, http://articles.chicagotribune.com/keyword/koran/featured/2; B. A. Robinson, 2002–Aug: University Dispute Re: Islamic Book," *ReligiousTolerance.org*, August 12, 2002, accessed February 10, 2016, http://www.religioustolerance.org/isl_unc.htm.

41. Andrea Garrett, "Academic Freedom? Intolerant Tolerance: AntiChristian Bigotry on Campus," *Christian Broadcast Network*, July 10, 2002, accessed February 11, 2016, http://www.freerepublic.com/focus/news/721143/posts.

42. Dan Flynn, "Temple U. Sued for Hauling Christian Student to Psychiatric Ward, Lawsuit: Administrators Banned Protest of Sacrilegious Play Then Assaulted Student," *Accuracy in Academia*, February 2001.

43. "UC Irvine Student Government Bans National Flags from Campus Areas" *Huffpost College*, March 6, 2015, accessed February 11, 2016, http:// www.huffingtonpost.com/2015/03/06/uc-irvine-ban-flag_n_6821316.html.

44. Naomi Schaefer Riley, *God on the Quad* (New York: St. Martin's Press, 2005), 169–170.

45. Jon Ward, "Lawmaker tells colleges to curb sex education," *Washington Times*, May 18, 2003.

46. Vigen Guroian, "Dorm Brothel," *Christianity Today*, February 2005, 46.

47. Ibid.

48. Ibid., 49.

49. Ibid., 46.

50. Simon J. Dahlman, "A Revealing Look at Academic Freedom," *Boundless.org*, 1999.

51. Kaitlin Mulhere, "Red-Faced Over Sex Weeks," *InsideHigherEd.com*, October 15, 2014, accessed February 11, 2016, https://www.insidehighered.com/news/2014/10/15/sex-week-events-draw-criticism-some-campuses.

52. Ibid.

53. Todd Starnes, "University of Tennessee Uses Student Fees to Host Lesbian Bondage Expert," *FoxNews.com*, March 14, 2013, accessed February 11, 2016, http://radio.foxnews.com/toddstarnes/top-stories/university-of-tennessee-uses-student-fees-to-host-lesbian-bondage-expert.html.

54. Ibid.

55. Ibid.

56. Ibid.

57. John Berk, "Survey Reveals Attitudes Toward Lifestyle Guides," *Lakeholm Viewer*, May 8, 2015, accessed February 11, 2016, http://www.lake holmviewer.com/#!Survey-reveals-attitudes-toward-lifestyle-guides/c4z2/554a2e030cf2487417142c73.

58. See www.thefire.org/about-us/mission/.

59. Ibid.

60. Ibid.

61. Alan Charles Kors and Harvey A. Silvergate, *The Shadow University: The Betrayal of Liberty on America's Campuses* (New York: Harper Perennial, 1999).

62. "FIRE's Twelve Worst Colleges for Free Speech in 2012," *FIRE.org*, March 27, 2012, accessed December 23, 2015, https://www.thefire.org/fires-12-worst-colleges-for-free-speech-in-2012/.

63. "Top Conservative Colleges," Young America's Foundation, accessed December 23, 2015, http://www.yaf.org/topconserva-tivecolleges.aspx.

Chapter 10: Black Robes Bring Dark Days

1. Matthew Spalding, *We Still Hold These Truths* (Wilmington, DE: ISI Books, 2009), 2.
2. "From Thomas Jefferson to Adamantios Coray, 31 October 1823," National Archives, Founders Online, accessed December 23, 2015, http:// founders.archives.gov/documents/Jefferson/98-01-02-3837.
3. Phyllis Schlafly, *The Supremacists: The Tyranny of Judges and How to Stop It* (Dallas, TX: Spence Publishing Company, 2004), ix–x.
4. Ibid., 4–5
5. *Board of County Commissioners v. Umbehr*, 518 US 668, 711 (1996, Scalia dissenting).
6. Barton, *Original Intent*, 56.
7. Ibid.
8. Ibid., 57.
9. *Vidal v. Girard's Executors*, 43 US 126, 132 (1844).
10. *Murphy v. Ramsey*, 144 US 15, 45 (1885).
11. *Zorach v. Clauson*, 343 US 306, 312–314 (1952).
12. Schlafly, *Supremacists*, 53.
13. Mark Levin, *Men in Black* (Washington, DC: Regnery Publishing, 2005), 74.
14. Levin, 74; see also *Bowers v. Hardwick*, 478 US 186, 191 (1986).
15. Levin, 19–20; see also *Lawrence v. Texas*, 123 S. Ct. 2472, 2481 (2003).
16. *Lawrence v. Texas*, citing *P. G. & J. H. v. United Kingdom*, App. No. 00044787/98, 56 (Eur. Ct. HR, Sept. 25, 2001); *Modinos v. Cyprus*, 259 Eur. Ct. HR (1993); *Norris v. Ireland*, 142 Eur. Ct. HR (1988).
17. Schlafly, *Supremacists*, 55–56.
18. Ibid., 56.

19. Ibid.
20. *Lawrence v. Texas.*
21. Robert H. Bork, *Coercing Virtue: The Worldwide Rule of Judges* (Washington, DC: The AEI Press, 2003), 52.
22. Ibid., 63.
23. Ibid.
24. Ibid.
25. Ibid.
26. *Roth v. United States* 354 U.S. 476 (1957).
27. Schlafly, *Supremacists*, 74–75.
28. Ibid., 75.
29. Bork, *Coercing Virtue*, 61; see also *Miller v. California*, 413 US 15 (1973).
30. Schlafly, *Supremacists*, 76.
31. Ibid., 79.
32. Ibid., 83.
33. Levin, *Men in Black*, 120–121.
34. Ibid., 157.
35. Bork, *Coercing Virtue*, 5–6.
36. Levin, *Men in Black*, 161; see also Fla. Stat. § 102.166(5) (2000).
37. Levin, *Men in Black*, 161.
38. Fla. Stat. § 102.111 (2000).
39. Levin, *Men in Black*, 161–162.
40. Ibid., 168.
41. Schlafly, *Supremacists*, 174.
42. Ibid., 174–175.
43. *Perry v. Schwarzenegger*, 2010 Westlaw 3025614 2010 US Dist. LEXIS 78817 Case No. C 09-2292.
44. Joe Eskenazi, "Prop. 8 Ruling: Judge Vaughn Walker's Most Scathing Language," *SF Weekly*, "The Snitch" (blog). August 4, 2010, accessed February 11, 2016, http://blogs.sfweekly.com/thesnitch/2010/08/prop_8_ruling_judge_vaughn_wal.php.
45. *Obergefell v. Hodges*, 576 US (2015).
46. Patrick Kampert, "Parents or Husband: Who Decides," *Chicago Tribune*, October 12, 2003, accessed February 12, 2016, http://

articles.chicago   tribune.com/2003-10-12/news/0310120378
_1_bob-and-mary-schindler-attorney-for-michael-schia-
vo-schindlers-attorney; "Background on the Schiavo Case,"
CNN Law Center, March 25, 2005, accessed February 12,
2016, http://www.cnn.com/2005/LAW/03/25/schiavo.qa/.
47. Levin, *Men in Black*, 116–121.
48. Ibid., 121; *Hamdi v. Rumsfeld*, 2004 U.S. LEXIS 4761, 20.
49. Levin, *Men in Black*, 129.
50. Jefferson, *The Writings of Thomas Jefferson*, vol. 15, 277.
51. Ibid., 213.
52. Thomas Jefferson, *The Writings of Thomas Jefferson*, vol. 4
(Washington, DC: Thomas Jefferson Memorial Association of
the United States, 1903), 27.

Chapter 11 — Fighting Back

1. Richard J. Neuhaus, *The Naked Public Square: Religion and
Democracy in America* (Grand Rapids, MI: Wm. B. Erdmans,
1984), ix.
2. Daniel Lapin, *America's Real War* (Sisters, OR: Multnomah,
1999), 57.
3. Erwin Lutzer, *Exploding the Myths That Could Destroy America*
(Chicago: Moody Press, 1986), 83.
4. Bruce, *The Death of Right and Wrong*, 107.
5. Rebecca Hagelin, *Home Invasion: Protecting Your Family in a
Culture That's Gone Stark Raving Mad* (Nashville, TN: Thomas
Nelson, 2005), 164.
6. Michael Medved and Diane Medved, *Saving Childhood:
Protecting Our Children from the National Assault on Innocence*
(New York: Harper Collins, 1998), 6–7.
7. As quoted in Tullian Tchividjian, *Unfashionable: Making a
Difference in the World by Being Different* (Colorado Springs,
CO: Multnomah, 2009), 64.
8. Kirsten Powers, *The Daily Beast*. "Yes, There Is a Gosnell Trial
CoverUp by Major News Organizations," April 16, 2013,
accessed February 11, 2016, http://www.thedailybeast.com /

articles/2013/04/16/yes-there-is-a-gosnell-trial-coverup-by-the-big-news-organizations.html.

9. Katie Yoder, "What? ABC Covers Cecil the Lion 15x More Than Abortion Videos," *NewsBusters*, July 31, 2015, accessed February 11, 2016, http://news-busters.org/blogs/culture/katie-yoder/2015/07/31/what-abc-covers-cecil-lion-15x-more-abortion-videos.

10. Bork, *Slouching Towards Gomorrah*, 337.

11. Ibid., 338–339.

12. Ibid., 339.

13. Ibid., 336.

14. "Evangelism Is Most Effective Among Kids," Barna Group, October 11, 2004, accessed February 11, 2016, https://www.barna.org/component/content/article/5-barna-update/45-barna-update-sp-657/196-evangelism-is-most-effective-among-kids#.VnK-dU_zyLU.

15. Limbaugh, *Persecution*, 352.

16. Bork, *Slouching Towards Gomorrah*, 336.

17. Ibid.

18. View the *War Room* movie trailer on YouTube at https://www.you tube.com/watch?v=mIl-XY9t_Lw.

19. Bork, *Slouching Towards Gomorrah*, 337.

20. Warner Todd Huston, "Pepsi… The Choice of the Angry Generation — (CEO gives middle finger to America!)," *Free Republic*, May 23, 2005, accessed December 23, 2015, http://freerepublic.com/focus/f-bloggers/1412025/posts.

21. Bork, *Slouching Towards Gomorrah*, 331.

22. Lapin, *America's Real War*, 31.

23. Laurie Goodstein and David D. Kirkpatrick, "On a Christian Mission to the Top," *New York Times*, May 22, 2005, accessed December 23, 2015, http://www.nytimes.com/2005/05/22/us/class/on-a-christian-mission-to-the-top.html.

24. Hope Yen, "Supreme Court Rules Cities May Seize Homes," *Free Republic*, June 23, 2005, accessed February 11, 2016, http://www.free republic.com/focus/news/1428929/posts.

25. Ibid.

26. Charles Colson with Anne Morse, "Worldview Boot Camp," *Christianity Today*, December 2004, 80.
27. Homeschooling parent, in communication with the authors, October 14, 2015.
28. As quoted in Donald R. McClarey, "Charles Carroll of Carrollton: Without Morals a Republic Cannot Subsist Any Length of Time," *American Catholic*, July 3, 2011, accessed January 23, 2016, http://the-american-catholic.com/2011/07/03/charles-carroll-of-carrollton-without-morals-a-republic-cannot-subsist-any-length-of-time/.

ABOUT THE AUTHORS

Steve Feazel an ordained minister who successfully planted two churches and served as an adjunct college professor in business. Now in retired status, he has produced three award winning, faith based documentaries on the topics of pornography (*Every Young Man's Battle*), abstinence (*Yellow Roses*) and abortion (*A Voice for Life*). He is an active writer and speaker and holds the following degrees: BA – Olivet Nazarene, M. Div. – Nazarene Theological Seminary and MBA – Arizona State. He and his wife, Edythe, have two grown sons and four grandchildren and reside in Gambier, Ohio. Website: www.visionword.com

Dr. Carol M. Swain, professor of political science and professor of law at Vanderbilt University, is an award-winning author and a widely recognized expert on race relations, immigration, and evangelical politics. She has published six books with Abduction being the 7th. Dr. Swain's books include B*lack Face, Black Interests: The Representation of African Americans in Congress, Be the People: A Call to Reclaim America's Faith and Promise, The New White Nationalism in America*; and *Debating Immigration*. She has appeared on thousands of national, local, and international radio and television programs. Her op-eds have appeared in The *New York Times*, The *Washington Post*, The *Wall Street Journal*, The *Washington Times*, and *USA Today*. She has served on the advisory board of the National Endowment for the Humanities. Dr. Swain is the creator of *Be the People TV*. Twitter: @carolmswain Facebook: Profcarolmswain Website: www.bethepeopletv.com

CPSIA information can be obtained
at www.ICGtesting.com
Printed in the USA
LVOW11s1213250717
542517LV00002B/331/P